Industrial and Organizational Psychology
Help the Vulnerable

Industrial and Organizational Psychology Help the Vulnerable

Serving the Underserved

Edited by

Walter Reichman
OrgVitality, Pleasantville, USA
Baruch College and The Graduate Center, The City University of New York, USA

First published 2014 by
PALGRAVE MACMILLAN

Palgrave Macmillan in the UK is an imprint of Macmillan Publishers Limited,
registered in England, company number 785998, of Houndmills, Basingstoke,
Hampshire RG21 6XS.

Palgrave Macmillan in the US is a division of St Martin's Press LLC,
175 Fifth Avenue, New York, NY 10010.

Palgrave Macmillan is the global academic imprint of the above companies
and has companies and representatives throughout the world.

Palgrave® and Macmillan® are registered trademarks in the United States,
the United Kingdom, Europe and other countries.

ISBN 978–1–137–32772–7

This book is printed on paper suitable for recycling and made from fully
managed and sustained forest sources. Logging, pulping and manufacturing
processes are expected to conform to the environmental regulations of the
country of origin.

A catalogue record for this book is available from the British Library.

Library of Congress Cataloging-in-Publication Data
Industrial and organizational psychology help the vulnerable : serving the
    underserved / edited by Walter Reichman.
       pages cm
    Includes bibliographical references.
    ISBN 978–1–137–32772–7
    1. Psychology, Industrial—Social aspects.   2. Industrial psychologists.
    3. Humanitarianism.   4. Volunteer workers in social service.
    I. Reichman, Walter.
    HF5548.8.I52325 2014
    158.7—dc23   2014019771

To the whip cream on the cake of life:

Lahra Gavriella Will-Reichman
my granddaughter

Lazer Shalom Reichman
my grandson

Contents

Figures and Tables

Figures

Tables

Acknowledgments

I want to acknowledge those who brought me along my career path and to this point in my life: Angelo Dispenzieri who opened my eyes to industrial and organizational (I-O) psychology when I was an undergraduate, Timothy Costello who showed me the joy of teaching, and Jeffrey Saltzman who gave me the opportunity to use I-O as a consultant.

There are many people who contributed to this book and helped me to edit it. I am grateful to Dr Allen Kraut who first suggested that I edit such a book and then was instrumental in developing the format and in suggesting chapter authors.

I am grateful beyond words in my vocabulary to the editors at Palgrave Macmillan for their valuable advice and direct assistance in the preparation of this book. Arvinth Ranganathan at Integra and Kirandeep Bolla are experts in their profession and provided great advice as well as direct assistance. I will always be grateful.

I appreciate the support of my colleagues at OrgVitality and the support and understanding of my wife, Marion; my son, Howard; daughter-in-law, Jill; and daughter, Judi, as I neglected them to devote time and energy to this book.

I am grateful to all the contributing authors for their understanding and acceptance of my vision for this book, their hard work in writing their chapters, and for the excellence of the work they reported in these chapters.

Contributors

Inusah Abdul-Nasiru is a PhD candidate in Industrial and Organizational (I-O) Psychology at the University of Ghana where he teaches I-O Psychology and Psychology and National Development. He was a visiting research scholar at North Carolina State University, USA, where he joined the IO Tech 4D lab in the Department of Psychology. He is a member of the Global Organization for Humanitarian Work Psychology and an international affiliate of the Society for Industrial and Organizational Psychology (SIOP). His special interest in serving humanity was borne out of his background and personal experience when growing up in rural Ghana.

Mary O'Neill Berry is an Organizational Psychologist and an independent consultant with 30 years of experience in organizational surveys, evaluation research, and management consultation. She was formerly Executive Vice President of Sirota Survey Research and Research Executive at Opinion Research Corporation. Among her clients were Action Against Hunger (USA), American Airlines, Mayo Clinic, The Office of the First Lady of Lesotho, and the *New York Times*. She serves as a non-governmental organization (NGO) representative to the United Nations (UN) Economic and Social Council (ECOSOC) and is the former co-chair of the Global Organization for Humanitarian Work Psychology. She holds a PhD degree in Social Psychology from Columbia University, USA.

Kim Marie Bischoff is a PhD student at Leuphana University of Lunsburg, Germany. She studied psychology at the University of Giessen, Germany. Her research interests are in the field of entrepreneurship. In particular, she is interested in entrepreneurship training, entrepreneurship in developing countries, education and training, and the interaction of individual characteristics and economic environmental factors in venture creation. She has conducted research in these areas in Uganda, Kenya, Tanzania, Rwanda, Liberia, and Ghana. She has also worked for consulting firms in the United Arab Emirates, China, and Germany. In Germany, she has also developed management training about intercultural competencies for enterprises and consulting companies.

Martin Butler is an educational psychologist in private practice and conducts research and writes on issues affecting the African American community. He serves as an NGO representative to the UN for the International Association of Applied Psychology and the International Council of Psychologists. He organized the workshop on "Sustainable Societies: Responsive Citizens" for the DPI/NGO Conference in Bonn, Germany, in 2011 and co-chaired Psychology Day at the UN in 2012. He has been active in Haiti relief efforts and chairs the task force on human trafficking for the NGO Committee on Migration. He has recently been appointed Liaison with to the UN DPI/NGO Office for the Psychology Coalition at the UN.

Kristie L. Campana is Assistant Professor at Minnesota State University (MSU), Mankato, USA. She received her PhD in I-O Psychology from the University of Minnesota, USA. Her research is on emotions in the workplace, new graduates' entry into the workplace, and unproctored Internet testing. She serves as a senior consultant at the Organizational Effectiveness Research Group, a student-run consulting organization at Minnesota State. She has also led the travel abroad program since 2012 and has accompanied student groups to Ecuador, Turkey, Belize, Vienna, Salzburg, Prague, and Budapest.

Stuart C. Carr is Professor of Psychology at Massey University, New Zealand, and coordinates the international and interdisciplinary Poverty Research Group. He co-led Project ADD-UP (Are Development Discrepancies Undermining Development?), a multi-country study of pay/remuneration diversity in developing economies. He co-edits the *Journal of Pacific Rim Psychology* which is focused on development. His books are among the first to examine poverty reduction from an I-O psychology perspective. He is the recipient of the APA/SIOP Presidential Coin for research excellence. This award recognizes those members who exhibit exemplary and extraordinary behavior in support of psychological science and practice. In 2013, he was a European Union Erasmus Mundus Scholar in Humanitarian Work Psychology at the Universitat de Valencia, Spain. His most recent book published in 2013 is *Anti-Poverty Psychology*.

Carol Lynn Courtney is President of Courtney Consulting Group and consults in the areas of executive coaching, executive selection, management selection, development assessment, and organization and team development. Prior to founding Courtney Consulting Group, Carol Lynn spent close to 20 years working as an internal and external consultant, staff and line contributor, and in various management and executive roles both in the United States and internationally. These experiences provided a strong foundation for linking each consulting engagement with the business goals and connecting with people at all levels.

Scott T. Fee is a faculty member in the Department of Construction Management at MSU, Mankato, USA. He is the past department chair and currently the Interim Dean of Online Learning and Extended Learning and Strategic Partnerships. He is Visiting Professor at Nelson Mandela Metropolitan University in Port Elizabeth, South Africa; a consulting faculty member to HAN University of Applied Sciences in the Netherlands; and a past recipient of the Greater Mankato Diversity Council's Martin Luther King Jr Pathfinder Award for connecting academics, professionals, and students in Minnesota with peers in South Africa.

Michael Frese holds a joint appointment at the NUS Business School at National University of Singapore, Singapore, and Leuphena University of Lueneburg, Germany. His research spans a wide range of basic and applied topics within organizational behavior and work psychology. Most recently, he has done studies on the concept of error management, innovation, and psychological training for increasing entrepreneurship and personal initiative as well as research that looks at psychological success factors in entrepreneurs in developing countries and in Europe. He is one of the most frequently cited authors and researchers in organizational psychology in Europe. He is a past President of the International Association of Applied Psychology.

Michael M. Gielnik is Junior Professor at Leuphana University in Luneburg, Germany. He studied Psychology at the University of Giessen, Germany, and received his PhD from Leuphana University. He conducts research on entrepreneurship, particularly entrepreneurial learning and training, the entrepreneurial process, and aging of entrepreneurs. He has taken a special interest in entrepreneurship in the developing context. He has conducted several research and practice projects on entrepreneurship in various countries in sub-Saharan Africa and Asia.

Alexander Gloss is a doctoral student in I-O Psychology at North Carolina State University, USA. He is interested in the study of organizational behavior in lower-income settings and in international development organizations. He is the recipient of the United States National Science Foundation's (NSF's) Graduate Research Fellowship and is researching the use of occupational information for societal development worldwide. He is one of the founders of the Global Organization for Humanitarian Work Psychology and sits on its executive board.

Jeffrey Godbout is a PhD candidate at Massey University in Aukland, New Zealand. To keep his academic–practitioner balance, he also works as a psychology consultant with not-for-profit and for-profit organizations. As a consultant, he worked with 360 assessment feedback, coaching, and leadership development and selection. Before beginning his doctoral work, he spent a year examining the relationship between aid organizations and the people they serve. His current research for his dissertation examines the fit between NGO projects and community expectations and the mediating role of human factors. His research seeks to hold aid and development organizations accountable to the communities they impact.

Binna Kandola, OBE (Order of the British Empire) is the senior partner at Pearn Kandola, a UK-based practice of business psychologists, where he specializes in diversity and inclusion. He is the author of several books, including *The Value of Difference: Eliminating Unconscious Bias at Work* and co-author of *The Invention of Difference: The Story of Gender Bias at Work*. He is Visiting Professor at Leeds University Business School. He was awarded an OBE in 2008 for services to diversity and disadvantaged people.

Judy Kuriansky is an internationally known clinical psychologist, humanitarian award-winning journalist, and well-known radio and television personality who is also on the faculty at Teachers College, Columbia University, USA, and an honorary professor at Peking University in China. Her many awards include the Humanitarian Award for Lifetime Achievement in Global Peace and Tolerance from the Friends of the UN. She has published many books related to bringing peace to the world and comments on news and relationships for media worldwide on her blog published in the *Huffington Post*. She is the founder of the Global Kids Connect Project and Stand Up For Peace Project, which organizes workshops and provides support for youth in Africa and post-natural disasters in Haiti, China, and Japan. She is the main NGO representative from the International Association of Applied Psychology to the UN.

Malcolm MacLachlan is Professor of Global Health and Director of Research in the School of Psychology, Trinity College Dublin, Ireland, and Extraordinary Professor of Rehabilitation at the Centre for Rehabilitation Studies, Stellenbosch University, South Africa. His research interests are in promoting inclusive global health – especially with regard to vulnerable and marginalized groups – and humanitarian work psychology. He is currently facilitating the knowledge management of two multi-country UN programs: the Partnership for the Rights of Persons with Disabilities and the International Labour Organization's (ILO's) Promoting Rights and Opportunities for People with Disabilities in Employment Through Legislation. He was awarded the American Psychological Association's International Humanitarian Award for 2014.

Leo Marai is completing his studies in the area of dual salary, work motivation, and health/well-being at the University of Papua New Guinea at Port Moresby. He teaches I-O Psychology courses and has published over 60 articles in peer-reviewed journals and is the co-editor of the *Journal of Pacific Rim Psychology.* He was co-chair of the Task Force on Humanitarian Work Psychology. His interests are in poverty reduction through humanitarian work psychology which includes dual salary, work motivation, and well-being of workers. He holds a master's degree in Social Psychology from Gadjah Mada University in Indonesia.

Jennifer Martineau is the Vice President for Research, Innovation, and Product Development for the Center for Creative Leadership (CCL). With over 20 years of experience in the leadership development field, she has served leaders, organizations, and communities globally, including health care, government, military, educational, community leadership, pharmaceuticals, and energy. She has a deep expertise in leadership research and how to apply it in practical, powerful ways for leaders and organizations. She has been published in both peer-reviewed and popular publications and co-edited CCL's *Handbook of Leadership Development Evaluation* and the second edition of CCL's *Evaluating the Impact of Leadership Development.*

Eilish McAuliffe is the founding Director of the Centre for Global Health established in 2004. She is Associate Professor of Health Policy and Management, Trinity College Dublin, UK. Her research is on strengthening health systems in middle- and low-income countries with particular focus on human resource crisis. She worked as a UNICEF/Irish Aid Research Fellow at the Centre for Social Research, University of Malawi, Malawi, and consults with governments, NGOs, and professional health-care bodies, contributing to many strategy and policy documents on health care in both high- and low-income countries. She currently leads the Support Train and Empower Management Project in Tanzania and Mozambique and is the Director of the Centre for Global Health at Trinity College Dublin.

Julene Nolan has a special interest and expertise in multicultural competence, particularly in assessment, consultation, coaching, and training. With more than 15 years of experience in working with diverse populations, both domestic and abroad, she brings unique skills in improving multicultural competence for professionals in education and the private sector. She is also dedicated to creating systems in the developing world to aid in equal access to education. Her most recent research findings were published in *School Psychology International* and *Education and Treatment of Children*.

Richard Olson is President and Founder of Olson Consulting Group and consults in the area of executive and management appraisal, selection testing, executive coaching, leadership development, and organizational change. With more than 20 years of experience in consulting, leveraging people's strengths in conjunction with addressing people's limitations serves as the underlying foundation of his work. Working both in the United States and internationally, he has provided innovative and practical approaches to business challenges.

Walter Reichman is Vice President and Partner in OrgVitality, a management consulting firm specializing in survey research, leadership development assessment, and coaching and training. He is also Emeritus Professor of Psychology at Baruch College and the Graduate Center of the City University of New York. He chaired the Department of Psychology at Baruch College for 17 years. He is also the main NGO representative to the United Nations Economic and Social Council from the International Association of Applied Psychology and co-chaired the 2013 Psychology Day at the UN. He was one of the founders of Humanitarian Work Psychology.

Tracey Rizzuto is an I-O Psychologist and Associate Professor of Human Resources and Leadership Development at Louisiana State University (LSU), USA. The focus of her research program is on developing human capital and organizational capacity through technology-mediated processes with the goal of increasing access to knowledge, expertise, and resources needed to manage change in the modern workplace. She has taken an active role in providing *pro bono* service to aid businesses in need. She has worked with organizations such as Baton Rouge Area Violence Elimination Project, Katrina Aid and Relief Effort, the Disaster Research Team, and Stephenson Disaster Management Institute at LSU. She is associated with over 7.5 million grant dollars from state and federal agencies, including the NSF, the Department of the Interior, and the Department of Justice. She has published in journals across multiple disciplines.

Daniel Sachau is Professor in the I-O Psychology Graduate Program at MSU, Mankato, USA. He is also the Director of Organizational Effectiveness Research Group at MSU. The Group provided human resource consulting services for regional and national organizations. His primary research interests include employee attitudes, intrinsic motivation, and impression management strategies. He attended The Graduate School at the University of Utah, USA.

Raymond Saner is co-founder of Centre for Socio-Eco-Nomic Development (CSEND), a Geneva-based non-governmental research and development organization and Director of CSEND's Diplomacy Dialogue branch. He teaches at Basle University, Switzerland, and at Sciences Po, Paris. His research and consulting focuses on conflict studies and international negotiations in the fields of employment and poverty reduction, human and social capital development, trade, as well as in the humanitarian field. He has pioneered the field of business diplomacy and contributes to the study of multi-stakeholder diplomacy within the field of diplomacy. He is a reviewer of the *Journal of Managerial Psychology, Journal of Applied Behavior*, and *Public Organization Review.*

Sarah Stawiski is a senior research associate at the CCL. Her work focuses on evaluating the impact of leadership development programs and understanding individual and organizational factors that influence workplace attitudes and behaviors. Other interests include small group processes, ethical decision-making, and corporate social responsibility.

Before coming to CCL, she worked for Press Ganey Associates, a healthcare quality-improvement firm. She holds a PhD in applied social psychology from Loyola University, Chicago.

Vicki V. Vandaveer is a coaching and consulting psychologist and founder and CEO of the Vandaveer Group, Inc. Her experience has spanned more than 30 years, 12 inside two Fortune 50 global companies and the past 20 years in national and international consulting with different cultures on five continents. She specializes in individual leader coaching, multicultural team leadership development, and advising senior management on behavioral aspects of organizational performance and change. She is a Fellow of several Divisions of the American Psychological Association. She has received several national awards for excellence in consulting as well as for her work on recovery from the devastating Louisiana hurricane which is described in her chapter in this book.

Telma Viale is the Director of Organizational Development, SRI Executive Search. Until the end of 2013, she was the Special Representative to the United Nations and Director of the ILO office in New York. Prior to that, she was leading the Human Resources Services for the ILO, based in Geneva. Prior to joining the ILO, she worked for the World Health Organization, The International Organization for Migration, and the World Meteorological Organization. She also held various posts in the United Nations Development Programme (UNDP) with field assignments in Afghanistan and Mozambique. She was also an NSF scholar with a grant to do research in psychology.

Lichia Yiu is the President of CSEND in Geneva, Switzerland. Her research and consulting focus on institutional performance and transformation in the field of poverty reduction, aid effectiveness, human capital development, and policy impact of multi-stakeholder engagement. She has taught at different universities and consulted corporations on leadership development, cross-cultural communication, and organizational change in Asia, North America, western Europe, and Africa. She works also with UN organizations and national governments on building internal capacities for transformation and performance improvement. She has published articles and books covering these topics. She is a reviewer for the *Journal of Managerial Psychology*, *Vision*, *The Journal of Business Perspectives*, and *Journal of Gestalt Review*.

1

Industrial and Organizational Psychology Encounters the World

Walter Reichman

What industrial and organizational psychology can accomplish

Industrial and organizational (I-O) psychology has the potential to improve the world. The theories, procedures, practices, and research of I-O psychology can be used, should be used, and, to a limited extent, are being used to heal the wounds of our civilization. These wounds are found in the vulnerable people in our world. They have been underserved by what we believe is an ethical, humanitarian science that has the ability to help the vulnerable.

Vulnerability is not restricted to a certain group of people in a particular part of the world but is among us, and each of us can become a member of that vulnerable group with a twist of fate. An illness, a hurricane, an earthquake, a fire, and a mad man with a gun can suddenly turn a whole happy community into a vulnerable group. There are too many people who at no fault of their own find themselves living in areas of war, civil unrest, and poverty. The recent economic recession, for example, resulted in millions losing their jobs and not being able to find work to support themselves and their families. Many families have lost their homes as a result of losing their livelihood and found themselves living in shelters for the homeless. Psychologists have documented the negative psychological effects on the breadwinners and their families of prolonged unemployment (APA, 2014).

The damage to the lives of hundreds of thousands of people around the world, resulting from natural and weather-related events, has been documented by the media. We read daily of thousands of refugees leaving their homes and often their countries in the hope of keeping alive during civil wars and wars between countries. As individuals, we desire

1

to help people who are suffering, and many of us offer some form of help and often wish we could do more.

As I-O psychologists, we often separate our profession and ourselves as professionals from the aid process. I have often thought, as I watched the catastrophes documented on television that if I were a physician, or a firefighter, or had the strength to search through the rubble of a collapsed building for survivors, then I could be of some use to those who were suffering. As an I-O psychologist, I have been an academic, a management consultant, and a representative to the United Nations (UN) from a non-governmental organization (NGO), the International Association of Applied Psychology (IAAP). In the latter capacity, I became familiar with the extent of suffering around the world resulting from poverty. I learned, for example, that three billion people, 50% of the world's population, live on less than $2.50 a day and that one billion children are living in poverty and that 22,000 of them die each day as a result of poverty (World Bank, 2014). I also learned two other things. The first was that there were dedicated people fighting against poverty and that the number of people living in poverty had declined by 50% since the year 2000, as a result, in part, of the Millennium Development Goals established by the UN (Chandy and Gertz, 2011). I also learned that I-O psychologists were in the forefront of some of the most important efforts to bring about poverty reduction (Carr, 2013).

As I tried to align my professional activities with the plight of the vulnerable in the world, I learned that many of my colleagues were way ahead of me and found ways of applying I-O psychology and other psychological disciplines to help heal our world. These colleagues were academics, consultants to companies, internal company consultants, and graduate students who had come to I-O psychology to better help them serve the vulnerable and underserved in the world because they experienced the need for such an education to continue their life's work. My pride and my joy in being a part of this discipline increased with each story I heard about the activities of these colleagues. I think the stories of their work should be made known to other I-O psychologists, as well as to those preparing for or considering a career in this field. This book will describe how I-O psychology is beginning to assume its responsibility to serve the needs of the vulnerable. It will present the stories of some of those people who have used I-O psychology to serve the needs of the vulnerable and thereby are showing the way to expand the boundaries of our field to include an option of using our science to help save our world. Each author was asked to tell the story of their work, what motivated them, the barriers they encountered, their successes, their failures, what they learned personally, how they used I-O principles and methods, and what I-O psychology can gain from their experiences to strengthen and expand our discipline.

In evaluating their work and its role in our discipline, it is important to remember that I-O psychology has been an independent field of psychology for fewer than 125 years. Its development was influenced by the school of Functionalism, which promoted the use of psychology to deal with problems faced by people as they attempted to survive, persevere, and prosper in the world in which they lived. Applied psychology owes its beginnings to the school of Functionalism that (Heidbreder, 1961). I-O psychology was developed to deal with the problems and issues faced by organizations, especially business organizations. Procedures and theories for selecting the "right" people for activities and jobs within the organization, training them, evaluating their performance, compensating them, motivating them, and managing them became the focus of I-O psychology. Our discipline was used most often to serve the needs of the business organization so as to improve their profitability. More peripheral elements such as job satisfaction/engagement, work–life balance, health, and safety were evaluated by the extent to which they served the goals of the organization, and only secondarily, if at all, as to whether they enhanced the well-being of the employee. As a result, I-O psychologists became known as the servants of business and the powerful (Lefkowitz, 1990). We were accused of neglecting the rights of workers by not being involved with unions; favoring white-majority men; and not being concerned with the well-being of racial and ethnic minorities, women, persons with disabilities, GLBT (gay, lesbian, bisexual, and transgendered), immigrants, etc. which resulted in these groups continuing to be marginalized in the world of work as businesses prospered in part due to our efforts. While we were reactive to government laws to prevent discrimination against such groups, we were not proactive. As a result, the actions of I-O psychologists were perceived as adjusting to the rules imposed on business in order to be sure that their profitability was kept intact. There is no doubt that promoting the goals of business and other organizations are legitimate aims of I-O psychologists, and there is no suggestion that they should not serve the interests of business organizations. However, when we recognize that the same methods, procedures, and theories can have a wider impact and can improve the lives of vulnerable people, it is appropriate to encourage the broader use of our skills. This is the direction that I-O psychology is now going.

Even while the majority of I-O psychologists were concerned with enhancing for-profit organizations, there were a number of psychologists who already had this wider view for using our science. Many of them are sharing their experiences by writing chapters for this book.

The experiences of the authors

Chapter 2 is written by a woman who at age 21 with a master's degree in I-O psychology began working for the UN and in a short time found herself in Afghanistan just after the withdrawal of Soviet troops and at a time when warlords were fighting each other for control of the country. The UN was there to provide humanitarian aid and find ways to end the conflicts. Her job was to provide administrative support for the office of the UN representative and to train the local staff on new software equipment. She was, in part, acting as a human resources professional responsible for both Afghan and UN personnel in an ongoing conflict in a nation recovering from a devastating war. After completing this assignment, she was sent to Mozambique at the end of their civil war that left one million dead. Her assignment was to arrange the logistics for UN-supervised elections throughout the country with little if any infrastructure intact. Her use of I-O psychology and what she learned from her experiences affected the remainder of her career.

Chapter 3 is written by two young I-O psychologists who took upon themselves the task of improving education in two areas of the world where education was almost completely lacking and the literacy rate was extremely low. The first author describes his work in his own country Ghana, where he was given the task of developing the capacity of a community to assume responsibility to control and improve their schools. The second author describes his work in South Africa as a Peace Corps worker charged with designing a program to increase the motivation of teachers in a school system that was failing its students. Both young men persisted in the face of conflict with those they were supposed to help, despite the lack of resources, terrible environmental conditions, and danger to their lives. Their work and accomplishments not only affected the educational systems they were working to improve but also set the course of their own professional lives.

The Rift Valley of Kenya is the scene for a project designed to turn young murderers into responsible citizens. The Rift Valley was a place of horrific tribal warfare that caused death of thousands with 70% of the killers being adolescents and young men. The Center for Creative

Leadership, a respected psychological organization in the United States, undertook the task of converting killers into responsible citizens and preventing other young people from becoming killers. The Center developed a leadership training procedure that was implemented by the authors of the third chapter in the Rift Valley. They used the theories, practices, and methods of developing and implementing training programs, the roots of which are in common with training that takes place in industry, to bring about change. In the Rift Valley, they changed young people who saw themselves as killers into young people who saw themselves as dedicated to peace and unity (Chapter 4).

The kingdom of Lesotho is a poor landlocked African country of extreme natural beauty that has one of the highest rates of HIV/AIDS in the world. Young women were particularly vulnerable to becoming HIV positive as a result of trading their bodies for money for their impoverished families which they often headed as a result of their parents having died from AIDS. At the behest of the First Lady of Lesotho, a multidisciplinary team consisting of an I-O psychologist, a clinician, and educational psychologist, along with the government of Lesotho, other aid organizations, the IAAP, and the government of Ireland developed, implemented, and evaluated a camp for vulnerable girls, designed to increase their empowerment, and enable them to develop income-generating activities to make them more financially independent and less vulnerable. The description of this endeavor supports the need for cooperation and collaboration among different psychology specialties as well as non-psychologists to bring the benefits of psychology to the vulnerable populations (Chapter 5).

It is generally accepted that the most effective way of reducing poverty in a country is to build profitable businesses that will employ workers and provide them with decent work and enough wages to adequately support their families. It takes entrepreneurs to build successful businesses. A question that has often been asked is whether entrepreneurship can be taught or whether it is an innate characteristic of the individual. Chapter 6 demonstrates that entrepreneurship can be successfully taught, and its principles can be acted upon to build successful businesses. The authors describe two cases from Uganda in which "job seekers were turned into job creators" as a result of participating in their unique training program. These authors not only developed and implemented an action-oriented entrepreneurial training program but also demonstrated that their training led to long-term business success. In this demonstration, they applied all the basic I-O psychology principles to turn the vulnerable into the successful.

There is probably nothing as motivating as a personal experience to set a goal for oneself, a research agenda and a program for activism. Chapter 7 is written by a psychologist who began teaching at a college in his own country and discovered that he was being paid less than others teaching the same type of courses. He discovered that the reason was a remnant law left since colonial times when foreigners were paid more money than local citizens for the same work. This unsettling discovery led him to research the effects of this dual salary system on motivation, productivity, social relationships, and mental and physical health. It provided a direction for his doctoral dissertation and for his advocacy efforts to change the system. You will see in later chapters that this dual salary system also has implications for effectively dealing with poverty reduction by organizations mandated to work to reduce poverty.

There are many organizations with explicit mandates to serve the vulnerable. They include such organizations as the Red Cross, Save the Children, UNICEF, and many more. Over the years, there has been criticism of many such NGOs for not delivering the aid they promised and at times for making matters worse for the people they intended to help. Aid organizations would probably benefit from having an organizational psychologist on their staff because they face the same problems that any business organization would face and probably a lot more. I-O psychologists could be of assistance to them. For this reason, there are a number of I-O psychologists who have researched the work of aid organizations and made suggestions to enhance their operations. One I-O psychologist with an interest in learning about the effectiveness of such organizations in helping vulnerable people after a disaster spent a year studying NGOs in Haiti. After the terrible earthquake of 2009 that wreaked havoc on the country, hundreds of aid agencies went to try to relieve the suffering. In Chapter 8, the author describes the good, the bad, and the ugly about aid organizations. His investigation also increased his appreciation for the role that I-O psychology can play in conducting humanitarian work.

Three of the most prolific researchers and theorists on poverty reduction and the operations of aid organizations as they endeavor to reduce poverty wrote Chapter 9. On the basis of their work, they conclude that the only way to reduce poverty is to empower poor people. The poor can be empowered by providing them decent work, education, and health care. In this chapter, they call upon I-O psychologists and business organizations to provide the power and the energy to bring about the needed change. They maintain that it is time for I-O community to "step up to the challenge of working with governments and organizations to achieve poverty reduction." Among the specific recommendations to governments and aid organizations is that they end the dual salary system that was described in Chapter 7, prevent social dominance, end the brain drain, and encourage "task shifting" as a means of bringing services to the vulnerable. Their provocative chapter is likely to have reverberations among those professionals working to reduce poverty. It is a contribution from the I-O community to poverty reduction efforts.

An NGO headed by a social and an organizational psychologist that has encountered governments in an effort to reduce poverty in their country is the Centre for Socio-Eco-Nomic Development (CSEND). In Chapter 10, these psychologists describe their efforts to incorporate the provisions for Decent Work into the poverty reduction strategies of countries. Decent Work has been defined by the International Labour Organization (ILO) as creating jobs, guaranteeing rights at work, extending social protection, and providing social dialogue between employers and worker (ILO, 2013). Member nations of the ILO agree to abide by the ILO conventions and incorporate their mandates into their government policies. The World Bank is also involved in poverty reduction and mandates that each country that receives aid from the World Bank to reduce poverty write a document describing its strategy to reduce poverty in their nation. The psychologists from CSEND work with the governments to incorporate the Decent Work mandate within its poverty reduction strategy. The authors describe their efforts and the problems they encounter in accomplishing this goal. They also describe a relatively new professional activity for I-O psychologists as advocating, networking, negotiating, and educating to bring about the changes within governments that will benefit the vulnerable. Training in these activities may become a part of the future I-O educational curriculum. As the authors state, there is a call for a new diplomacy to change the attitudes of those in power to focus on humanitarian endeavors. It is likely that this will be a skill in demand for future I-O psychologists as they take their place among the ranks of professionals working to provide for the vulnerable.

So far, the chapters described deal with vulnerable people in developing countries mostly in Africa. To be sure, there is no lack of vulnerable people in developed countries who can utilize the expertise of I-O psychologists. For example, the global recession of 2008–2009 resulted in an increase of 34% of homeless people living in shelters in the United Kingdom (Chapter 11). Their homelessness was due to loss of employment and not to addiction or illness or anything else that can be attributed to their behavior. A very successful I-O psychology consulting firm Pearn

Kandola decided to take action to bring help to some of the homeless shelters in their area. When they visited the shelter, they concluded that what people needed more than monetary donations was psychological services that an I-O psychologist could provide. They developed a unique training program to address what this vulnerable group needed: more confidence, greater resilience, and guidance in seeking employment. As part of the training, they invented a fictional character named Toki who finds himself in situations that are familiar to the homeless and unemployed. They build strategies to deal effectively with these situations. Training has always been an I-O activity to improve performance within an organization. This I-O psychologist adapted it to the needs of a vulnerable group to help develop them into effective employees who could build a good life for themselves and contribute to the well-being of their community.

New Orleans was hit by a horrific hurricane with 125-mile-an-hour winds destroying most of the city. The first responders came in to save the lives of those in danger of losing their lives. When the immediate emergency had ended, there had been an enormous amount of destruction and disruption especially to businesses. At that time, the second responders came in to provide assistance in recovery. Among this second group of responders were I-O psychologists who traveled from their home states to New Orleans. Among these second responders are the authors of Chapter 12. They describe in detail how they made the decision to help, the resistance they encountered, the difficulties they overcame, and then detailed how they put an organization back on its feet and thereby saved the lives of hundreds of animals. This description also brings into focus the positive aspects of I-O psychologists cooperating with other psychologists and other professionals to bring help to those suddenly made vulnerable by a disaster. The chapter also provides a good description of the recovery process of people from personal devastation to productive functioning and the role that I-O psychology can play in the process. There is no question that terrible events occur, and the need for I-O psychology to assist in recovery will continue. This chapter can be a template for preparation to cope under such circumstances. It suggests that while I-O psychologists may not be able to treat the wounded or search through the rubble right after a disaster, we can come along after the initial responders to help build resilience and return life to a level of normality.

The new role for I-O psychology is becoming evident in the field work courses being taught in master's and doctoral courses. For example, Minnesota State University has two courses that give students field work opportunities to deal with vulnerable people and vulnerable institutions. These two courses are described in the last two chapters (Chapters 13 and 14). The first is a service-learning course in developing nations. The authors describe students working in a Black Economic Empowerment Project in South Africa. Students, their advisors, and consultants from Minnesota State University worked with students in South Africa, teaching them job-seeking skills, business planning, resume writing, and means of starting a business. The goal of the program was to teach entrepreneurial skills that the young people could take back to their villages and thereby be able to make a living. In another project, the Minnesota students went to schools in the Amazon jungle of Ecuador to help young people there develop skills that could sustain them financially. They also consulted with the school administrator on succession planning and institutional maintenance to be sure the school would continue to function successfully after the retirement of the current administrator.

The program also developed unique procedures in which the students from Minnesota and the students in South Africa and Ecuador saw themselves as equals working together for the sake of both groups. The mutual understanding of the various cultures and what it takes to be a successful helper of the vulnerable will serve them as professionals throughout their career. Ability to serve the vulnerable will be a part of their professional repertoire (Chapter 13).

The second course describes students conducting research and evaluation for a non-profit major health-care provider in a developed country. They applied what they had learned in textbooks to solving a real problem that had implications for the success of the enterprise with which they were consulting. How do you evaluate the success of a non-profit organization, how do you deal with controversy and ethical principles as a consultant in I-O psychology, and how do you use statistics so as to reach a meaningful conclusion that will be useful to the lay leaders of the organization and that will help them make decisions about running their organization? These are real-life issues faced by I-O psychologists that must be resolved to achieve success. The author of Chapter 14 challenges her students to deal effectively with these issues as they solve a real-life problem in their community.

The themes of the experiences and the future of I-O psychology

There are two essential themes that run through all of these stories of serving the underserved. The first theme is that I-O psychology can utilize its procedures and practices to help vulnerable people to empower themselves. The second theme is that psychologists can only help vulnerable people empower themselves when they respect them, treat them as equals, and recognize their humanity and potential to change and grow. We cannot help people become empowered when we perceive them as inferior in any way or perceive our role as one who has to control the other person or situation in order to "save" them. A person or group that is empowered perceives themselves as being able to make a difference in their lives or community, having a range of behavioral options, able to find and use information, able to be assertive, and not feel that they are alone but are a part of a group in which they are accepted as equal (Chamberlin, 2014).

I believe the experiences described in these chapters demonstrate the ability of I-O psychologists to enhance the lives of the vulnerable by serving the underserved with the methods developed to serve business and other organizations. The work of these I-O psychologists portends the beginning of I-O psychologists influencing the world and helping the vulnerable. These authors are leading by examples, and as a result of their examples, procedures for helping the vulnerable will become a part of the curriculum of graduate programs in I-O psychology. New professionals will have more opportunities open to them and will have the capacity to move back and forth between serving private for-profit, nonprofit, and aid organizations. This overlap of opportunities will affect the way the vulnerable are treated. As I-O psychologists working in private industry, I anticipate that they will advocate for their organizations to engage in corporate social responsibility and devote some of their energy and resources for humanitarian activities. I-O psychologists, for example, could influence their companies to join the Global Compact, a UN-affiliated organization that encourages the private and public sector to cooperate to resolve some of the world's most pressing problems such as poverty reduction, energy efficiency, and climate change. There is a growing recognition that involvement of industry is essential if there is to be any lasting resolution to world problems. I-O psychologists can become the link between the involvement of private, public, and government resources in enhancing services to the vulnerable. There is evidence that I-O psychologists are interested in assuming this role. For example, in 2012 a new international organization of I-O psychologists, called the Global Organization for Humanitarian Work Psychology (GOHWP), was formed. This new organization is attracting members from I-O psychology and related disciplines in developed, emerging, and developing countries. It has the support of major psychology associations such as the Society for Industrial and Organizational Psychology

(SIOP) and the Organizational Division of IAAP. Both SIOP and IAAP have consultative status with the United Nations Economic and Social Council, thus allowing I-O psychology to be brought to the deliberations of the UN, the primary world organization mandated to be concerned with the vulnerable people in our world. I-O psychology is taking its rightful place in this effort.

References

American Psychological Association (APA) (2014). Psychological effects of unemployment. Retrieved December 5, 2014, from www.apa.org/abook/gr/issues/socioeconomic/unemployment.aspx.

Carr, C. (2013). *Anti-pverty psychologies*. New York: Springer.

Chamberlin, J. (2014). A working definition of empowerment, national empowerment center-articles. Retrieved from www.powqer2u.org/articles/empower/working_def.html.

Chandy, L., & Gertz, C. (2011). Poverty in numbers: The changing state of global poverty from 2005–2015. *The Brookings Institute*. www.Brookings.edu/research/papers/2011/01/global-poverty-chandy, 2–23.

Heidbreder, E (1961). *Seven psychologies*. Englewood Cliffs, New Jersey, Prentice Hall.

ILO (2013). Triparte constituants in *About the ILO structure*. http.//www.ilo.org/global/about-the-ilo/who-we-are/tripart.te-constituents/lang-en/index.htm.

Lefkowitz, J. (1990). The scientist-practitioner model is not enough. *The Industrial Organizational Psychologist*, 28, 47–52.

The World Bank (2014). Poverty facts and stats-global issues. Retrieved December 2014 from www.worldbank/en/topic/poverty.

2
Challenges of the Ultimate Messengers

Telma Viale

I am writing this chapter from the eyes of a psychologist, not in a clinical sense, but in the sense of somebody who is constantly trying to understand what shapes human behavior and what impresses people's minds when they make a judgment and decide to act, or not to act, upon a decision. I was 21 years old when I joined the United Nations (UN), and little did I know that it would open up the doors of the world for me. Over the years, I have held a variety of positions, performing work ranging from administrative tasks to director of human resources in large international organizations. I also write from the perspective of a woman from El Salvador who has witnessed poverty and years of a war. This motivated my desire to understand people and their environment and ultimately led me to study psychology specializing in organizational change.

Through some observations, anecdotes, and my voice I would like to invite you to some of the places that forever changed my understanding of human suffering, beyond that of my own land, and enriched my knowledge about the people we are trying to help, as well as the helpers. I will also reflect upon the kinds of resources that organizations have for identifying and selecting the right people, as well for tackling the challenges that UN staff members face in their journey when trying to deliver the mandates for which they are called upon. In doing so, I will hopefully shed light on areas where industrial and organizational (I-O) psychologists could further contribute.

Afghanistan

That morning in Kabul in 1991, about seven women came to work at the UN premises, veiled and dressed in black. It was my last day at work after an administrative assignment that lasted half a year. At such a sight, my heart jumped at the thought that another child had been killed or that some tragic event had hit one of their loved ones. But no, they came into my office and said, "Telma jan, today it is a day of mourning for us since we know in our heart that we will never see you again. Afghanistan is a forgotten land and we doubt that you will ever come back here, but we will pray to see you in heaven" I recall that words failed me, but I made the gesture of gratitude they had taught me, my hand over my heart and a slight nod, and I remember a chill in my entire body at such a sincere and deep expression of love.

If there is one memory that traveled with me after I left Afghanistan, it is the gaze of the Afghans. Each time our paths crossed, I instinctively turned my eyes in search of theirs, and so I learned about the deep messages in their unique silent language. Whether it was the nostalgic look of the 10-year-old boy longing for childhood while watching his younger brothers playing, or the sad look of the 15-year-old girl meeting the husband chosen by her father for the first time, or the humble aged office clerk bowing while hand delivering photocopies and shyly raising his eyes in search of a sign of gratitude, my heart stopped every time that those powerful hidden messages would hit me. There was nothing to say but much to understand and to learn from those people I had come to serve.

Context of Afghanistan in the early 1990s and role of the UN

The almost ten-year-long Soviet war in Afghanistan had recently ended; the final troop withdrawal had taken place about a year ago. People had witnessed the death of hundreds of thousands of Afghans, both military and civilians. But the devastation was not over. Roads were mined, making access difficult and dangerous. While the country was officially ruled by Najibullah, former Chief of Intelligence during the Soviet Union's occupation, he was perceived as a foreign imposition, and there was resistance to accept him. Therefore, internal groups that had made up the resistance against the occupation continued a civil war, a few of these groups were the followers of Gulbuddin Hekmatiar (Pashtun origin), or of Ahmad Sha Massoud alias the "Lion of Panjshir" (Tajik origin), or of Abdul Rashid Dostum (Uzbek origin), and they were driving rocket bombardments in their fight for power. So the city of Kabul was hit by rockets that randomly fell in the various urban neighborhoods on a daily basis.

I lived in the Wazir Akbar Khan neighborhood, one of the traditionally wealthiest parts of Kabul where the few remaining foreign embassies were located. Neighboring countries had more diplomatic representation than other non-neighboring countries. Some even had resorted to appoint representatives in their embassies from nationals of their countries who had either married Afghans or had chosen to stay despite the conflict. As my Afghan colleagues said to me, Afghanistan was a forgotten land. After the Soviets left, the civil war was a silent one for world news, yet the sound of rockets was heard daily in Kabul. I recall one day a rocket hit the backyard of a house a block down from mine. The situation was far worse for Afghans, who had rockets and also scarcity of basic goods. Kerosene, for instance, which was the primary domestic energy fuel, was expensive, and without it cooking was not possible, and the harsh winters of Afghanistan were unbearable. The main meal for most Afghans was "chaa" and "naan" (tea and bread), with sugar only when available. Their delicious "pallaw" (a rice plate) remained a taste for special occasions. Hospitals were full of wounded civilians, amputated men and women, and many children missing their limbs. Fortunately, the UN was there, the Red Cross was there, and some humanitarian agencies were trying to help. But resources to help were scarce.

The UN was meant to provide humanitarian aid and seek paths to peace. And with all its challenges, it also worked toward capacity building, bearing in mind that after years of conflict many of their talented professionals had fled the country. My role was to provide administrative support to the Resident Representative's office and to train local staff on a new software system. There were staff security restrictions which did not allow us to travel outside a certain radius within the city of Kabul, and there were also language barriers hindering communication with most Afghans. Therefore, my interactions with local staff were my only first-hand opportunity to understand the realities of the Afghans.

Days in the life of . . .

The 24th October is considered the UN day. It marks the anniversary of the enforcement of the UN Charter, and the words rang to me, "WE THE PEOPLES OF THE UNITED NATIONS DETERMINED to save succeeding generations from the scourge of war . . . to reaffirm faith in fundamental human rights, in the dignity and worth of the human person, in the equal rights of men and women and of nations large and small . . ." And there we were organizing a reception for the government officials to celebrate this founding document, meant to fundamentally change the state of the world. I had noticed at other occasions when food was served that nothing, not one crumb, was left on the tables. This must have been due to the preciousness of food in such a scarce environment. At the time, most of the officials were men who wore suits, and I had noticed that they would even put food in their pockets, probably to take it home. So I looked around me, having become familiarized with the lives of the local staff, their large households, their hardship, and the limited ways in which these could be alleviated, and I decided to organize something for them for that day, something that would be warm and human in the midst of so much suffering. There are no resources allocated for staff parties at the UN, therefore we had to be resourceful. So I wrote to the international staff asking them for any voluntary contribution to make a staff party on UN day that would involve the local staff and their children. The response was surprisingly generous, so I just had to put in organizational and networking skills to make it happen. At the time, even with money one could not buy any toys in Kabul, so I sent for them in Islamabad. I also called upon a local singer who was very famous among Afghans, and she agreed to sing for free. Then we invited the staff and two of their children, a girl and a boy, and also gave them an age range – there was no other way possible since families often had more than 20 members including many children. The party was a success; our premises were filled with the beautiful bright colors of Afghan dresses that children wear. It was a day of joy with music, food, salty and sweet, and toys for the children. Only later did I learn what this gesture had meant for the Afghans, my judgment for pulling it together was not only purely intuitive but also within the realms of creativity, given the resources that we had.

But the days following this happy event were less pleasant. One morning I heard screaming outside the office premises, there were fights in the entrance between the security, the staff doctor, and a local staff member who was trying to get into the compound with his seven-year-old girl who had just been crushed by a military truck. Hospitals had lines waiting for help and meager capacity to help, so he wanted our staff doctor to care for his daughter. At the same time, guards and the doctor himself, who was a very young volunteer on his first assignment abroad, were concerned about liabilities for taking on somebody so badly injured and about responsibilities in case of death. In the eyes of this very young doctor, I could see great distress and confusion, but at the same time there was not much time to think, nor much to think about. A man was holding his bleeding child in his arms, both were crying for help. It was astonishing how administrative consequences were paralyzing the judgment of this doctor to move and help. There were no higher level officials in the compound at the moment to make that decision for him, but I reminded the doctor of the Hippocratic Oath.

I just wanted the doctor to uphold the highest professional ethical standards and move. The girl was finally taken in but nothing could be done with her little body crushed completely by the tires of a huge military truck. I knew the wife of the staff member and speechlessly accompanied them through their mourning. There I learned that many Afghan mothers have no way of escaping the pain of losing a child in such dramatic circumstances. Indeed, Afghan children are common victims of physical injury. As described in the study cited below, serious physical, psycho-social, interpersonal, and economic consequences are faced by survivors and their families.

Independent study

The effects of amputation for an Afghan child

During my time in Afghanistan, I was particularly impressed by the number of children in the streets. In the midst of taupe colors so characteristic of Kabul, children running around, showing off the bright colors of their dresses were the most hopeful sight of the city. At the time, Afghan children aged 0–14 years represented 47% of the total population of around 19.6 million (The World Bank, 2013a, 2013b). It is interesting to note that in 2011, Afghan children were over 46% of the population, the difference being that in nearly two decades the population has almost doubled to around 35 million (The World Bank, 2013a, 2013b). So I decided to take up an independent study, a first-hand observation on my own time about the seriousness and tragedy of war on the most defenseless of Afghanistan, the children. As many children of war, Afghan children are common victims of physical injury. Due to the lack of economic means, common in war-torn countries, the treatment and rehabilitation of these children is extremely poor, if any. Afghanistan, arguably among the poorest countries in the world, and having struggled through a decade of war, was far from providing appropriate medical assistance to its war-injured children, and it could not provide the psychological assistance needed by the injured and their families. I am here sharing my considerations, based on my observations during the time in Afghanistan, and focusing on the psychological effects of amputation for an Afghan child.

Obviously, the psychological impact of amputation is dependent on a large variety of factors, the most important one being the individual make-up of each child. However, being such a difficult factor to observe and analyze in the described circumstances, I chose to restrict my study to three more observable sets of factors: the resources of their environment, the culture, and the events to which they are exposed.

Of course, this self-limitation entails a limitation in the "reach" of my observation. I will come back to that later.

Environment

Environmental conditions are key to determining the extent to which a child can rehabilitate and integrate back into society. In 1991, out of every 1,000 children in Afghanistan, 184 died before reaching the age of five (The World Bank, 2013c). Safe drinking water supply systems were lacking in both urban and rural areas, and vitamin A deficiency and nutritional anemia were major children health problems; in 2011, 101 out of every 1,000 children died before the age of five (The World Bank, 2013c). Despite the telling figures and most urgent needs, in the early 1990's, there was only one national institution for children's health in all of Afghanistan, the "Indira Gandhi Institute of Child Health." In order to find out what kind of assistance amputated children received, I interviewed the head of the pediatrics orthopedic department. Unfortunately, the hospital did not provide any rehabilitation specially designed for children, so these were referred to a center at the Wazir Akbar Khan General Hospital which treated adults as well as children. In view of this, the International Committee of the Red Cross (ICRC) had opened an orthopedics and rehabilitation center. In the center, there was a waiting list of over 2,500 patients, and although children and women were given priority, only a small percentage of children in need of treatment had access to the advanced technology, qualified prosthetics, and physiotherapists available at the center. It was explained to me at the time that even the best quality prostheses available needed to be changed approximately every two years, but for children who outgrow their artificial limb, the change is needed almost every year. This was a particular problem for families living in the provinces, for whom a trip to Kabul is costly and often made once in a lifetime. Due to the continuing war in both rural and urban areas, schools had been opening sporadically. They also lacked skilled teachers, appropriate teaching aids, class-room supplies, furniture, etc. The substantial limitations in terms of sanitary, health, and educational assistance were evident for children in Afghanistan. For children with disabilities who share the same environment while having special needs – as is the case for children with amputations – these limitations were even more severe. From interviews with doctors and physiotherapists at the ICRC Orthopedic Center, it appeared that the main desire of children was to be able to walk again. When they saw other children in the rehabilitation process, they looked anxious for their turn. Once the children started to walk again, the doctors reported observing a drastic change in their facial expression and also in the personality.

Culture

The lifestyle of Afghans and the way in which they interpret a physical handicap also shaped the children's perception of their own condition. Afghans form a very heterogeneous society. However, for all their differences, a majority of them share similar occupations, common religion, and undergo economic pressures which in the end account to a large extent for their psychological interpretations. Doctors and therapists at the ICRC Orthopedic Center and at the Indira Gandhi Institute, who treated patients coming from all provinces of Afghanistan, reported that the families of amputated children expressed three major concerns: first, the fear of the reaction of their fellow villagers toward them or their child. The thought that they or the child would be demeaned because of their fate seemed to be a deep preoccupation. Second, the concern about the little productivity of the disabled child and the disadvantage that they would face as parents at old age having to care for a non-productive child. Most Afghans are farmers or laborers (cultivators, carpet weavers, etc.) and mainly rely on their physical fitness to earn a living (according to the World Bank 2011 data, 76% of the Afghan population is rural). In addition, children start working at an early age. Sub-teen boys assist their fathers in the fields and girls assist their mothers to fetch water, cook, wash clothes, etc. One major feature of child-socialization, mainly in the Afghan non-urban society, is that children have no adolescence; the young Afghan moves directly into an adult world (Dupree, 1980). According to the 2013 UNICEF (United Nations International Children's Emergency Fund) report on the state of the world's children, 10% of children aged 5–14 in Afghanistan were involved in child labor between 2002 and 2011 (UNICEF, 2013). Consequently, children are perceived as productive and a profitable source of income, and later as a social security for old age. In contrast to modern Western culture with its emphasis on the intellectual ability of children at school, Afghans tend to stress their children's ability to produce wealth. While the child's functionality in one society is primarily limited to school performance, in Afghanistan functionality means the ability to perform hard work. Therefore, amputation would seem even more physically impairing in Afghanistan than in Western cultures. On the other hand, physiotherapists brought to my attention the observation that children seemed to be less self-conscious as far as their physical appearance was concerned. Perhaps less bombarded by advertising and demands to be young and beautiful, and more pressured by the needs to perform physical work, it seemed that amputation was less traumatizing for Afghan children in relation to their "looks," but more in relation to the physical "impairment" that amputation entailed. Third, families expressed the concern that the amputated child was unlikely to get married. It should be noted that for most groups in Afghanistan, marriage is strongly related to productivity. Acquisition of wealth seems to be a primary condition for males to envisage marriage and the ability to perform heavy housework is essential for women, both activities emphasizing physical work. However, according to the concerns reported by the Afghans visiting the Center, the possibilities of marriage for amputated men were better than those for amputated women. As long as men can find a way to earn enough money for the "bride's price" and to buy clothes, carpets, dishes, and jewelry for the bride, they can get married. As for amputated women, they were seldom chosen to raise a family.

Life events

But the drama of amputated children did not stop there. Those who suffered stressful events were exposed to greater psychological consequences. Many war children had witnessed bombardment, dead bodies, and other war-related violence. Many had also lost their parents or guardians or suffered abuse. Yet, anxiety, depression, or fear was often coupled with infectious diseases (i.e., malaria, TB, gastro-intestinal problems) caused by the long hot season and improper basic sanitation. These were just some of the variables that had to be added to the observation of these children. There was a sense of helplessness conveyed by the few doctors and therapists that were working with these children, but it was also witnessed by the families, and consequently by the children. And there I was recording everyone's sense of helplessness, including mine. I recall that during the winter months, while I was tracking the notes of my study, a colleague who worked with UNICEF grew quieter than usual during the dinners that we used to share. Only later I learned that he could not sleep thinking of the children who camped before dawn in the line outside the bakery, and about one in particular that he had carried in his arms, frozen to death, due to hours waiting in extreme cold temperatures. This was not child labor but the epitome of poverty and war. Yet, this dead child had been carried and was being remembered with the utmost love and compassion.

Conclusions

My observations concluded that because Afghan society puts a major emphasis on physical functionality, amputation represents a major trauma for the child. Second, because rehabilitation facilities were so scarce and inaccessible, no support was available from social institutions to effectively alleviate that trauma. Third, amputated children were likely to face other stressful situations brought about by the war. In view of that, it became more understandable to me why so many parents, when asked to authorize amputations, requested doctors to let the child die. Interestingly, despite the above-mentioned odds against the child's survival, there were no records of suicide as a result of amputation. Quite the contrary, doctors, and therapists reported that Afghan children in treatment showed a remarkably strong will to overcome their handicap. In addition, the children's cheerful attitude brought joy to their work. Therefore, no matter how devastating the amputation may be, there is a coping mechanism strong enough to allow the children to adjust to a totally new condition. I had no choice but to limit my analysis to the more readily observable factors. While numerous question marks regarding the psychological effects of amputation still remain, I gathered that there is so much to learn about the extraordinary coping mechanism that so many Afghan children displayed. With prostheses, I saw children climbing trees and smiling at me.

Life in the compound continued, this time with the preparation for the visit of a high-level official from headquarters. In the midst of the stress around it, I learned that our local engineer in charge of the maintenance of our regenerator had resigned. In view of the visible lack of skilled engineers in Kabul, his departure had put us in trouble since we largely depended on the regenerator for electrical power. In light of the good contact established with local staff, I was asked to speak to the engineer in question to change his mind. I learned that his sudden resignation had been motivated by an unpleasant exchange with a senior staff member. Apparently, his chief, who was an international staff member, had raised the voice to the engineer, which was unacceptable for him. When approached, he said to me that he was grateful for the work he had and for the better life that he was providing to his family because of it, but that he could not bear the dissonance of going back to his home at the end of the day and being the chief of a large honorable family if his work required him to accept humiliation from his chief. He reiterated to me that he needed the job, yet that his family also knew how to live with "chaa" and "naan" if that is what was necessary to maintain their dignity.

Fortunately, this time, apologies from the staff member concerned and assurances that it would not happen again were sufficient to get the engineer and the regenerator working again. When the high-level official finally arrived, our local staff watched every step that this official took. Yet, in the cloud of conversations that were entertained with the few high-level officials who permanently accompanied her, the high-level official failed to turn her eyes to the local staff to greet them. Ironically, from the visit of such an important person that was meant to help Afghans have a better life, and who certainly made great efforts for that, the local Afghan staff retained the image of someone who did not even show them the respect of an acknowledgment.

The consideration demonstrated by the local Afghan staff contrasted starkly with the treatment they received from the high-level official. A few days before my scheduled departure, I received an invitation for a lunch that had been organized by the local staff at their own initiative. I was impressed at the sight of the table they had put together. There was an abundance of food, various types of "pallaw" prepared at their homes, sweets, and more. And they had also bought a small carpet as a gift for me. I was amazed because I knew what this meant for them in view of their situation and their needs. I recall that not much of what I had in my wardrobe met the standards for their dress code, so during my entire mission I had opted to wear their colorful taffeta punjabes. Was it this gesture that made me more accepted? I had organized that staff party; was it a way of giving back to me what I had sought for them? Who knows? But for sure they conveyed the message that they cared for me. Understanding what was important for them was enough to be accepted among them, to the point of making sure that I knew that my presence mattered.

Mozambique

A military plane landed at the airport of Nampula, the northern headquarters of ONUMOZ (UN Operation in Mozambique), the peace-keeping mission where I had been assigned to coordinate logistics and administration for the northernmost province, bordering Tanzania: Cabo Delgado. I was met by a civil police officer, part of the UN team, and was taken to the regional headquarters for a day briefing. Basically I was given a UN flag, a map, and was informed that I had to open a headquarters in the provincial capital, plus 16 district offices to prepare for the elections scheduled for October 1994. Everything was meant to happen in less than a year. But everything was also so foreign to me. The town was ruined and crumbling, one could see the physical dev-astation of war, but there were also many young men grouped in the street corners with little hope in their eyes. For most of my time there, I had opted for a dress code of khaki pants and a white UN T-shirt to blend in as much as possible with the UN male personnel; but although nobody spoke to me in the streets, looks were direct, deep, and curious. I felt somewhat daunted and recall that when I finally reached my hotel room I prayed for wisdom and strength to carry out my assignment. I recall not only the light and warmth that pierced through my window that afternoon in that remote town of Africa, but also the overwhelming comfort that the sunset light brought to me. In my entire life, it is the only memory that I have of sleeping in the hollow of God's hand.

Context of Mozambique 1994 and role of the UN

Mozambique is arguably among the poorest countries in the world. Shortly after gaining independence from Portugal in 1975, a civil war began between the ruling party, the Front for Liberation of Mozambique (FRELIMO), and the Mozambique Resistance Movement (RENAMO), which was largely supported by South Africa. The legacy from that war that lasted about 16 years was about one million people dead, five million civilians displaced, and many amputees because of landmines (Reibel, 2010; Weinstein, 2002). In 1992, a general peace agreement was signed in Rome between FRELIMO and RENAMO. In accordance with the agreement, the UN peacekeeping mission ONUMOZ was established to implement the accords.

The ONUMOZ mandate covered four important elements: political, military, electoral, and humanitarian. Their interrelationship was crucial. Besides the complexity of the political element under the direct responsibility of the Special Representative of the Secretary-General, the military component was huge. It was meant to monitor and verify the ceasefire, the separation, and concentration of the two party forces; the demobilization of soldiers and the collection, storage, and destruction of weapons; to monitor and verify the complete withdrawal of foreign forces and to provide security in the transport corridors; to monitor and verify the disbanding of private and irregular armed groups; and to authorize security arrangements for vital infrastructures, while providing security for UN and other international activities in support of the peace process. The security aspects were also enhanced with the addition of a civil police element. The humanitarian team was in charge of coordinating and monitoring humanitarian assistance operations; aid was meant not only to be an instrument of reconciliation, but also to assist refugees, internally displaced persons, demobilized military personnel, and the affected local population. Last but not least, there was a need to create the conditions for elections since the mission would be in charge of monitoring and verifying all aspects and stages of the electoral process which would be organized by the National Elections Commission. The electoral team was therefore in charge of providing technical assistance and monitoring the entire electoral process. In order to accomplish its mission, ONUMOZ had an authorized strength of 6,625 troops and military support personnel, 354 military observers, 1,144 civil police officers, 355 international staff, 506 local staff, and 900 election observers (United Nations, 2013). My task was to lead administrative and logistical services in the province of Cabo Delgado to support the civil police, the humanitarian, and the electoral teams, while setting up 17 offices to host elections, prepare transportation, facilitate accommodation for the 200 electoral staff and observers that would be deployed throughout the province for the elections, and handle their medical evacuations as needed.

Days in the life of...

Another civil police officer was waiting for me at the small airport of Cabo Delgado and took me to the guest house in downtown Pemba. A few hours later he took me back to the airport to show me where my vehicle was and handed me the keys. It was a pickup truck that apparently had been waiting there for months, just as the civil police themselves had been anxiously waiting for an administrative chief to arrive. I had a New York driver's license and was used to driving automatic vehicles. Learning to move a stick shift pickup truck in the sandy roads of Cabo Delgado was the first self-taught activity of my mission. Part of my work was to identify the premises where we would set up the provincial headquarters, and in the meantime, we had a room rented to us by an international agency settled there. The room had one table and two stools and a big cardboard box serving as the desk for an electrical typewriter. While I read the accumulated "pouch" mail coming from the mission's headquarters in Maputo, full of instructions on administrative procedures, I saw the civil police officer who had picked me up at the airport totally concentrated on writing up a memorandum. After a few minutes he finished it, signed it, sealed it in an envelope and hand-carried it to me. It contained complaints about the lack of logistic and administrative support that they had had since their arrival months ago and included a list of all the things that they needed in order to operate, ranging from pencils to vehicle repairs. I smiled and said "thank you for putting it so tidily on paper."

The entire province of Cabo Delgado has an area of 77,867 km^2. Pemba is the capital, and it is divided into 16 districts. Access was difficult not only because of landmines but also because of the poor road conditions, coupled with the strain of torrential rains during cyclone season. October had been selected for elections, precisely because it followed the best dry season of August and September. Hotels or guest houses were often a good choice for office premises since they resemble the infrastructure of an office building, and with some repairs and upgrading these were soon operational. The guesthouse that I found for rent in Pemba could take up to 200 people and with some imagination and creativity was converted within a few weeks into an accessible and well-equipped provincial headquarters. Every single material had to be ordered and brought from South Africa, through Maputo and through the regional office of Nampula, ranging from nails to office furniture to medical supplies. I also received 200 4 × 4 vehicles, set up a car garage, and hired a chief mechanic for its maintenance.

But the establishment of the district offices was a different story. Each district needed an exploratory mission to determine whether or not a house could be repaired or a tent camp was the only feasible way for an electoral center. There was a general agreement that the government facilitates the use of office premises, and if available provides a house for the electoral center. However, when word was out that ONUMOZ repaired the houses and left them anew, the houses in the worst of conditions were made available. No matter how good negotiation skills were, some of the houses provided were so bad, full of rodents and snakes, that it was far better to identify an accessible open space for a tent-camp.

Because of the difficult road access, some exploratory missions had to be made by helicopter, which were sent from the regional headquarters in Nampula. I had completed the evaluation of all the districts with the exception of Mueda, the northernmost town bordering Tanzania, next to the Rovuma river. Because of its difficult access, it was the last one on my list. As was the case for each of these trips, two civil police officers were at all times with me, together with an interpreter. In Mueda, the main language was Shimaconde, but they also spoke Emakhua, Kisuahili, Makue, Yao, and Ngoni e Kimuane. The town of Mueda was the center of the Makonde culture, known for the most beautiful ebony sculptures. Makonde were known as loyal, fierce, and strong people. In fact, to guard the small house by the sea where I lived, all had recommended to hire a Makua (i.e., someone from Makonde), namely because of the qualities so inherent in them. It turned out that one night my house and I were under attack, but the guard managed to take the rifles off of three men who were surrounding the house and left with only a few scratches. Under Portuguese rule, the Makonde nationalists organized a demonstration in front of the Mueda town square demanding independence – a protest that ended in a massacre, but also generated the birth of the guerrilla FRELIMO. Popular accounts said that during colonial times, they would self-inflict amputations to escape being taken as slaves. Mueda had also been the site of Portuguese operations against FRELIMO and had suffered great devastation. It did not have the breathtaking light of the Indian Ocean but an imperial river line. From the helicopter, one could only see bushes and sand, groups of huts (*aldeias*), and more bushes and sand. Today, the Mueda district has 15% urbanization, water is scarce because of its sandy soil, there is one sanitary unit for every 22,000 people, and one bed for every 2,800 people (Perfis Distritais, 2005); but back in 1994, the square had only one visible house, that of the Administrator. It was clear already from the helicopter sight that in this town we could only have a tent-camp, but we had to land.

What I will describe is not an accident but an unforgettable image that brought to my mind a perspective of the real task at hand. From the desolated sights of bushes and sand, I could see hundreds of people coming out of their huts to witness the arrival of the white helicopter. Children, youth, and the elderly – yes, the elderly of such admirable warriors – were all gathered in front of the square to see us land. In the midst of sand whirlpools caused by the helicopter, the scene was apocalyptic, yet what was I bringing? Peace? Democracy? Hope? When the doors of the helicopter opened, the crowd was surrounding us to the point of suffocation and had no idea about what in the world we meant. With great effort, we made our way to the house of the Administrator who ran back into his house when he saw us, but reappeared a few minutes later, with a huge tie and some broken eye glasses. I followed the protocol of explaining the reason for the visit, and together we identified what would be the best place for a tent-camp. The visit lasted a few minutes, enough to recover my heart not only from the desolation I had witnessed but also from the fact that I had so little to offer.

In the months ahead, the offices were prepared and staffed. Road access continued to be a big problem, but the civil police visited, in advance, the areas where the election centers would later be set up. In preparation for the arrival of the observers, they familiarized themselves with the grounds to help determine what resources were available. The civil police force consisted of personnel from various nations of the world who contributed to the peacekeeping effort by sending people to join the UN effort. It was the most diverse group imaginable; they came from Europe, Asia, Africa, Latin America, and from the Arab states. I remember colleagues from Norway, Spain, Portugal, Ghana, Bangladesh, Malaysia, Jordan, and Brazil. The cultural differences were so evident in the way in which each one of them understood their mandate. One day I sent an ambassador to one of the districts; he had come to observe the preparation of the district offices. He reported that in one district office a civil police officer was waiting at the air strip in his uniform since 7 a.m.; in another one, he found the police under a tree, drinking tea, with *capulanas* wrapped around them. (*Capulanas* are a sort of sarong made in Mozambique.)

But there was a delicate and complex dimension to the civil police presence. They were meant to patrol the villages and bring a sense of security to the local population. However, the roads being often sandy and unknown to the officers, car accidents were at times unavoidable, particularly since children would tend to run to the roads, simply to see the 4 × 4 patrol vehicle passing by. In view of the deplorable state of hospitals, chances of survival from car accidents were next to none. Therefore, whenever accidents did happen, the situation was tragic. Naturally, this evoked contradictions on the "protective" nature of the role of the civil police. I recall that at one of the meetings with the governor and the entire district administrators, I was given the floor to brief them about the plans for the electoral district offices. On that occasion, I was not introduced as part of the solution but as part of the problem. The relations with the local authorities were smoothed over time, but it took a comprehensive effort to identify areas of collaboration that had value for them.

When election time finally arrived, a vehicle equipped with meals ready to eat (MREs), water, petrol, tents, first-aid, a local driver, a civil police officer, and a translator awaited each one of the teams. Having drivers was the best way not only to avoid further accidents but also facilitated access to the remote areas of destination, with maps that were only approximate sketches of the main roads. As daunting as it sounds, the best briefing that I could think of was a step-by-step account of what would happen to them if a car accident took place – starting from the radio message that they would send, hopefully with a somewhat accurate identification of their location, the time span of getting a helicopter to them, an evacuation to Maputo, etc. I concluded that the accident rate objective was zero since their survival chances were also zero. I also emphasized that it was better to go in at funeral pace through the roads, but to avoid anyone's funeral. In the end, zero accidents were reported and all 200 staff and observers did an outstanding job. They were sent back safely to Maputo, reporting only one case of MRE food poisoning and two cases of malaria, including my own.

Reflections

For the purposes of a psychological discussion, pretend that you have landed from these journeys and want to put some order into your thinking, with a view to reflect on what is and can be the best contribution of I-O psychology to these type of assignments. My experiences in Afghanistan and later in Mozambique illustrate that work does not exist in a vacuum. It is not a discrete event separate from and devoid of life events. Also, workers are not merely employees. They are at the same time women, fathers, heads of households, and friends, whose non-work life spheres (family, religion, relationships, physical and mental health, and basic needs) affect and are affected by work. Viewing the worker as just a worker and not a whole person limits I-O psychology research, theory, and practice in non-Western contexts. A related concern is the distinct boundary that often exists between I-O and clinical psychology. For many reasons, the field of I-O psychology tends to stay away from clinical psychology "turf." Yet, a grasp of clinical psychology is likely to enhance I-O psychologists' understanding of work, workers, and working. So the first reflection that I make on the days in the life of humanitarian workers and the people they are trying to help is that the demarcations we have created between I-O and clinical psychology are possibly too artificially distinct, especially among workers dealing with trauma and its aftermath.

Consider the independent study on the effects of amputation on an Afghan child. What at first blush may seem to be an investigation unrelated to I-O psychology turned out to have important implications for work and thus for Humanitarian Work Psychology (HWP). By limiting work prospects, the amputation limited other prospects including opportunities for marriage, parenthood, social security, and sometimes even life itself in the case where parents chose death over amputation when faced with a seemingly non-productive child. The perceived capacity to work mended the tragic consequences of amputation, impacting on other important areas of life. Helping amputees and their families overcome the stigmas and challenges associated with the loss of a limb, and find work suited to their capabilities, could translate into productivity and well-being. The issue then becomes how to better integrate the vulnerable and people with disabilities in developing settings when they are often perceived as doomed for life. Hence the question: how is I-O psychology, with its tradition of maximizing fit between workers and work through psychometric assessments and work analysis, playing a role in helping to solve this problem, that is also loaded with cultural and social stigmas?

In 2008, a special issue of the *Journal of Organizational Behavior* posed the statement, "To prosper, organizational psychology should..." and asked authors complete this sentence. Gelfand, Leslie, and Fehr (2008) responded with an article summarized in four words: "adopt a global perspective." The authors point out that the field of I-O psychology was born out of a largely individualistic, Western, capitalist tradition, leading to a science that does not necessarily reflect the values, realities, priorities, and needs of the non-Western world. In other words, the very research questions that I-O psychologists ask are often based on assumptions that do not hold in many parts of the world. For example, the assumption that people are largely independent and have freedom of choice leads organizational research and theory to – at times inappropriately – prioritize the importance of self-actualization over the fulfillment of basic needs. In addition, "the assumptions of highly distinct boundaries among spheres of life, leads to the neglect of research questions that prioritize the overlap of family, friendship, and religion with organizational life as found in Non-Western cultures" (Gelfand et al., 2008, p. 495).

Gelfand et al. (2008) focused on the need for I-O psychology research and theory to adopt a global perspective. Of course, that is only part of the equation. If I-O psychology and HWP follow the scientist-practitioner model, meaning they apply research knowledge to their work, what, then, does all of this mean for the HWP practitioner? Which specific skills and competencies are needed to be a successful I-O psychologist across a variety of contexts? In its guidelines for education and training in I-O psychology, the Society for Industrial and Organizational Psychology discusses the importance of communication skills and facility at developing interpersonal relationships, as well as sensitivity to social and cultural diversity (Society for Industrial and Organizational Psychology, 1994, 1999). The need for such skills is evident for expatriate workforces, as is the need for characteristics deemed important for expatriate managers, such as cultural openness, adaptability, and stress tolerance (Mendenhall and Oddou, 1985; Templer, 2010).

Such qualities were required throughout the assignments in Afghanistan and Mozambique. Consider, for example, the engineer in Afghanistan whose chief's angry outburst profoundly violated his sense of honor and threatened his role as head of household. What could have been a minor incident in some cultures escalated to the point of resignation. Interpersonal skills and cultural sensitivity were needed to avoid and later diffuse this situation and resolve the problem. Likewise, leading the effort to prepare the province of Cabo Delgado for elections also necessitated a variety of competencies important from the HWP viewpoint. Soft skills as well as knowledge of core areas of I-O psychology (e.g., training, motivation) were needed to deal effectively with police demonstrating varying levels of engagement, to negotiate accommodations, to establish constructive working relations with the local populations and authorities, and to persuade drivers and election teams to avoid accidents and prepare for unexpected contingencies.

Yet, it is within administrative budgets that are being perpetually cut that the human resources challenges to ensure the presence of this workforce is managed within international organizations. Of course, think tanks of psychologists are not affordable. But there is a competent I-O psychologist community out there, more and more interested in making a difference in the lives of the underserved. After a glimpse into these two journeys, and some understanding of the dimension of the mandates, the huge administrative and logistics burdens, the tight deadlines and constrained resources, how can I-O psychologists better address the complexity of the human resource dimension of the task at hand? From the purely HR (human resources) viewpoint, global talent management is for sure one key area, that is, selecting, preparing, and managing the international staff for these environments. So are values and psychological fitness. Besides the skill-set that they bring, what are the uncompromising values and psychological fitness that they must travel with, and which tools could be used to measure them and support them? How does one measure the abilities that will be needed on a daily basis to cope efficiently with the complex and dynamic environments which people working in these environments have to face?

Assuming that one needs the right leadership, internal culture, and skills to effectively lead organizations, a reflection on these key areas is needed for the contexts in question. And if culture is largely based on beliefs and values, understanding how people form beliefs may be a starting point of training for the staff who take on these assignments. And if personal experience is an important factor to shape beliefs and values, how can organizations facilitate the reality checks that have the potential of changing people's beliefs? Bearing in mind the high personal cost that these assignments may have on the lives of the staff, HR departments need a formula of gain to attract the best staff, one that is beyond financial incentives. Then, how does one evaluate the value that these missions will bring to the staff and the benefit they will bring to the people they are called to serve? How does one measure often intangible results?

Nobody will deny the importance of culture in the elaboration of assessment and training tools for the international workforce, yet less argument is made on the crucial relevance of psychology. It is still a myth. Both need to take a larger role in selection and staff development. In any case, framing the cultural and psychological context before an assignment is taken on is not as straightforward a task as one may think. It is not merely describing what matters in the culture, but understanding the complexity of cultural and psychological effects in war and post-war environments, for instance. And most importantly, it is about providing elements for understanding the dynamics of such changing environments. Being able to reflect on how people form beliefs, and what impressions resonate in people's minds more than others (the heuristics in the case of the official who did not greet the people); or basic knowledge about interactions between an individual and his or her environment (the case of amputated children); or about the differences in appreciation that certain things bring to people (the example of toys for Afghan children), depending on whether or not they have been lacking them for a long time; or the way in which people remember what struck them, understanding how people process episodes of their life – lengthy or short-lived ones, happy or sad – are just among the few things that could sensitize interventions in such highly complex environments and be the best travel advisor for the staff in these humanitarian assignments. This workforce also has to prepare to deal with emotionally charged issues in a difficult world and be able to provide comfort for others. Empirical methods to develop the most appropriate language and approach for the multicultural workforce that undertakes these tasks in all parts of the world are also some examples of what the I-O community can think about. That and more . . .

In the end, whatever was valuable to the peoples in such difficult situations as the ones described in Afghanistan or Mozambique, bringing aid to them entailed challenges of all kinds. While one can always question the extent to which one is able to change their realities for the better, one cannot question the crucial importance of the ultimate messengers of the mandates coming from the UN and its numerous bodies. Indeed, I think of UN staff in the field as the ultimate messengers since so many steps precede the day on which they finally land on the ground and roll up their sleeves for whatever their individual and collective task. But also because they are the closest hand to the people the UN is called to serve. There is also no doubt that all those involved along the way, from staff working on administrative procedures or highly skilled political negotiators, rely on those ultimate messengers to carry out the work, to fly the blue flag. So what is their message about? And who are these messengers? Let me rephrase it, who should be these messengers?

I would argue that their mere presence is a message of hope and courage. While everything else that follows their presence is of importance, the fact that they are not absent in the places where help is most needed is in itself a sign of hope. And shortening the distance between contemplative perspectives as well as the lands where others are suffering is also a message of courage. It is no longer seeing the world from outside but as actors inside the world we are in, at whichever point in time. It is not without personal sacrifice that staff members come to serve in these non-family duty stations. Any blame stemming from not doing things as efficiently and effectively as possible cannot compare to the potential blame and guilt stemming from remaining absent. Presence meets half of the challenge, and they need all the help they can get for the other half. As for the ultimate messengers, may I ask the readers to complete this sentence: "To fly the blue flag, the ultimate messengers should be . . ."

References

Dupree, L. (1980). *Afghanistan*. Princeton, NJ: Princeton University Press.

Gelfand, M. J., Leslie, L. M., & Fehr, R. (2008). To prosper, organizational psychology should . . . adopt a global perspective. *Journal of Organizational Behavior*, 29, 493–517.

Mendenhall, M., & Oddou, G. (1985). The dimensions of expatriate acculturation: A review. *Academy of Management Review*, 10, 39–47.

Perfis Distritais (2005). *Ministerio da Administracao Estatal de Mozambique*.

Reibel, A. J. (2010). An African success story: Civil society and the "Mozambican miracle". *Africana*, 4(1), 78–102.

Society for Industrial and Organizational Psychology, Inc. (1994). *Guidelines for Education and Training at the Master's Level in Industrial-Organizational Psychology*. Arlington Heights, IL: Author.

Society for Industrial and Organizational Psychology, Inc. (1999). *Guidelines for Education and Training at the Doctoral Level in Industrial-Organizational Psychology*. Bowling Green, OH: Author.

Templer, K. J. (2010). Personal attributes of expatriate managers, subordinate ethnocentrism, and expatriate success: A host-country perspective. *The International Journal of Human Resource Management*, 21, 1754–1768.

The World Bank (2013a). Population ages 0–14 (% of total): 1988–1992. World Development Indicators. Retrieved June 25, 2013, from http://data.worldbank.org/indicator/SP.POP.0014.TO.ZS?page=4.

The World Bank (2013b). Population, total: 1988–1992. World Development Indicators. Retrieved June 25, 2013, from http://data.worldbank.org/indicator/SP.POP.TOTL?page=4.

The World Bank (2013c). Mortality rate, under 5 (per 1,000 live births): 1988–1992. World Development Indicators. Retrieved June 25, 2013, from http://data.worldbank.org/indicator/SH.DYN.MORT?page=4.

UNICEF (2013). The state of the world's children 2013: Children with disabilities. New York: United Nations Children's Fund (UNICEF). Retrieved June 25, 2013, from http://www.unicef.org/sowc2013/files/SWCR2013_ENG_Lo_res_24_Apr_2013.pdf.

United Nations (2013). Mozambique – ONUMOZ: Facts and figures. Retrieved June 25, 2013, from http://www.un.org/en/peacekeeping/missions/past/onumozF.html.

Weinstein, J. M. (2002). Mozambique: A fading UN success story. *Journal of Democracy*, 13(1), 141–156.

3
International Development and I-O Psychology in Sub-Saharan Africa: Perspectives from Local and Expatriate Standpoints

Inusah Abdul-Nasiru and Alexander E. Gloss

Summary

This chapter describes the work of the two authors who served separately to help improve the quality of education in different sub-Saharan African countries: Ghana and South Africa. While both authors were not I-O psychologists at the time, their experiences involved applying industrial and organizational (I-O) psychology principles and helped shaped their current perspectives, and careers, as I-O psychologists. While both authors were associated with development initiatives tied to the United States, their perspectives represent different sides of traditional development projects as one brought the perspective of someone from the United States to South Africa while the other brought a local Ghanaian perspective and expertise to his project in Ghana. The authors' projects involved a range of topics from I-O psychology including motivation and organizational development, but they highlight select challenges and priorities that are frequently prominent in development work, namely, communication difficulties, the importance of strengthening relationships between stakeholders, and physical security. They discuss and explore the ramifications of these challenges and priorities, including how they reflect on the importance of issues of identity, power, and justice in international development work.

Introduction

Many forms of work contain at least the implicit goal of improving or "developing" others. From teachers to business consultants, improving the welfare of other people is frequently an important goal of many occupations. People in these occupations deal with a host of psychological issues that pertain to the dynamics of one person helping another to improve, including learning, training, self-efficacy, and empowerment. The complexity of forms of work devoted to developing others increases only when the social, political, historical, economic, linguistic, or cultural identity of one person involved in the process is different from others. This complexity rises further as entire organizations, communities, and nations become involved either as those providing development assistance or as targets of that assistance. Finally, these forms of work take on especially unique, and potentially perilous, dynamics when particularly marginalized and vulnerable populations are targeted as the recipients of assistance.

International development work typically combines all of the sources of complexity mentioned above. This chapter contains two case studies of the authors' divergent, yet related, experiences in conducting work within the international development system. We highlight our experiences because they both led and have influenced our careers and interests in I-O psychology. More importantly, we believe these experiences include examples of important challenges and priorities that are often salient in international development work. In particular, we highlight the frequent challenges inherent in communication across boundaries of sociocultural identity and in settings with limited transportation and communication infrastructure. Moreover, we also highlight the importance of building strong and respectful relationships with a diverse range of stakeholders in development projects. Furthermore, we mention and discuss the difficulties that both authors had in accessing relevant research from I-O psychology germane to their settings and forms of work. Finally, through comparisons of the experiences of both authors, we highlight the important distinction between expatriates and host-country nationals and the associated role of identity, justice, and power in international development work. The authors hope that the topics considered in this chapter will give the reader a more thorough understanding of the synthesis of I-O psychology's topics and methods with international development work in lower-income settings which house the vast majority of the world's population.

Before discussing the work that both authors undertook, it is useful to give some additional background both on international development and on how the authors came to be involved in this work.

International development

Broadly speaking, the international development system is concerned with the deliberate widespread enhancement of human welfare. The enhancement of human welfare, or human "development," is often conceptualized along three basic and seemingly universally valued dimensions: health, education, and income (United Nations Development Programme, 2010). That is, development can be measured in part by a person's or people's life expectancy, years of education, and financial income. Efforts to enhance or accelerate development can be characterized based upon whether they are more short term and/or crisis related, or whether they are more long term and better integrated into everyday activities. The former efforts are commonly referred to as humanitarian aid while the latter efforts are known as development work. For example, a response to a natural disaster by a non-governmental organization like the Red Cross or Red Crescent would be characterized as a form of humanitarian aid while a long-term project by an intergovernmental organization like the United Nations to supply clean water to lower-income nations would be considered development work. The work of both authors of this chapter is perhaps best considered to be a form of international development work.

Humanitarian aid and development work are carried out by a broad variety of actors operating both within individual countries and internationally. Distinctions between the organizations involved can be made based upon whether they are public (e.g., country governments), for-profit private businesses (e.g., Land Rover), non-profit and non-governmental (e.g., Save the Children), or part of partnerships or agreements between country governments (e.g., the United Nations). Another distinction can be made between aid and development efforts that are carried out by fully salaried professionals, by volunteers with varying degrees of qualifications or training, or by individuals mandated to serve for a specified period of time.

As an estimate of the size of the professional humanitarian aid and development system, the Active Learning Network for Accountability and Performance in Humanitarian Action (2011) estimates that the flow of finances to humanitarian emergencies totaled $16 billion in 2010 and involved over 274,000 field staff. These figures notably do not include non-emergency outflows of funding and support nor do they reflect the number of people involved in supporting those field staff. Getting a picture of the number of people involved in volunteering efforts related to international development and humanitarian aid proves more difficult, but two statistics reflect the tremendous number of people and resources involved. In 2011, 17% of the US population or approximately 52 million people, were engaged in travel related to volunteering for civic and religious activities on a given weekend or holiday (Bureau of Labor Statistics, 2012). While many of the people might not be traditionally considered engaged in a form of humanitarian aid or development work, the act of assisting in the improvement of the welfare of others is obviously quite common and widespread. While many people volunteer to provide humanitarian or development assistance, many others are mandated by various governmental authorities to serve their communities or the communities of others. For example, in Ghana, university graduates are required to complete a one-year term of community service that doubles as a chance to gain work experience related to their education. During the 2010–2011 time period, approximately 53,420 individuals were enrolled in this program (Ghana National Service Scheme, 2013). Non-military mandatory service schemes also exist in other countries from Nigeria's National Youth Service Scheme to Israel's Sherut Leumi program.

Civic service

Like many who have participated in the international development system, both authors of this chapter found themselves in international development work through civic service programs organized by the governments of their home countries. Inusah joined Ghana's National Service Scheme while Alexander joined the US Peace Corps. In Ghana, students who graduate from tertiary institutions are required under law to complete one year of civic service. With an undergraduate degree in psychology and interest in community development, Inusah was selected to work as a district facilitator on the Community School Alliance (CSA) project led by the Education Development Centre (EDC) – an international non-profit specializing in education, health, and economic development. The CSA project in Ghana is devoted to improving the effectiveness of primary education by building community participation with those schools. The project is funded from a prominent development donor organization – the United States Agency for International Development (USAID) – which is the United States' official entity for foreign development assistance.

In contrast with the system in Ghana, the United States does not make civil service a mandatory requirement for its youth or tertiary graduates. Instead, a wide range of options are available for voluntary service within the country or around the world through both private and public civil-service organizations. One major public entity that provides opportunities for civic service abroad is the US Peace Corps. Founded in 1961, the Peace Corps is an independent agency in the US government that is charged with the threefold mission of providing technical assistance to foreign countries, helping people outside of the United States to understand US culture, and helping US citizens to understand the cultures of other countries (www.peacecorp.gov). After completing his undergraduate education in international relations, Alexander chose to undertake the US Peace Corps' standard 27-month assignment and was appointed to work in the School and Community Resource Program in the Republic of South Africa. Similar to the CSA project, this program has as its aim the enhancement of education via the direct support of schools with technical assistance and the building of stronger community participation with schools.

Our experiences

To give an in-depth understanding of the work of both authors, we provide narrative accounts of our work in Ghana and South Africa. Following these narratives, we reflect on their potential broader implications for international development work and organizations in developing settings.

Community School Alliance Project, Kadjebi District, Volta Region, Ghana: Inusah Abdul-Nasiru

Daily life and objectives

I worked as a Cohort-IV District Facilitator with the CSA project. CSA was responsible for community mobilization toward education development and was a key component of USAID's Quality Improvement in Primary Schools (QUIPS) project. At CSA, I worked with selected primary schools in five communities in the Kadjebi District, located in the Volta Region of Ghana. To begin my work, I had moved from Accra, the capital of the country, some 200 kilometers away. However, I was familiar with the rural and remote environment of the area because I had grown up in Chinderi, a small town in another district in the same region of the country. While in the Kadjebi District, I lived in one community and would then spend a night or two in other communities in order to successfully complete an initiative. This was necessary because transportation between the various communities was a major challenge.

The communities were more than ten kilometers apart, and the road network was very poor and vehicles were often either unable or unavailable to provide transport between my schools. There were instances when projects and trips to communities had to be cancelled due to transportation issues. On some occasions, I would have to walk several kilometers through the bush using farm paths to be able to make it to some of the partnership school communities. In addition, using phones was frequently difficult; in fact, at the time, there was only one public telephone booth, serving the towns and communities in the whole district, and this comes with its challenges – having to queue for several hours to be able to place a call and then to wait for feedback. Other modes of communication like videoconferencing were impossible.

As a project, our general objective was to build the capacity of community members to participate in, and take ownership of, the educational system. In general, I served as the link between the CSA and several stakeholders, including school administrators, community chiefs/elders, parents, teachers, pupils, and general community members in the communities surrounding our partnership schools. Our ultimate aim was an improvement in the number of contact hours between teachers and students and an improvement in the quality of the learning and teaching environment at the school. Put another way, we were seeking to bring about change in the fundamentals of schooling: ensuring that children came to school on a daily basis, stayed in school from year to year, and enjoyed an environment at school where they could learn. These are particularly important goals in Ghana because the education system in the country is struggling to tackle large social issues – consider, for instance, that the literacy rate for men is 78.3%, and 65.3% for women (Central Intelligence Agency, 2013). On a national and big-picture level, my activities were designed to meet two overlapping purposes: helping to make the projects of the CSA sustainable, and helping realize aspects of the Ghanaian government's goals of providing and requiring free and compulsory universal basic education.

On a daily basis, I concentrated my efforts on supporting the specific objectives in each community's School Performance Improvement Plans (SPIPs) that were drafted, reviewed, and approved jointly by community members and the CSA. In order to support community members in achieving the goals set in the various SPIPs, I participated in everything from planning community meetings (known as *durbar*), holding training sessions, helping to run school drama performances, and inducing communal labor activities toward school developmental projects. In addition, I occasionally organized training sessions in a number of topics, including, building trust in the school system, improving relationship between teachers and community members, monitoring school pupils' performance, and improving collaboration between community members and district authorities. As a specific example of a challenge that I faced, at least one of the schools I worked at had identified that pupils' reading and mathematics abilities far behind where they needed to be. We believed that part of the problem was that children were not spending enough time working on homework when they returned home from school. We formed committees of parents and community leaders that helped to find and promote ways to get children to study.

Building community ties

The success of my job revolved around my ability to win the confidence of a wide number of different stakeholders. The CSA project involved people of all sorts – from expatriates from Western nations, and Ghanaians from all over the country, to members of the very communities we were working in. While it was helpful that I was a Ghanaian, and could speak the local dialect, it was not always easy to build trust with local community members. It should be mentioned that my background in psychology and appreciation of 'individual differences' helped in handling some of these challenges. Moreover, regular communication was challenging in the sense that because of communication-infrastructure limitations, once I left a community, it was extremely difficult to stay in touch until I returned there physically. This situation was only exacerbated by the difficulty in transportation mentioned earlier.

Winning the confidence of stakeholders became easier during the course of my one year as a district facilitator. I found that I was more successful when, in conjunction with stakeholders, we set specific goals and then worked together with those stakeholders to accomplish those goals. Only in reflecting back on these behaviors as an I-O psychologist do I now fully understand what it was that I was doing – namely, I was employing goal-setting techniques and adopting the participant-observer method to both understand and change the behavior of those I was working with. This method was helpful because it allowed me to build and develop both rapport with community members and maintain a sense of progress.

Performance management

A big part of my role was monitoring the success of the various initiatives that I was engaged in. In turn, every month I would communicate these results to the CSA project headquarters in the form of official reports. One of our most important measures of success was pupil learning as evaluated on standardized tests. However, these test scores would not capture all of the change that was taking place in the schools and communities that I worked in. On a daily basis, my visits to schools would involve monitoring progress made on different initiatives – like those meant to sharpen the management skills of school administrations as well as improvement in relationships between teachers on one hand and community members on the other. In addition, we would collect feedback on our initiatives from the community by bringing parents and community leaders together in durbars. Despite these metrics and sources of feedback, it was not always easy to evaluate the success of my work – especially when it came to individual training projects on topics that were more interpersonal than concrete (e.g., trainings designed to improve collaboration between community members and district authorities).

Reflection

Personally, I place great importance on being part of positive social change and the values and objectives of the CSA were in alignment with this desire. My experiences as a district facilitator during my national service were a major turning point in my life. It was this service that interested me in improving my skills in areas such as training and performance management. I had only limited exposure to I-O psychology through undergraduate courses, and when combined with some basic insights from my course in community psychology, I could see how important an understanding of psychology's role in work at the interface of formal organizations and the community could be for the sake of regional development. Not only did I see the important role of topics like training in the welfare of my entire nation, but I also saw that the development of that welfare, and movement on important metrics like literacy, was dependent on a holistic approach that included a broad swatch of stakeholders like community leaders that might not otherwise be included in a training program.

During the course of my service, I decided to enroll in a graduate program in I-O psychology. I knew that a greater understanding of I-O psychology and its tools could help me, as well as others, to do an even better job helping to serve the underserved. However, I-O psychology had not fully taken root in Ghana – indeed, while there are gifted professors with backgrounds in I-O psychology, there are currently none that had been educated in Ghana beyond the masters' level – the few with PhD qualifications were educated outside of Ghana. At the time of writing up this piece, I am likely to become the first doctoral student in I-O psychology to graduate from a university in Ghana. I hope many more will follow me and will devote their efforts to tackling many of the issues that our society faces.

The School and Community Resource Program, Northern Cape Province, South Africa: Alexander E. Gloss

Daily life and objectives

I lived and worked for 27 months in the Northern Cape Province of South Africa for the US Peace Corps' School and Community Resource Program. On a typical day, I would wake up in the room my host family had generously lent me for the duration of my stay. My accommodations were modest, but comfortable. My room was approximately 3×3 meters and covered by a tin roof. I lived in a densely populated community known as a township – a planned community which was formed under the racist apartheid regime as a place to house non-white South Africans. The township I lived in, which housed approximately 100,000 people, was not only a bustling and vibrant place, but also riddled by extremely high levels of violence and crime. According to the rules of the Peace Corps, I could not drive a car to work – so after eating breakfast, I would set out on my bicycle for a half-an-hour ride to make rounds at one or more of the three local primary and secondary schools I was charged with assisting. This mode of transportation was helpful because it meant I was not reliant on others to provide me a ride and could move quickly between schools – attending to a number of different priorities in an efficient fashion. Despite its benefits however, this mode of transportation was also problematic. On two separate occasions during the first two years of my service, I was physically assaulted on my bicycle; luckily both times I managed to escape with minor bumps and bruises. The motivations of my attackers were unclear, but because of the attacks Peace Corps moved my residence from the township to a neighboring predominately white and affluent neighborhood. After the move, I kept working in the township schools and commuting on bicycle, but I had lost much of my connection to my host family in the township.

Normally I would try and visit at least two schools per day. I would typically arrive and greet the school management and office staff and begin work on any number of initiatives that we had jointly agreed to undertake. My mission from Peace Corps was deliberately vague and they strongly encouraged me to spend at least several weeks observing, speaking with, and learning from the school management, teachers, and district officials before my specific projects were solidified. At some schools, it was decided that I should try and undertake a collaborative school-management reform initiative wherein I would assist the school principal to hold regular meetings devoted to reforming the school's constitution, revamping its management plans and policies, and strengthening channels for communication with and management of the school's teachers. At other schools, it was identified that teachers desired further assistance in the delivery of their mathematics curriculum.

Challenges and resources

Having scant pedagogical training or education, and having only recently graduated from university, I knew that I was hopelessly unqualified to engage in this work by myself. Yet being an outsider and foreigner, it seemed that many people deferred to my opinion, trusted me, and were usually ready and willing to listen to and try my suggestions. To overcome my lack of experience, and to maximize the effect of my role as an outsider, I worked closely with the principals and managers at the schools I was assigned to and helped them to carry out their reform agendas. In practice, this meant everything from drafting policies and plans, designing a new supplementary mathematics curriculum and training program, to convening school meetings as an impartial moderator. Without a background in education or I-O psychology, approaching these tasks proved to be especially difficult as they required conducting customized research into curriculum development, training, and motivational interventions. Unfortunately, locating research customized to a non-Western or lower-income setting was extremely difficult and often best-practices from Western and high-income countries like the United States were used in lieu of more contextualized solutions.

Drawing upon best-practices and research from places like the United States proved problematic as many of the realities present in the schools I was assigned were dramatically different from the educational settings that were assumed in the literature I was able to locate. Outside of questions of local culture and traditions, a large share of students came from families living in deep poverty and faced profound social issues like one of the world's highest prevalence of HIV/AIDS and high levels of shockingly brutal violence and crime. School facilities were often dilapidated due to neglect and an inefficient use of funds. Worse, a culture of learning and teaching was often entirely absent. A large segment of teachers would actively teach for far less than half of the school day and large numbers of children would be wandering the school grounds aimlessly at any given time. Nevertheless, many teachers would frequently demonstrate great passion, talent, and devotion to their profession in the face of overwhelming obstacles including a lack of resources and students who had been passed on through the years without having learned to read, write, and conduct simple arithmetic.

Motivation

As my time in South Africa wore on, I began to pay greater attention to the issue of teacher motivation. I had identified that South Africa, by many measures the most prosperous country on the continent, spends well above the global average on education in relation to their gross domestic product but it lags far behind many African countries on basic measures of literacy and numeracy (South African Human Resource Development Council, 2010). This gap between expenditure and performance was quite perplexing and, based upon existing research from the field of economics (e.g., Van der Berg et al., 2011) and my own observation, I began to put a large share of the blame on often poorly trained and disillusioned teachers who were frequently neither supported nor held accountable by the managers of their institutions. Another reason for my increased focus on motivation was my realization that the teaching and management resources and systems that I, and many others, had helped to developed were often ineffectual or useless without being adopted by a stakeholder who was both able and interested in implementing them.

To tackle the issue of motivation, I developed and video-recorded a motivational presentation and workshop. Without a deeper understanding of motivational theories, I appealed to the social justice sensibilities of the teachers I was working with (many of whom helped to lead the historic fight against the apartheid regime) by highlighting the degree to which educational disparities were creating new social inequalities in the post-racial democratic South Africa. Through an evocative imagery and compelling statistics (e.g., that unemployment for South Africans who had not completed their secondary education was over 66% in 2007 while only 0.7% for South Africans with a university degree; South African Human Resource Development Council, 2010) I made the case that the country's teachers were the new freedom fighters for South Africa's impoverished, predominately black African, youth. I argued that freedom and opportunity were no longer inhibited by racist laws – they were now inhibited by illiteracy and economic inequality and the resulting social ills of disease, crime, and social discord.

Identity and inequality

For some time I had begun to notice that my identity as a young and white man from the United States was a barrier to my work. This was the case for two reasons; first, I realized that my understanding of many situations and issues were skewed by my own background and cultural assumptions about the work-related norms, values, and priorities of the people I was working with and second, many of the teachers and school managers I interacted with dismissed initiatives I was involved in as arising from an irrelevant or inappropriate foreign perspective. Despite the fact that many aspects of the projects I was engaged in were developed by the managers I was working with, my identity sometimes became an excuse, and other times a legitimate reason, for inaction or opposition.

Unfortunately, the realities of the interlocking matrix of educational failure, inequality, and the high levels of crime and violence that South Africa was plagued with intervened in my own life toward the end of my Peace Corps service. While riding my bicycle to deliver the second part of my two-part motivation workshop at one of the secondary schools I was working at, I was ambushed by three gang-members just meters away from the school entrance. They had intended to murder me as an initiation ritual but luckily I managed to escape with serious but not life-threating knife wounds. Out of a concern for my safety, Peace Corps removed me from my site entirely and relocated me to their headquarters in the capital of the country. Two of the three gang-members were arrested, the third one having been killed in a neighboring township, so I was asked to stay for the duration of my service to testify against them in trial. This allowed me to finish some, but not all, of my work with the schools. During the trial, I learned that one of my attackers was a former student at the school I was traveling to when I was assaulted. He was only a teenager, and despite having made it to secondary school, he was functionally illiterate. The failures of the schooling system in South Africa had quite literally nearly cost me my life and undermined the support I was providing to those very schools.

Reflection

My experience in South Africa convinced me that the issues covered by I-O psychology are crucial to the development of nations. I set out on an entirely new career track to pursue study in the newly founded sub-discipline of Humanitarian Work Psychology which promised to integrate perspectives and priorities from lower-income settings with the broader discipline's set of theories and tools.

I-O psychology's engagement with international development

Reflecting on the narratives of our experiences working to assist the education systems in two countries in sub-Saharan Africa, we were both struck by the many similarities and important differences. Focusing first on the similarities, both authors were connected to, and in ways employed by, programs from the United States to enhance the performance of schools in challenged educational systems. Both authors were working relatively underprepared to deal with the issues they faced in these systems and were charged with engaging alongside a diversity of stakeholders in their schools and communities.

By looking at these narratives we can see at least three important common themes. First, in both Ghana and South Africa, the authors encountered difficulties in communication with project stakeholders; second, a key element in both authors' projects was the importance of building connections to a variety of stakeholders; and third, both authors ran up against limitations of existing literature and theories in I-O psychology in relation to the work they were conducting.

The course of both authors' projects were shaped by the inability to communicate effectively, but this inability emerged from different sources. While Inusah was hindered by a lack of efficient transportation and communication infrastructure, Alexander was prevented from the most efficient collaboration due to the intersecting divisions of nationality, culture, race, and age. Both of these communication limitations are representative of the types of challenges often found in international development work. We look more closely into each in turn.

In Alexander's case, communication was limited by various aspects of personal identity, including nationality, culture, race, and age. Some of these limitations to effective communication and collaboration – that is, culture – are relatively well researched in the field of I-O psychology (see, e.g., Erez, 2011). What seems to be less appreciated in organizational psychology's consideration of international forms of work are potential limitations to communication and collaboration that emerge from socioeconomics and power. The socioeconomic and power aspects of differences in identity might not be as obviously manifest as race, nationality, and age – but they are certainly important underlying dynamics in interpersonal relations in a country with incredibly high rates of poverty, extreme socioeconomic inequality, and a long history of racial oppression. Alexander is a young Caucasian man with a livelihood secured by the US Peace Corps – a branch of a government that once actively supported the racist apartheid policies of the South African state. While many of the precise issues mentioned above are somewhat unique to the South Africa–US bilateral relationship, they are broadly indicative of trends within international development scenarios wherein former colonial powers send volunteer and professional assistance to lower-income countries. MacLachlan, Carr, and McAuliffe (2010) highlight both power and identity as two of three fundamental dynamics that can inhibit effective international development work. The third dynamic – that of justice – was perhaps no less present in Alexander's case. Perceptions of justice – especially from the standpoint of teachers whose jobs might have been affected by his work are likely to have been strong determinants of interpersonal relations at the schools where he worked. Continued research into the aspects of interpersonal work relations that result from socioeconomics and historical injustice will go a long way toward a better understanding of interpersonal dynamics in international development work.

In Inusah's case, the ability to build trust, rapport, and accountability was not constrained as much by differences in identity as by limited transportation and communication infrastructure. Again, this seems to be broadly representative of many forms of work in lower-income settings. In terms of communication infrastructure, despite extraordinary growth in many communication media, a divide in information and communication technology (ICT) prevalence remains deep between lower- and higher-income countries (International Telecommunications Union, 2010) and an advanced and efficient transportation infrastructure is closely tied to levels of economic modernization and industrialization often not present in some lower-income settings. A great deal of research in I-O psychology has sought to understood the ramifications of ICTs on the workplace – especially in forms of work that involve great physical distance (see, e.g., Leung and Peterson, 2011). However, Inusah did not encounter difficulties emerging from particularly great amounts of physical distance, but instead, physical divides that were particularly difficult to efficiently traverse either physically or virtually. Greater research into the effects of limitations in transportation and communication infrastructure will go some way to better understanding the unique challenges to forms of work in lower-income settings.

In addition to difficulties in communication, both narratives reflected the importance of building ties between multiple stakeholders, both inside schools and within the broader community. The need to conduct work with a complex and diverse group of stakeholders is certainly not unique to international development work. What is perhaps somewhat unique is the relative importance of the ties between those stakeholders to the outcomes of such work. Often, the strengthening of community and organizational ties are both a means to an end and an end in themselves. Indeed, these ties are often important components in the socio-structural elements of individual, group, and community empowerment (Spreitzer, 2008). The importance of working cooperatively with, and aligning one's efforts to the priorities of, a diverse range of stakeholders is highlighted by important standards of best-practice within the humanitarian/international development community – including the Organisation for Economic Co-operation and Development's Paris Declaration on Aid Effectiveness. This declaration, adopted in 2005 by over 100 countries, "defines the principles and commitments by which donors and partner governments intend to ensure that aid is as effective as possible in contributing to the Millennium Development Goals and other internationally agreed objectives" (Organisation for Economic Co-operation and Development, 2009, p. 3). The declaration includes five principles of best-practice, including the need for "harmonization" and "alignment" which mandate the coordination of any humanitarian/development initiatives with existing efforts and the orientation of those efforts toward the goals of relevant stakeholders. As the Paris Declaration makes clear, the efficient management of humanitarian/development work, and its effectiveness in accomplishing tangible project outcomes like the improvement of student homework performance, is only one important consideration in a project's success. A project's ability to have capacitated community empowerment through stronger social ties is often a second, and critically important, outcome. As seen in Inusah's case, international development work can focus explicitly upon the ties between a formal organization and the broader community. Increased research in I-O psychology has begun to be conducted on this subject through the guise of triple bottom-line accounting which emphasizes the social impact of an organization on its community (see, e.g., Aguinis, 2011). We call for increased research on the nature of these organizational-community ties and the ways to enhance them that maximize the empowerment of stakeholders and the effectiveness of development projects.

Alongside the themes of communication difficulties and the importance of ties between stakeholders, both authors' narratives also highlighted the limitations of research in I-O psychology. Both authors found existing work in I-O psychology to be of limited relevance to their work because it often did not account for the unique cultural and socioeconomic dynamics of the settings in which they were engaging and because it did not account for the unique nature of the work in which they were engaging. This assertion is simply a reflection that, as has been pointed out above, research in I-O psychology has not substantially engaged with organizational dynamics in lower-income settings, with work that involves individuals from higher- and lower-income countries, and with work that emphasizes building social ties and empowerment as an end in itself. Part of this claim was echoed by Gelfand, Leslie, and Fehr (2008) in their reflection on the limitations of the field. There, they pointed out that organizational psychology has limited its attention to concerns and realities of the predominately high-income "post-materialist" world where material and physical security are better established than in lower-income settings.

In addition to the similarities and common themes, there were also several important differences in our experiences. One author worked in a distinctly rural environment while another operated in a dense urban environment. In addition, the narratives noted the prominence of concern for physical security in South Africa and the relatively absence of such a concern in Ghana. Finally, and perhaps most fundamentally, Alexander engaged in his work from the standpoint of an expatriate while Inusah worked in his home country alongside other host-country nationals. Perhaps just as importantly, Alexander's identity was that of someone from a nation traditionally responsible for providing international development assistance, whereas Inusah's identity was that of someone from a nation who traditionally receives such assistance.

As highlighted in Alexander's narrative, but not as prominent in Inusah's, lower-income settings are not merely defined by limitations in physical security (United Nations Development Programme, 1994). This includes issues of warfare, crime, and political instability. As is obvious from Alexander's case, these issues can directly affect the course of international development work. However, considerations of physical security can also directly affect organizational behavior in important ways. For example, in the case in South Africa, considerations for students' and teachers' physical safety were concerns that necessarily defined the work setting and overrode other considerations such as task performance and job satisfaction. While issues like job satisfaction and organizational commitment are likely important in any setting, they are likely to be greatly influenced by variation in physical security of the surrounding community. Existing research on military personnel and others operating in physically insecure conditions might yield important insight in this regard but more direct research in lower-income settings that suffer from physical insecurity will be key to properly understanding international development work.

While the motives of all of Alexander's attackers were never fully determined – it was clear that his identity as a white man in a predominately black African area contributed to him being targeted. However, issues of identity in Alexander's case were not limited to race as his national background and age also helped to shape unique dynamics of power and privilege between him and those he worked with in his schools. In this way, Alexander's narrative provides a useful example of the difficulties inherent in development work that involves expatriates. In contrast, Inusah's narrative – while certainly not determinative evidence – is a good example of how challenges relating to identity might be avoided by employing host-country nationals in international development projects. The importance of the distinction between expatriate and host-country national is not accidental; this distinction is central to the dynamics of power, identity, and justice that Carr et al. (2012) put forward as central to the success of international development work. Research into the implications of the expatriate/host-country national for organizational behavior has begun to play a more prominent role in I-O psychology (see, e.g., Carr et al., 2011).

Conclusion

As demonstrated through the narratives of our authors' experiences in civic service in the education sector in sub-Saharan Africa, international development work is often complex, challenging, and potentially perilous. Yet, this work serves as a way to potentially benefit some of the world's most marginalized populations. As has been demonstrated through our personal experiences, there are a number of issues that I-O psychology needs to consider for it to most usefully engage with international development work and work in lower-income settings in general. These considerations include the impact of a region's transportation and communication infrastructure, the importance of building ties between multiple stakeholders, physical security, and the implications of the expatriate/host-country national distinction.

References

Active Learning Network for Accountability and Performance in Humanitarian Action (2011). The state of the humanitarian system: Assessing performance and progress. Retrieved from www.alnap.org/stateofsystem.

Aguinis, H. (2011). Organizational responsibility: Doing good and doing well. In S. Zedeck (Ed.), *APA Handbook of Industrial and Organizational Psychology,* Vol 3: Maintaining, expanding, and contracting the organization (pp. 855–879). Washington, DC: American Psychological Association. doi: 10.1037/12171-024.

Bureau of Labor Statistics (2012). Organizational, civic, and religious activities. Retrieved from http://www.bls.gov/tus/current/volunteer.htm.

Carr, S.C., Legatt-Cook, C., Clarke, M., MscLachlan, M., Papola, T.S., Pais, J., Thomas, S., Normand, C.J., & McAuliffe, E. (2011).

Carr, S.C., MacLachlan, M., & Furnham, A. (Eds.) (2012). Humanitarian work psychology, Basingtoke, Palgrave Macmillan.

Central Intelligence Agency (2013). Ghana. Retrieved from https://www.cia.gov/library/publications/the-world-factbook/geos/gh.html.

Erez, M. (2011). Cross-cultural and global issues in organizational psychology. In S. Zedeck (Ed.), *APA Handbook of Industrial and Organizational Psychology, Vol 3: Maintaining, Expanding, and Contracting the Organization. APA Handbooks in Psychology* (pp. 807–854). Washington, DC: American Psychological Association.

Gelfand, M.J., Leslie, L.M. & Fehr, R. (2008). To prosper organizational psychology should adopt a global perspective. *Journal of Organizational Behavior, 29*(4) 493–517.

Ghana National Service Scheme (2013). Mandate of the national service scheme. Retrieved from http://196.201.43.251/index.php?option=com_content&view=article&id=78&Itemid=88.

International Telecommunications Union (2010). World telecommunication/ICT development report 2010: Monitoring the WSIS targets. Retrieved from http://www.itu.int/dms_pub/itu-d/opb/ind/D-IND-WTDR-2010-PDF-E.pdf.

Leung, K., & Peterson, M. F. (2011). Managing a globally distributed workforce: Social and interpersonal issues. In S. Zedeck (Ed.), *APA handbook of industrial and organizational psychology: Maintaining, expanding, and contracting the organization* (pp. 771–805). Washington, DC: American Psychological Association.

MacLachlan, M., Carr, S. C., & McAuliffe, E. (2010). *The Aid Triangle: Recognizing the Human Dynamics of Dominance, Justice and Identity.* New York, NY: Zed Books.

McWha, I. (2011). The roles of, and relationships between, expatriates, volunteers, and local development workers. *Development in Practice,* 21(1), 29–40.

Organization for Economic Co-operation and Development (2009). Better Aid: Aid effectiveness: A progress report on implementing the Paris Declaration. Retrieved from http://www.oecdbookshop.org/oecd/display.asp?CID=oecd&LANG=en&SF1=DI&ST1=5KSQFBRSSCHF#OtherThings.

South African Human Resource Development Council (2010). Human resource development South Africa: Strategy for discussion 2010–2030. Retrieved from http://www.hrdcsa.org.za/document/hrcdsa-strategy-document.

Spreitzer, G. (2008). Taking stock: A review of more than twenty years of research and empowerment at work. In J. Barling, & C. L. Cooper (Eds.), *The SAGE handbook of organizational behavior.* Los Angeles, CA: SAGE.

United Nations Development Programme (1994). Human development report 1994: New dimensions of human security. Retrieved from http://hdr.undp.org/en/reports/global/hdr1994/.

United Nations Development Programme (2010). Human development report 2010: The real wealth of nations – pathways to human development. Retrieved from http://hdr.undp.org/en/reports/global/hdr2010/.

Van der Berg, S., Taylor, S., Gustafsson, M., Spaull, N., & Armstrong, P. (2011). Improving education quality in South Africa (Report for the National Planning Commission). Retrieved from http://resep.sun.ac.za/wp-content/uploads/2012/10/2011-Report-for-NPC.pdf.

4

Developing Young Leaders in Kenya's Rift Valley

Sarah Stawiski and Jennifer Martineau

Leadership is a topic that has been studied formally by social scientists for nearly 100 years, and from a number of different angles. For instance, the field has tackled topics including leader selection, leading teams to maximize effectiveness and performance, motivating a workforce, and, of course, development of leaders. At the time the Center for Creative Leadership (CCL) was founded in 1970, there was a general notion that "leaders are born, not made." However, advancements in theory helped the field move away from trait-based leadership and toward the importance of certain skills for effective leadership. With this shift, there was recognition that leaders can in fact be "made" or, in our terms, developed. Further, all people have the potential to be effective at leading, in some situation or another. And, there is an opportunity (and a need) for individuals throughout organizations, and communities, to step up and take a leading role, regardless of whether they have a formal leadership position.

CCL, of course, was originally founded by a businessman to help businesses achieve success. And given the strong roots that leadership development has within industrial and organizational (I-O) psychology, much of the research in the field has had a focus on business or workplace applications. However, if leadership development can help executive teams run more effective organizations, couldn't it also be useful in solving community problems? And as a non-profit organization with a mission to advance the understanding and practice of leadership worldwide, it was our belief that we should share our expertise beyond just those in white-collar positions employed by companies with healthy learning and development budgets.

Hence, CCL launched a global initiative called Leadership Beyond Boundaries (LBB). Through this initiative, CCL can further its mission of advancing the understanding, development, and practice of leadership for the benefit of society worldwide. Working in more than 20 countries, LBB builds on decades of research and experience from the field, as well as CCL's specific tools and resources, to provide accessible, low-cost but equally high-quality leadership development at the grass roots. Through LBB, leadership development opportunities are made available to audiences that do not fit the mold of the corporate executive; audiences that include children in Indian slums, migrant farm workers in Cambodia, and young people from rural and economically distressed communities in North Carolina, just to name a few. To say the least, CCL's models have been applied in some profoundly different contexts than was typical of our past.

Therefore, when presented with the opportunity to bring leadership development to young people in Kenya's Rift Valley, CCL was ready and willing to take it. The youth of the Rift Valley are vulnerable in a number of ways. They are living in a region prone to violence and conflict and, in many cases, extreme poverty. They often have strong beliefs about out-group tribes that have been profoundly shaped by history and social influence, and they have not typically developed the resources and skills to know how to make a difference in their situation. Leadership development is crucial in empowering youth toward increasing their participation in democratic processes, particularly in the reform agenda (changes proposed in Kenya to promote fairness in the political and electoral system). Among other skills, leadership development equips youth with good communication, decision making, critical thinking and problem solving skills. They learn to appreciate and accommodate diverse views and perspectives, to prevent conflict from occurring, and to manage and resolve conflict constructively when it occurs.

In this chapter, we will describe the Youth Leadership Development for Reforms project, starting with a brief overview of the relevant context and recent history of the Rift Valley. The description will also highlight some of the principles from I-O psychology that were applied in the design and delivery of the program. Then, we will briefly discuss the efforts made to evaluate this program and understand the impact it had on the target audiences. Finally, we will conclude with a discussion of how this work informs the field of I-O psychology as well as gaps in our understanding that may be filled through future work and research.

The context

On March 4, 2013, Kenyans flocked to the election polls to cast their votes for a new president. As the largest economy in eastern Africa, millions around the world were watching. This was the first general election since 2007–2008 when a dispute about the results led to an eruption of violence which claimed the lives of more than 1,000 Kenyans. To be sure, there was interest and anxiety about the outcome of the election. Of the two front-runner candidates, would it be Prime Minister Raila Odinga or Uhuru Kenyatta who next lead the country? However, another central question on everyone's minds' was whether the election would be peaceful or if Kenya would once again witness great upheaval and violence in the aftermath.

After the 2007 elections, much of the violence took place in the Rift Valley Region of Kenya. Gangs primarily from Kalenjin and Kikuyu tribes engaged in looting, rioting, and killings in parts of the Rift Valley. It is estimated that as a result of these acts, 1,500 Kenyans were dead, 3,000 women were raped, and 300,000 were displaced from their homes. The reasons behind the violence are complex and go well beyond the scope of this chapter. However, it is important to note that it was the *youth* of the region that were at the forefront of the violence, both as perpetrators and as victims. In fact, over 70% of the perpetrators were estimated to be Kenyan youth (Mercy Corps, 2011). At the core of much of the violence was a long and deep history of conflict between the tribes of the region.

So, what happened after the 2013 elections in Kenya? There has been a great deal of controversy surrounding the elections, given that the newly elected President, Uhuru Kenyatta, is also facing indictments for crimes associated with the 2007 election violence. On a positive note, however, there were far fewer reports of violence this time around, and certainly nothing close to what took place in 2007–2008. The outcome can be attributed in part to the reforms that were initiated after the previous election. These reforms relied on awareness, engagement, and leadership from a diverse range of Kenyans, including youth like those who participated in the Youth Leadership Development for Reforms project that we will describe in this chapter.

In thinking about this context and how to overcome some of the challenges faced by the Rift Valley, I-O psychology may not be the first connection that comes to mind. However, the field of I-O psychology has produced knowledge and solutions that are indeed quite relevant. To make progress toward peace in a region that has a profound history of tribal conflict, it would be up to the young people to play a significant role in leading change. It would require a shift in their beliefs and mental models, skills for collaborating effectively with others, and an ability to envision and create change in their communities. In short, effective leadership would be necessary for change to occur. And clearly there are strong ties between the study of leadership (and its development) and I-O psychology.

The case

The Youth Leadership Development for Reforms Project was implemented jointly in Kenya by the Center for Transformational Leadership (CTL) and the CCL, supported by a grant from USAID/DAI (United States Agency for International Development/Development Alternative Inc.). The project objectives were (1) to help young people in the Rift Valley have a greater appreciation for themselves and others and a greater understanding of leadership principles; (2) to support young people to work constructively in teams with peers from other tribes and boost youth participation and contribution to the reform agenda; and (3) to enable youth to enact civic service project(s) that advance the social good and improve relations in the community. This project involved youth from Egerton University, Njoro Campus, and ten selected high schools across three districts, Molo, Nakuru, and Njoro.

The key activities under this project included youth mentorship and leadership training, action learning program and civic engagement programs. Through trainings, some 289 youth were reached directly, equipping them with leadership skills and increasing their knowledge of the reform agenda. A further 1,950 young people were reached through six distinct civic engagement events held throughout the project. See Figure 4.1 for an overview of the model and the number

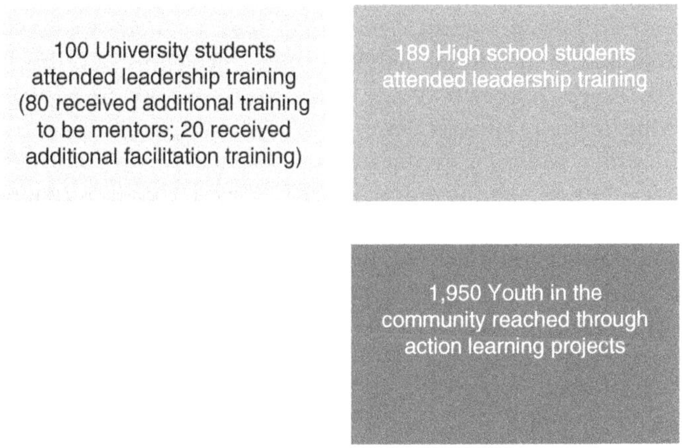

100 University students attended leadership training (80 received additional training to be mentors; 20 received additional facilitation training)

189 High school students attended leadership training

1,950 Youth in the community reached through action learning projects

Figure 4.1 Overview of the program model

of people reached. Through a formal program evaluation, CTL and CCL captured the project impacts and outcomes, and a summary of those is contained here.

University students were recruited through a questionnaire that was designed to provide CTL with critical information including personal details, past leadership experience, the student's motivation to participate in the project, and previous engagement in civic activities. CTL used criteria of school location and classification of the schools to select ten high schools across the three project districts. CTL preferred public schools over private schools due to the fact that public schools draw their student population from middle- and low-income families. CTL selected schools located within neighborhoods that were hot spots during the post-election violence. Within these ten schools, CTL created criteria to guide high school administrators in selecting high school students to reflect the diversity of the community in the final group.

Training

Three types of training occurred as part of this project: (1) college student leadership training including mentor training and (2) a training-of-trainers to enable college students to facilitate the same leadership program for high school students. These training programs were followed by (3) high school leadership sessions conducted by a team of 20 trainers.

College student leadership training

CTL and CCL used practical and interactive tools in the delivery of and in all of these programs. Techniques used included group discussions, dialogue, experiential activities, and storytelling. Content areas included several frameworks and tools developed by CCL including what it means to be a leader, leveraging personal strengths, values, and social identity as a leader, giving feedback and working with others. The college leadership training was delivered to approximately 100 college students, regardless of their intent to subsequently mentor or facilitate leadership development with high school students. We will focus in this chapter on the training that prepared college students to work with high school students.

Mentor training

The three-day youth mentorship program was intended to develop mentorship skills for the university students to enable them to support the high school students in developing and implementing civic engagement projects in different villages/estates across the three project districts. The training design borrowed heavily from CCL's Leadership Essentials/Mentorship training developed to help leaders and mentors at all levels understand and unlock their leadership potential. The content of the mentor training may be classified into three sub-sections: Reform agenda, leadership concepts, and conflict mitigation.

Reform agenda

Through group discussions, participants brainstormed on the role of the youth in the reform process and practical ways in which they can actively participate. The discussion revolved around five reform issues – (1) constitutional reforms; (2) poverty, inequalities, and regional imbalances; (3) youth unemployment; (4) national cohesion integration; and (5) transparency, accountability, and impunity – with youth generating lists of ideas regarding what youth can do to address each critical issue.

Leadership concepts

The students were taught essential elements of leadership and key drivers of leadership development combined with the attributes of good mentorship. Tools and techniques for acquiring deeper self-insight and discovering one's own leadership strengths and challenges were used. Several principles of psychology inform the concepts covered, for example, developing self-awareness and understanding social identity.

Developing self-awareness is considered a core element of developing as a leader. Typically, this concept has been defined as an understanding of one's resources and an understanding of how one is perceived by others (Taylor, 2010). Research suggests that by becoming more self-aware leaders have a better idea of what areas they need to develop most (Avolio, 2005).

Social identity is also an important concept to have awareness around when developing as a leader. We base our identity not only on our own individual characteristics, experience, and preferences, but also on our group memberships (Tajfel and Turner's social identity theory, 1986). Our group memberships can be very powerful forces driving our behavior, because, we want to protect that aspect of our identity at (almost) all costs. The program helped young leaders connect with different aspects of their identities – from their core values to "given" attributes (such as race or gender) to chosen aspects (e.g., careers, hobbies). When individuals understand their social identities, and the social identities of others, they not only see what makes them unique and what drives their own actions, but, they often find remarkable similarities with others, particularly in the core values that they may share. As humans, we have two needs when it comes to our identities – the need for differentiation and the need for belonging (Brewer, 2001). In the case of the young Kenyans going through the program, they may see that they are members of different tribes, but they may also see that they all value loyalty, family, and peace (examples only).

Conflict mitigation

In a study conducted by Mercy Corps, there were several factors that were correlated with non-participation in violence in this region. Young people with employment and income generation, as well as conflict management skills and social integration were less likely to engage in the violence (Mercy Corps, 2011). Through experiential exercises, sessions on conflict mitigation and management helped participants understand how distorted information, lack of information, stereotypes, and blowing up small issues can ignite violence in our communities. Sharing the tips for constructive conflict, facilitators prepared participants to sensitize and motivate their mentees and peers on the importance of the reform process, and the active leadership role the youth need to play in this process thus helping to safeguard a future of stability, peace, and prosperity for Kenya. The content covered in this section also draws from psychology, for example, challenging mental models and stereotypes.

Mental models are simply the way that we organize our thoughts about the world. Stereotypes are one specific type of mental model – a set of beliefs about the personal attributes of a group of people, which are sometimes overgeneralized, untrue, and hard to change (Myers, 2002, p. 328). Conflict situations, such as the one in Kenya, have a multitude of factors at play. However, negative stereotypes about out-group tribes are likely one of the cognitive factors contributing to the upheaval. Helping young people understand what stereotypes are, and encouraging them to challenge their own beliefs about others is an important step toward peace.

Train-the-trainer program

The train-the-trainer program was a three-day program delivered to university students to equip them with facilitation skills to enable them to deliver leadership training to the 200 high school students. The training covered key components including planning for training sessions, facilitation of dialogue among participants, time management and climate management in the room. CTL and CCL facilitators helped participants understand four tips for effective facilitations, which are (1) use of space, (2) engaging in active dialogue through "putting something in the middle" (i.e., photos, physical artifacts, or other visual items used to spark creativity in dialogue), (3) identifying what constitutes good facilitation process, and (4) experiential learning.

High school training

CTL then organized one-day training programs in each of the ten high schools participating in the project. Each program was delivered by a pair of the college student trainers. The high school students were trained in selected leadership concepts including social identity, mental models, and conflict resolution. The students were also trained on the contents of the reform agenda and the role of the youth in the reform process.

Action learning program

The action learning program which followed these trainings can be characterized as a mentorship process that lasted for a period of one month. It provided an opportunity for the trained college mentors to interact and support the high school students in (i) understanding the issues contained in reform agenda, (ii) identifying issues of concern in their local communities and linking them with an issue in the reform agenda, (iii) identify practical ways for youth to address issues at community level, and (iv) packaging the reform message in creative and attractive ways to sensitize youth on the contents of the reform agenda and the role of youth in the reform process.

Mentors worked with their high school mentees for four consecutive weekends. Over the course of the four weekends, students moved through the phases of an action learning project using a variety of activities. For instance, in the first week, students used the visual explorer tool (a deck of picture cards) to facilitate dialogue about issues within their local communities that are of concern to them. In the second week, mentors supported students in identifying ways of packaging the reform message. In this week, mentees started writing skits, songs, dance, choral verses, narratives, and poems aimed at sensitizing youth on the reform agenda as well as calling them into active participation in the reform process. In the third week, the focus was polishing and practicing presentations, followed by actually conducting the presentations in the final week. Activities included organizing high school students for presentations, preparation of event programs, notifying and acquiring relevant permits, conducting public processions, and running the main events. A closer look at some of these projects is presented below.

Flamingo secondary school event

This was the first civic event to be carried out and reached an estimated 200 youths. The event was held within Nakuru Town and showcased creative presentations staged by a group of 20 enthusiastic students from Flamingo secondary school. The event drew youths from surrounding estates including Bondeni, Kivumbini, Shauri Yako, Manyani, Kaloleni, Flamingo, and Phase II Estates. During the 2007/2008 post-election violence, these estates were among the areas that bore the brunt of violence with youths blocking roads and sending members of minority tribes packing in Nakuru Town. The issues that are of concern to the youth in these areas are first and foremost youth unemployment; the rate of youth unemployment is very high in these estates and, due to idleness, they spend time indulging in drinking and drugs.

With the rate of youth unemployment high, there are insecurity and poverty concerns. The presentations made by the students called youth to shun tribalism, corruption, and violence and instead utilize their unique talents and gifts to make a living through self-employment. Salma, one of the students, showcased how she utilizes her artistic talent to make a living by decorating brides through drawings. Other self-employment case studies were presented by three youth groups that use art to earn a living through staged drama and dances.

These case studies were a true presentation of how the youth venture into self-employment, avoid idleness, and contribute positively in their communities. In addition to these, the students challenged youth to shun tribalism through skits and poems. A skit that stood out with a clear message on tribalism showed how a family fired their household help because she was from a different tribe. Later, the lady of the house was involved in a road accident and the same girl who she had chased away donated blood and saved her life. The students staged a moving scene with a clear message on building national unity, a key issue contained in the Reform Agenda.

Hillcrest secondary school event

This event was held in Free Area in the outskirts of Nakuru Town. During the post-election violence, Free Area was one of the estates that was seriously affected in Nakuru with deaths and burning of houses belonging to tribes perceived to be "enemies." Youth unemployment and poverty in these areas is very high, leading to a rise in cases of insecurity and youth indulging in alcohol abuse. Presentations made by high school students focused mainly on how tribalism and corruption in according job opportunities affects the youth. In a well-staged play, the students showed how well-educated youths opt to join militia gangs to earn a living after experiencing frustrations in the job market as bosses prefer to employ less qualified staff either because they belong to the same tribe or can afford bribes. The play proceeded to show how youths can reach out to their frustrated peers and help them regain hope by forming themselves into formal groups, identify sources of capital such as the youth development fund, and pursue business ideas that would enable them to improve their living standards. Other presentations made during this event called on the youths to shun corruption and embrace positive values that will move the country forward.

Kiamaina secondary school event

This was a joint event organized and hosted by mentors and students from Kiamaina and Upper Hill secondary schools. In sharing the message of reform, the students presented a well-constructed skit that spoke against tribalism, corruption, and encouraged reconciliation among communities over the sharing of scarce resources. Among other moving presentations was the poem "The Kenya We Want" that gave a reflection of what youth want to see happen in their country – to become a country that is secure and politically stable where there is economic growth and people live in peace and unity. Another Swahili poem, "Vijana tujenge Kenya Pamoja," called on youth to join hands and build Kenya into a better country. Other reform issues addressed in this event include constitution, youth unemployment, national unity and transparency, accountability, and impunity.

Evaluation process

In order to monitor the success of the program, CTL and a CCL Evaluation team worked together to design and implement a system that monitored and evaluated project impacts. The evaluation design focused *primarily* on self-report data, and therefore has limitations in terms of assessing impact from the perspectives of multiple stakeholders. However, we did hear from adults at each of the school who were in a position to assess program impact, and we utilized multiple data collection methods. The formative evaluation utilized the end of program surveys (EOP) completed immediately at the end of each training component. The project evaluation measured both short- and long-term impacts expected from participation in the project activities. In November 2010, CTL and CCL conducted follow-up meetings with university students. Evaluation focus groups were conducted at Egerton University and in three of the participating high schools. At each school, the lead evaluator and project director met with the students who had participated in the program and interviewed adults at two of the schools.

In addition to the tangible outcomes collected at the school and community level (such as number of youths trained in leadership, number of youths reached through the youth mentoring program), the surveys, interviews, and focus groups focused on what the students had learned as a result of participating in the training, what they were doing differently as individuals, how the school and community benefited from their participation, and the opportunities they see in the future due to having participated.

Program impact

Recognizing the limitations of the evaluation and the primary focus on self-report data, evaluation findings indicate at least some tentative evidence that impact was realized at multiple levels:

- impact on university students and university community;
- impact on high school students and surrounding communities.

Impact on university students and community

General reactions

First, we observed a very favorable reaction to the program by the university students. For instance, the newly trained university student mentors reported a very high level of satisfaction with the workshops they attended. Based on survey results, 96% indicated that their "perspective on the process of mentorship and leadership changed." Mentor trainees ratings of the extent intended outcomes of the workshop were met were very high, ranging from 4.32 to 4.67 on a one-to-five rating scale (with five being the most positive rating). The students participating in the train-the-trainer workshop also rated the experience positively, with average ratings on program outcomes ranging from 3.90 to 4.85.

Increase in confidence and self-perception as leaders

In focus groups, the level of awareness demonstrated by the university students regarding their own leadership capabilities and responsibilities was profound. Having worked with many youth and senior level groups over a career spanning 20 years, the level of accountability these students communicated feeling is significantly higher than the typical group of either youth or senior leaders. Perhaps due to the extreme violence and its effects that they have experienced at the hands of adults who use youth to carry out their deeds, these students are committed to creating a different Kenya from the one in which they currently live.

Students talked about realizing they have abilities and talents, and feeling more empowered, and speaking up when they see something happening that is wrong.

> At first I thought that I did not have the ability to work with others well but I have realized that I can organize a group of people and have a discussion that will impact their lives. Now I believe that given any task to perform, I have what it takes to do it.

Their definition of what a leader is also changed and broadened. The negative connotation about leaders as someone who exploits others started to shift. They also saw leaders as more than just those with positional power:

> Initially, the definition of a leader was someone who exploits others; the norm was to do some things in school but we don't know the implications; mentorship – brought these issues into the perspective, now we see things differently.

Willingness to challenge mental models

Students reported a shift in their thinking and a willingness to challenge their beliefs about others. They spoke specifically about tribalism and not labeling others. They began to see themselves as one groups rather than multiple, competing tribes:

> My perception of other people really changed a lot as I got to work with people from different ethnic backgrounds. I became more comfortable being with them, am now able to relate with anyone regardless of their ethnic background.

Ability to resolve conflict

Students reported being asked to help resolve conflicts and proactively bringing people together when experiencing disagreement.

Community building

There was a very powerful impact on the Egerton University community that was not directly a part of the program's design but was instead a natural outcome of the development of 80 university students, in addition to nine university student leaders. That is, the university community gained at least one group focused on leadership in the university ("Champions of Leadership"), founded by participants in this program. Other indications of broader impact on the university community include:

- The establishment of a chapter of Students in Free Enterprise. The group's constitution was being revised at the time of the focus groups, and there were 15 members.
- Realizing the importance of voting in university elections and mobilizing other voters; people are voting today which will influence students in the future.
- Recognizing the need to foster what they really want – not keeping quiet or blaming those elected for their problems.

Impact on high school students and community

General reactions

The high school students were also asked to evaluate the program on a series of objectives regarding its performance. The overall ratings for these objectives ranged from 4.44 to 4.77. This assessment indicates that high school students largely agreed that the initial training workshop ran smoothly and met their needs. High school students also evaluated the intended outcomes of the workshop. Their average ratings ranged from 4.35 to 4.75, indicating that the workshop achieved its intended outcomes for impact.

Lessons learned by high school students were relevant to multiple realms of life. We asked the students to indicate where they thought they'd be most likely to use the leadership concepts they were taught (they could select multiple options). The responses varied – 86% indicated they would apply the lessons at school, 43% would use it at home, 62% reported "with friends," and 58% said "other." When examples were provided for the "other" response, students primarily indicated "at church," "in my community or village." High school student mentees experienced growth at different levels through the action learning program. The following are the major areas of impact reported for the mentees.

Ability to work together

Mentees' level of cooperation, respect for one another and discipline worked well during the preparation of civic events. Like the university students, the high schoolers resonated significantly with the "mental models" component of the program. In each high school, students shared stories illustrating how they were able to see themselves and others differently as leaders as a result of the training. For example, we heard many times in focus groups that the students now understand people from tribes other than their own differently than in the past. Where they previously had automatically believed the stereotypes of other tribes, they now understand that the mental models they have learned are not necessarily true. They have learned to question the "truths" spoken by adults and think of people as individuals and Kenyans first, rather than as members of other tribes. This awakening of awareness motivated the students to understand themselves to be leaders of today who must work from this point forward to change the stereotypical attitudes held by many youth and adults.

Ownership of the reform process

The mentees felt that they were also part of the reform agenda and had a role to play. At first, they thought it was only meant for their parents and elders, but they realized later that they could also make a difference.

Increased confidence and self-discovery

Compared to the start of the project, the mentees were more confident, able to interact, and ready to contribute constructively to the reform agenda debate by the time the project came to completion. There was discovery of new talents and abilities among the students and their level of maturity rose amazingly:

> I thought that leadership is all about giving orders and expecting them to be obeyed but now I learnt to respect and listen to other people's opinions. I am now able to identify myself in the society, I know what I can do better and I know how to resolve a conflict. I also know how to come up with a viable means of communicating.

Students also started to see themselves as leaders: "We learnt to become today's and tomorrow's leaders" was a common thread we heard from the high school students. The realization that they are not only the leaders of tomorrow but the leaders of today was striking for the students. Social identity was another theme that was clearly learned. Students told us that they now understand that they can "appreciate my given, core, and chosen attributes" as well as those of others. Rather than using mental models that all people have chosen to be who they are, they learned that people are given some aspects of their identity (e.g., into which tribe they were born) and can choose others (e.g., whether they spend their time idle, work hard in school, or begin to learn a trade).

Another common theme was that students have built more confidence and understanding of their abilities and role in leading others. They spoke of leading in terms of helping others understand something by understanding others first. One of the students used the metaphor of a mirror, saying, "It is like a mirror – I can see myself in others and learn about how I am through others. Transparency is important – we must be open and frank with each other, and help others do that." They have learned to socialize with others by taking time to understand them rather than making judgments about others.

Students also see themselves as being better able to cope with the challenges that they face – their courage and self-confidence keeps them going. They have learned that leaders must love those that they lead in order to effectively influence them.

Community building

Students repeatedly spoke of how important coexistence is to building national cohesion, and that they have a deeper understanding of how the differences between themselves and other students can be valuable by bringing diversity to a community. They realized that youth were used by politicians during the post-election violence. Using their talents, young people can be engaged in productive activities to change their communities and the country. Such activities include planting trees, planning of progress projects, and utilizing their talents to encourage other youth to engage in constructive activities.

The high school students with whom we met were very animated when they spoke of the work they'd done in their communities through the civic engagement events. After the events, some of the high school students met with the youths who attended their events – these youths reported wanting more of these types of events. The community youth have been sharing the message to others through their church groups and in their villages.

As we spoke with the high school students, it was clear that their motivation from the program will continue to have an influence on their communities and on society, especially through the reform agenda. They intended to do so through finishing school and gaining self-employment; maximizing the use of resources they have available to them. They wanted to educate their families and others on reform issues. There was a great deal of energy for spreading the message by organizing additional events, drawing students from other schools into the events, and writing educative songs about positive change.

The students also have a growing passion for filling leadership positions with other youths who are educated and not corrupt. They plan to run for constitutional leadership positions, pursue law degrees to become judges and help realize justice for the poor in their society, and take responsibility for reporting injustice and corruption. They shared with us that they refuse to be corrupt.

Discussion

Lessons learned

The model used in this initiative – preparing university students to train and mentor high school students, who would in turn serve as role models for other youth in their community – was a powerful and sustainable approach to developing a large number of youth in a given community. The lessons learned from this model indicate its strengths:

- Youth are an appropriate audience to work with to effect change because they are creative, energetic, and willing to take the risk of going an extra mile.
- Youth responded well to youthful mentors. Because of the closeness in age, the mentorship relationship became more impactful.
- Young people are not inherently tribal; it is their minds which have been negatively influenced by older generations. When their consciousness about stereotypes is raised, they are able to think beyond ethnic lines. One university student suggested leadership development like this program should start in primary school, as "clay is easier to twist when it is soft."

A grounded knowledge of self builds confidence at self and collective level, causing young people to work well in teams and achieve more.

How this helps inform the field of leadership development and I-O psychology

The field of leadership development, through both research and practice, certainly has the potential to make a significant contribution to the lives of the vulnerable. And the reverse is true as well. By applying what we know in so many new and diverse contexts, we also learn lessons that helps strengthen the field.

For one, we learn about how to scale. To be able to reach and make a positive impact in the lives of the vulnerable, traditional delivery methods are not always affordable and sustainable. Therefore, CCL and the LBB initiative in particular have employed innovative methods for scaling, most notably in the form of train-the-trainer models, as was utilized with the Youth Leadership Development for Reforms Project. These models can be useful in more traditional leadership development settings as well. For instance, in a recent meeting, we discussed how to a meet a corporate client's need (in the oil and gas industry) to scale leadership development in its rapidly expanding company, with hundreds of new leaders expected to join or rise up the ranks in the next few years. The organization wants to have an impact on the development of all its leaders in a very deep and meaningful way while being mindful of cost and sustainability. Further, the company wants to build its own capacity for developing its people rather than always being dependent on another party to design and implement developmental experiences. Since we have accumulated several years of experience in train-the-trainer models, we can apply aspects of the model to help this company achieve its goals. Therefore, the work we are doing with the vulnerable is simultaneously helping us meet the needs of our more traditional (corporate) client base.

Similarly, bringing leadership development opportunities to vulnerable populations helps us to get to the essence of the intent of the developmental experience. When working with very limited budgets, perhaps in situations where technology is not readily available and with large numbers of people, some of the more sophisticated tools that we have access to are not viable. For instance, 360 feedback assessments are not always possible, but they also are not always necessary, either. We recently delivered a program to more than 200 business students in India. The students and the program supporters greatly valued the opportunity to use assessment and feedback data as part of the program, but using traditional platforms was not affordable or scalable and therefore was not incorporated into the design. Instead, groups of peers who had been working on projects in teams of eight provided feedback to one another on a handwritten form. Then, facilitators helped the teams process the feedback and support one another through the process. This simple exercise got to the essence of what the students needed – feedback from peers about their leadership performance, without any reliance on an expensive 360 platform. It was one of the highest rated and most praised parts of the six month program for these students.

It also informs the field about how effective leadership is conceptualized and developed. The vast majority of studies in our field have focused on Western concepts of leadership and how it plays out in the workplace. By applying our models and approaches outside of this realm, we can test which aspects are universally accepted, and which are subject to change as a function of context.

Ongoing challenges

There is a great need for leadership development, yet, even the most efficient and cost-effective models can be too burdensome for some populations to bear. It is still a luxury for some audiences to be involved in a leadership program. Millions of people around the world struggle to meet basic needs such as clothing, shelter, and sustenance. Others have barriers such as gender role constraints or work–family obligations that would make it very difficult to participate in a typical leadership development experience. Therefore, the field needs to continue to innovate in the area of scalability. Developments in technology are promising.

For instance, one creative solution developed by the LBB team was intended to meet the needs of women in rural Ethiopia. Despite the potential for leadership in rural woman, there are huge challenges in reaching this audience. For one, they often have substantial work responsibilities that do not allow them the time to get an education. Relatedly, they often cannot read. Therefore, the team developed a women's leadership audio toolkit. It's a small, solar-powered audio device that has a ten module training program. The modules (and the picture-based book that accompanies it) help women understand themselves, set goals, work with others more effectively and creatively, and work toward a vision for a changed community.

There is also the challenge of quality control. The success of the train-the-trainer model relies on the effective cascading of quality over time. While we can be fairly confident that when we send in an experienced trainer to use tried-and-true (and research-based) methods for developing leaders, we can expect to meet most of the learning objectives of the initiative. However, what happens when those trained go back into their communities and try to teach others? From an evaluation perspective, follow-up with the original participants (the newly trained "trainers") is very challenging. We know very little about how much of what they learned sticks enough to deliver a similar-quality program to another group of leaders; and we know even less about the impact on the participants that are trained by these trainers.

What more we need to know

There is an ever-growing body of research about the contextual factors at play in defining, developing, and executing effective leadership (e.g., House, Hanges, Javidan, Dorfman, and Gupta, 2004). Yet, little is known about the specific developmental needs of vulnerable populations; how do other competing needs get in the way of learning and developing as a leader? Therefore, there is an opportunity to more systematically study what methods work best for various populations. How do cultural differences play a part in meeting these unique audiences? This question was not examined in this study; rather, both the design and facilitation of the leadership development initiative and the subsequent evaluation were informed specifically by the cultural influences of the target audience and the Rift Valley area in which they lived. The question of cultural differences remains for another study.

Further, we do not know very much about the motivation and personal readiness of various vulnerable populations to develop as leaders. We hear anecdotally from our work around the world that there is a "hunger" for this type of development. Yet, we also hear that leadership is a dirty word in some parts of the world, with certain populations of people. We need to understand more about beliefs about leaders and leadership in general from the Cambodian migrant farm workers to the at-risk US high school students. The more we know about where individuals are in their journeys as developing leaders, the more we can help them confront their unique challenges and circumstances.

For the past five years, CCL has collected data from professionals and managers around the world via the World Leadership Survey (for more information, see http://www.ccl.org/Leadership/research/worldsurvey. aspx) to help answer these questions. Through this work, we are learning more about what individuals in different countries believe helps and hinders effective leadership (e.g., Deal, Stawiski, Graves, Gentry, Ruderman, and Weber, 2012). Further, in the past year, a version of the World Leadership Survey has been launched for students. These data allow us to understand differences in the belief about whether leaders are born or made, what images best represent their idea of leadership, and what characteristics are most closely associated with effective leadership. To date, the majority of the data collected come from African, Indian, and US students. We hope to soon be able to collect data from a more diverse group of young people, which can ultimately have implications for our work with young people around the world.

Conclusions

The field of I-O psychology has generated an enormous body of knowledge that has and will continue to make a positive impact on individuals, organizations, and communities. And the field of leadership development – while influenced and shaped by a multitude of academic fields – has strong roots in I-O psychology. The theories developed in I-O psychology as well as the long history of rigorous empirical research have certainly influenced what we know about how to best develop leaders. And with each new experience we have in developing leaders, we can build on this knowledge and improve our practices.

For instance, building on the work of the program described here, CCL has recently initiated another program in partnership with CLT for a similar audience, using a similar model, to continue to develop the individual and collective leadership abilities of the young people in this region. Youth Voices for Peace (YV4P), a 15-month, four-phase program funded by the US Institute for Peace (USIP), built on the concepts of Youth Leadership Development for Reform Project. Preliminary evaluation results suggest that students are increasing their knowledge of leadership concepts and have been able to apply them at school and at home. With each new opportunity to work with young people in the Rift Valley as well as other vulnerable populations, we better understand their unique leadership development needs and we become more effective at meeting those needs.

For obvious reasons, leadership and leadership development has had a strong focus in a fairly narrow setting: the traditional, Western workplace. However, in this case and in our work in general with hugely diverse audiences around the world, we know that even the "unlikeliest of suspects" can grow and learn as leaders. In fact, those most vulnerable – for instance, youth who have witnessed and become used to the uncertainties of violence and poverty surrounding them – develop as leaders through their own unique experiences and struggles before ever stepping foot into a leadership classroom. For having lived under and survived these circumstances of uncertainty, risk, and great conflict, these young people likely have already developed skills related to resilience, empathy, and courage, all important in effective leadership. Understanding how experiences outside of the workplace can accelerate one's development is an area ripe for future study. But we know one thing already – leadership development holds promise well beyond the potential to make business leaders more effective and corporations more successful; it can make a difference in the lives of the most vulnerable people all around the world. The young men and women in Kenya's Rift Valley can attest to that.

References

Avolio, B. J. (2005). *Leadership Development in Balance: MADE/Born*. Mahwah, NJ: Erlbaum.

Deal, J., Stawiski, S., Graves, L. M., Gentry, W. A., Ruderman, R., & Weber, T. J. (2012). Perceptions of authority and leadership: a cross-national, cross-generational investigation. In E. S. Ng, S. T. Lyons, & L. Schweitzer (Eds.), *Managing the New Workforce: International Perspectives on the Millennial Generation*. Cheltenham: Edward Elgar Publishing, 241–259.

House, R. J., Hanges, P. J., Javidan, M., Dorfman, P. W., & Gupta, V. (Eds.) (2004). *Culture, Leadership, and Organizations. The GLOBE Study of 62 Societies*. Thousand Oaks, CA: Sage Publications, Inc.

Lewin, K., Lippit, R., & White, R. K. (1939). Patterns of aggressive behavior in experimentally created social climates. *Journal of Social Psychology*, 10, 271–301.

Mercy Corps (2011). Understanding political violence among youth: Evidence from Kenya. Retrieved from http://www.mercycorps.org/sites/default/files/full_report_-_kenya_youth_and_conflict_study.pdf.

Myers, D. (2002). *Social Psychology*. 7th Edition. New York: McGraw Hill.

Tajfel, H., & Turner, J. C. (1986). The social identity theory of intergroup behaviour. In S. Worchel, & W. G. Austin (Eds.), *Psychology of Intergroup Relations* (pp. 7–24). Chicago, IL: Nelson-Hall.

Taylor, S. N. (2010). Redefining leader self-awareness by integrating the second component of self-awareness. *Journal of Leadership Studies*, 3(4), 57–68.

Zaccaro, S. J., Heinen, B., & Shuffler, M. (2009). Team leadership and team effectiveness. In E. Salas, G. F. Goodwin, & C. Burke (Eds.), *Team Effectiveness in Complex Organizations: Cross-Disciplinary Perspectives and Approaches* (pp. 83–111). New York, NY: Routledge/Taylor & Francis Group.

5

A Multidisciplinary Approach to Solving Global Problems: The Case of Psychologists Collaborating on a Girls Empowerment Program in Africa

Mary O'Neill Berry, Judy Kuriansky, and Martin Butler

Introduction

It is often said that "It takes a village," meaning that many partners are necessary to get a project done. This principle applies when it comes to developing and implementing large-scale programs and evaluations in the field of psychology, with several psychologists collaborating on such projects. Consistent with this, the present chapter describes how a non-governmental organization (NGO) accredited to the United Nations assisted in the development and evaluation of a camp program in Lesotho, Africa, to help orphans and vulnerable young girls living in poverty and at risk for HIV/AIDS. The emphasis in this chapter is on the collaboration of the NGO team members trained in different psychological disciplines, combining their skills to work together. This approach, called by the authors a Multidisciplinary Psychology Team (MDPT), is deemed important since various perspectives are often needed in order to develop, implement, and also evaluate programs on local, national, and, certainly, international levels. A multidisciplinary team is often necessary to effectively address the mission of the program, and to design the elements that will best achieve the intended goals (Housley, 2003; Kuriansky and Corsini, 2009). The multidisciplinary team model has often been used in medical care, referring to different fields of medical and social service (Patkar et al., 2011); this paper is one of the first of its kind to focus on the team cooperation from professionals in different specialties within the same field, psychology.

The development of a project in an international setting, particularly in a nation with an emerging economy, considered a "developing country," requires significant consideration of many factors regarding the practicality of its application in the setting and with the particular population. Sensitivity to the clinical issues in the cohort is necessary. Additionally, education is almost universally either a part of the program or a recommendation of its outcome. A major consideration, too, must be the culture of the particular locale. Furthermore, many local and international partners may be involved; these can be governmental as well civil society actors from the public and private sectors. These issues, respectively, require the expertise of clinical, educational, and industrial-organizational (I-O) psychology – exactly the disciplines reported about in this collaboration.

Many intervention programs in the public health field that have been implemented in developing countries have not been systematically evaluated by validated questionnaires or other scientific methodology that would attest to their effectiveness. Yet, experts recognize, in the "Limitations" section in their papers, the need for such evaluation (Rychetnik et al., 2002). It is recommended that such evaluations be done on both quantitative and qualitative bases. To address this issue, the project described in this paper included an evaluation on both dimensions. Given the description of the program in the preceding paragraph, the development of such an evaluation protocol required the collaboration of those psychological experts in different disciplines to participate in the protocol design.

In the current case, the team that came together to achieve these goals – both the development of the program and the evaluation of the intervention – represented the three psychological disciplines mentioned above, specifically, a clinical psychologist, an I-O psychologist and an educational psychologist. This chapter describes what each of these individuals contributed from their different perspectives as well as the project itself, and some outcomes of the evaluation. The intention of the chapter is to present a model for the reader, and particularly students and early career professionals, about how professionals can collaborate effectively from varied perspectives to develop and evaluate an intervention that addresses global problems.

The project

The specific project discussed in this paper relates to a program that addresses the empowerment of young girls in Africa, called the Girls

Empowerment Programme (GEP), with its main activity being a residential camp for girls. The NGO that led the project is the International Association of Applied Psychology (IAAP), which is accredited to the United Nations Economic and Social Council (ECOSOC) and affiliated with the Department of Public Information (DPI). The objective of IAAP is to promote the science and practice of applied psychology and to facilitate interaction and communication about applied psychology around the world (www.iaapsy.com). The objective of ECOSOC is to coordinate the economic, social, and related work of all UN-specialized agencies, functional, and regional commissions; its central concern is the world's economic, social, and environmental challenges, and it is the forum where such issues are discussed and debated, and policy recommendations issued. The objective of DPI is to assist the NGO community to gain access to, and disseminate information about, UN issues.

The main IAAP representative at the UN is Dr Judy Kuriansky, a clinical psychologist, one of the authors of this paper, and a participant in the MDPT described in this chapter. Two other chapter authors, Dr. Mary O'Neill Berry and Dr. Martin Butler, are IAAP team members and also MDPT members of the project described in this chapter. Dr. Kuriansky brought the project to the IAAP team, who agreed that it is in alignment with their mission, as well as with the goals and objectives of ECOSOC and DPI. NGOs accredited to ECOSOC and/or affiliated with DPI are oriented toward projects that address the current Millennium Development Goals (MDGs) of the UN, agreed by the UN member states to achieve by the year 2015 (http://www.un.org/millenniumgoals/). The MDGs also intersect with topics addressed in the field of psychology, for example, MDG #1, eradicate extreme poverty; MDG#3, promote gender equality and empower women; MDG#6, combat HIV/AIDS; and MDG#8, develop a global partnership for development (Kuriansky and Berry, 2010).

Our project started with Dr Kuriansky's participation on the Board of Directors of US Doctors for Africa (USDFA), a non-profit organization that hosted a Summit of the First Ladies of Africa in Los Angeles in 2009, focused on health issues (McBride, 2009). One of the first ladies in attendance at the summit, the then First Lady of Lesotho, Ms. Mathato Mosisili, asked Dr Kuriansky for assistance in enhancing a camp program for youth which had been run by the staff of her office for several years. A major focus of the earlier camp program was teaching the girls life skills in the service of coping with bereavement, since many of the attendees had lost family and community members to HIV/AIDS. The First Lady was also committed to a scientific evaluation of the effectiveness and outcome of the program, as only anecdotal evidence and minimal qualitative and quantitative measures had previously been collected about the girls participating in the camp. The First Lady had been a teacher, and thus she was aware of the importance of measuring the outcome of the program.

The background to the content of the GEP is the continued extremely high rate of HIV/AIDS in Lesotho: estimated at 23% for adults, 15–49 years, nationwide in 2007 and 2011 (UNAIDS, 2012; UNICEF, 2009), with gender disparity, that is, approximately 60% of all HIV-positive adults and children were female (UNAIDS, 2012). An estimated 18.3% of young women age 15–24 were infected with HIV/AIDS (UNAIDS, 2012) – the same age group as the youth who attended the First Lady's camps. In addition to this high rate of illness, the death rate is also high – although it has declined from 2008 to 2011 (UNAIDS, 2012) – resulting in many young people losing one or both parents and having to become the caretaker in the family, including for siblings. Many such young people, especially girls, have to drop out of school, either to directly look after their families, or because the family can no longer afford to send them to school (secondary school is fee-paying in Lesotho). The situation of lack of education for girls is complicated by gender inequity, including that preference is given to boys for financial resources for education (UN Millennium Project, 2005).

Additionally, families are typically very poor, with little opportunity to pull themselves out of poverty; these circumstances cause many young girls to turn to transactional sex in order to make money, despite the risks involved of contracting HIV/AIDS or other sexually transmitted diseases.

Further, there is a remarkable amount of myths as well as denial in the country about the realities of HIV/AIDS, and the tendency is to downplay the widespread nature of the disease and the likelihood of becoming one of its victims.

As a result, it was vital that the GEP raise awareness of, and knowledge about, the consequences of risky behavior, and provide some alternative avenue for young girls to achieve some modicum of financial support for themselves.

The IAAP team began work to assemble a set of suitable evaluation instruments. As mentioned above, the three members of the IAAP UN team who particularly worked on the Lesotho project included psychologists in the clinical, I-O, and educational arenas. Each of these disciplines has a perspective to contribute with regard to the content of such evaluation protocols. In this regard, it is relevant to point out some details of the background of these team members, which con-tributed to their personal commitment to the project and the expertise they each respectively brought to it. Dr. Kuriansky, the clinical psy-chologist on the team, teaches in the Department of Counseling and Clinical Psychology at Columbia University Teachers College and is an honorary professor at the Health Sciences Center in Beijing, China. She has developed and implemented many clinical training programs in dif-ferent cultures, and has also co-founded the Global Kids Connect Project which addresses trauma recovery and needs of children at risk in vari-ous countries around the world (Kuriansky and Jean-Charles, 2012). The I-O psychologist in the team is Dr. Mary O'Neill Berry, who worked for many years conducting survey and evaluation research at a global consulting firm, Sirota; she is also an executive board member of the Global Organization for Humanitarian Work Psychology, which seeks to apply organization psychology to deliberate and systematic efforts to enhance human welfare. The educational psychologist on the team is Dr. Martin Butler, who has a graduate degree in educational psychology from City University of New York, and works as an independent consul-tant conducting evaluations and assessments. He has a sub-specialty in test construction, and was invaluable in researching tests and scales that would be the most appropriate for use in the proposed camp setting.

The IAAP team had to expand the existing modules of the camp pro-gram that had been used by the Office of the First Lady (OFL) over the previous five years. This required consideration of the various experi-ences that members of the team had in designing other programs for at-risk teams. Dr. Kuriansky's vast experience in developing programs for teens and in teaching about HIV/AIDS was valuable in adding to the specific exercises already in the camp program (Kuriansky et al., 2009a). Kuriansky was further familiar with other programs for HIV education in other countries in Africa (Kuriansky, 2009; Kuriansky, Spencer and Tatem, 2009b). As the clinical psychologist on the team, Dr. Kuriansky focused on the psychosocial aspects of the program, including the var-ious dimensions that had been a part of other programs for teens' empowerment and HIV/AIDS education. Important aspects included self-esteem, relationships with others, knowledge of sexuality, and sexu-ally transmitted diseases. The exercises that address these issues already in the camp program were examined, and others that had been pre-viously used by Dr. Kuriansky in other settings were included, when deemed culturally appropriate.

The protocol also had to evaluate other modules that were incorpo-rated into the program that were introduced by a partner in the project,

Global Camps Africa (GCA), whose collaboration is described below. These were included as they focused on very similar objectives, and also had been shown to be culturally relevant (since they had been applied in the neighboring South Africa, and over many years). Other constructs to be evaluated included self-esteem and self-efficacy. These have been deemed as important in evaluating any intervention for skills building (Mann et al., 2004). Although many measures of a construct such as self-esteem are available, few had been applied in the African setting.

Dr Berry, the I-O psychologist, focused on the entrepreneurial training component, referred to as Income-Generating activities (IGA). Questions addressing this component in the final instrument was developed specifically for the GEP and consisted of a number of scaled items as well as several open-ended items. Dr Berry also worked on "knitting together" the entire set of instruments and analyses as a pilot effort in this first round of the newly revamped camp program. In addition, research by Dr. Berry, with her organizational psychology background in bringing together partners, led to the connection with Global Camps Africa, and collaboration with its director, Phil Lilienthal, on enhancing the camp program (www.gca.org). This resulted in the First Ladies' staff being trained by trainers from GCA. In addition, GCA trainers joined the OFL staff team onsite in implementing the newly developed camp.

Dr. Butler, the educational psychologist, focused on selection of the instruments that were already available for program evaluation that could be applied in this context, and the identification of depression scales that could be included in the protocol. The focus on the measurement of depression was in order to provide empirical evidence of the impression that the girls were less depressed about their life situation after going through the camp. This is important given the research that shows that depression is a major factor in health risks for youth (Washington University, 2013). Dr. Butler's specialization in test construction was crucial in building the evaluation protocol itself.

The intention was to develop a protocol consisting of a battery of evaluation instruments – including some measures already in existence and some that would need to be constructed specifically for the specific intervention in Lesotho. The multidisciplinary team was invaluable in exploring what had already been done in similar evaluations. The Lesotho evaluations would need to assess the content of the major components of the planned GEP. These components included Life Skills, to build self-confidence, self-esteem, self-efficacy, assertiveness, and awareness of and knowledge about HIV/AIDS and other sexually transmitted diseases, and income-generating activities, which refers to basic entrepreneurial training, to provide an alternative to transactional sex as a means to secure financial independence.

The instruments had to be culturally sensitive and easily translatable. It was preferable that these have proven reliability and validity. The scales also had to test the various constraints that would reveal the effectiveness and impact of the camp experience and learning by the participants.

A lengthy and intensive review was conducted of the literature of scales that would assess the educational impact of the camp experience. The reviews revealed that few scientific evaluations of a pre-post intervention nature have been implemented and that few reliable and valid instruments were available that could be immediately be applied in the current setting. Additionally, few methodologically sound evaluations had been carried out on interventions with African populations, including ones that address psychosocial issues and even in situations where programs had received federal funding, exemplifying myriad problems with the evaluation of intervention development programs that have been pointed out (Bamberger, 2000; Ebbutt, 1998; Mertens and Wilson, 2012).

The final instruments used were selected on the basis of the following criteria:

(1) related to the camp activities and intentions, for example, HIV risk reduction, skill building and assessment of income-generating activities;

(2) developed by reliable institutions, for example, the United States National Institute of Mental Health;

(3) to include some questions from other instruments that had been used in similar settings with similar interventions that could potentially show change and that could serve as comparison data, for example, risk reduction peer education camps run by a South African Peer Education Center in collaboration with Harvard School of Public Health, and teen peer sexuality education groups conducted by Dr. Judy Kuriansky in conjunction with Planned Parenthood in America;

(4) broadly used in other research projects to serve as comparison data, the Rosenberg Self-Esteem Scale, which has shown a stable factor structure across multiple populations, including several in sub-Saharan Africa (Schmitt and Allik, 2005);

(5) other questions devised by the team that appeared relevant to the intervention material;

(6) discussions with, and recommendations by, experts in the field who have worked in Africa settings and with youth, from institutions like Harvard School of Public Health, Tulane University, Duke University and UNICEF.

Contact was also made with psychological test publishing companies in America, corporations who had worked with female adolescents, and HIV/AIDS groups in Africa. Questions included quantitative and qualitative items.

Once the battery of scales was assembled, they were presented to and reviewed by the IAAP team, as well as with the staff of the Office of the First Lady of Lesotho, who were responsible for running the camp. Discussions with local Lesotho professionals and stakeholders resulted in adaptations of some of the questions, the language was simplified in order to be comprehensible at the basic literacy levels prevalent among the attendees; the draft content was also modified to best fit local community conditions; and items previously used by the local camp partners in earlier camp programs were integrated into the current camp content. These discussions also involved some re-tooling of the draft program and timetable to be more appropriate to the experience level of the trainers, as well as to integrate input from the multi-stakeholder group (the IAAP team, GCA, and the local partners).

Eventually, an acceptable battery of tests was assembled. This included the Rosenberg Self-Esteem Scale (1965), CES-D Depression Scale (Locke and Putnam, 1971), Assertiveness Scale (UNICEF), Confidence Scale (UNICEF), Self-Efficacy Scale, the Income-Generating Activities Scale (Kuriansky and Berry, 2010), and the KB Psychosocial Scale (Kuriansky and Berry, 2010). The latter two were developed specifically for the GEP.

The team's multidisciplinary collaboration resulted in a more robust evaluation protocol than would otherwise have been the case.

Meetings of the Multidisciplinary Psychology Team

Many projects in current times are carried out by partners via technological connections, given that partners may be in different locations, or even unavailable to meet in person. The present team members each had particular expertise that they "brought to the table" for the project, thus they were able to work independently to some extent in the initial phases of the development. But eventually it was deemed preferable to meet together in person to review the plans. This was fortunately possible as the three team members were all in the New York area.

This process is important, given that many teams use electronic features, from e-mail to dropbox, to google, to exchange information about projects. While this is helpful, the MDPT determined that it was optimal to also have face-to-face exchange. Additionally, meetings were held with diplomats from the US Mission of the Kingdom of Lesotho in New York.

It is also important to point out that the MDPT had to interact with the main team "on the ground," that is, the staff of the OFL. Working out the details of such communication is essential for projects of this nature, where there is international collaboration.

This communication required much more effort, given the time zone differences and also availability of the team, and further, the need for clarification of the questions and issues to be resolved and agreed upon. The MDPT had to identify one member who would be the major point-of-contact on this side (in the United States), and another team member on the Lesotho team who would be the major point of contact. Besides e-mails, several discussions also took place by various electronic media.

Such issues have to be identified and worked out among the MDPT in order to insure smooth communication and exchange among the internal and external teams.

The fact-finding visit to ensure multiple stakeholder involvement

Close collaboration of the MDPT members in the United States with the OFL team in Africa was considered essential in identifying any other members of the final team "on the ground." For the program to run smoothly, it was important for the bilateral team members to make a joint assessment of any other partners in-country that might participate in the project. Of course, the OFL and their partners who were already in place would be involved. But the MDPT determined that it would be helpful to assess the activities of other organizations in the region and potentially bring in other partners to insure the best design for the program design and evaluation.

It was also necessary to meet with the existing partners identified by the OFL, to make sure they were "on the same page" for the new version of the camp program and also were willing and able to "buy into" the new evaluation process, which would require time, and thus a session before and after the camp, which had not been planned in previous camps.

Further, the MDPT had to vet other potential new partners, who would become part of the international collaboration team. This required the MDPT working together, to research and then interview, these potential partners. Specifically, this required in-person visits on site in Lesotho.

It was therefore deemed crucial to make a site visit to Lesotho. It would have been optimal for the three members of the team to make this visit but because of schedule, availability and practical issues (e.g., that the team members would have to invest personal funds for the trip), two of the three-person team went on the site visit.

Such issues are important to plan and recognize in the execution of such a project as the present one.

To prepare for the site visit, the two team members who were going to visit Lesotho identified potential partners who needed to be seen, and set up meetings with the assistance of the OFL staff for this to happen. Partners were considered who might provide input about cultural specificity, applicable modules of activities, assessment tools and funding. It is important to note that additional potential partners became evident during discussions held in the course of the site visit, and therefore, meetings had to be set up with these new potential partners during the site visit.

The collaboration and discussions about these potential partners amongst the two MDPT members who were on the visit were important. Long hours of discussions that lasted late into the night centered on these partners and their potential contributions, and also keeping careful records of their contacts. These discussions then had to be factored into further meetings with the OFL. Meetings were therefore held with numerous potential partner groups, in order to explore whether they could contribute to the camp project either in terms of financial support or human capital.

These organizations included the Millennium Challenge Corporation, United Nations Development Programme, International AIDS Care and Treatment Program (in conjunction with the Columbia University School of Public Health), the Clinton Foundation, and the Lesotho Country Director for the US Centers for Disease Control. The team also met with past partners of the OFL, including Lesotho Durham Link, the NGO Coalition of Rights of the Child, the Salvation Army, the Lesotho Child Counseling Unit, and the Lesotho Nutrition Department. The IAAP team also met with the Open Society Initiative of Southern Africa and the Center for Support of Peer Education in Johannesburg. While all of these were potentially valuable partners, many either had very specific alternative support strategies (e.g., mother-to-child transmission, the development and distribution of vaccines) or were fully engaged in their own project schedules and were unable to take on the camp project as well, or what they had to offer was already incorporated in the new program.

The final partners in the conduct of the April 2010 Camp were the OFL of Lesotho; the Lesotho Ministry for Gender, Youth, Sports, and Recreation; the Lesotho Girl Guides Association (members of which had been prior partners of the OFL, and who assisted in the delivery of the Camp program), Global Camps Africa (who both provided training to the OFL staff as well as assisting in the on-site delivery of the Camp program), US Doctors for Africa, and IAAP, with modest financial support provided by the Irish Embassy in Lesotho and IAAP. This represents a unique collaboration between multiple NGOs and multiple government departments – a sort of "public-public partnership."

It should be noted that not every project like this one needs to involve a large cast, but a thorough review of available partners and relevant projects is advisable, leading to a group of well-chosen relevant contributors.

Funding

Funding is an important issue for such a major project. In this case, the costs of the camp were borne by the OFL, as they had done in the past. The MDPT contributed their expertise and time pro bono, as part of their volunteering for the IAAP UN team. Some reimbursement of expenses was contributed by IAAP but the largest part of the hard costs of their trips to the site was absorbed by the team members themselves, out of commitment to the project. Major fundraising was not possible in the time constraints to launch and implement the project. Some meetings were held during the course of this planning visit to explore with potential partners the means and possibilities of funding which could be given to the OFL, given that IAAP is not a formal charitable organization that can receive funds. As mentioned above, the then Irish Ambassador to Lesotho donated some financial support; though very enthusiastic about the work, due to the last-minute nature of our contact, he was able to contribute only a very small amount from his "discretionary fund" for this project.

The camp design

The attendees at the 2010 Camp were 40 girls, predominantly aged 17–22 years and drop-outs from secondary school (primarily for economic reasons – as mentioned above, secondary school is fee-based in Lesotho). They had been selected for participation by local community leaders and village Chiefs, the criterion being that they had already demonstrated some leadership ability in their villages. The major focus of the 2010 Camp was on HIV/AIDS prevention and risk reduction, as well as some initial training about how to start a business, addressed by the camp component on Income-Generating Activities. The latter is considered "crucial for the girls to resist being seduced into 'transactional sex,' exchanging sexual favors for money for food, clothes, or school," notes Dr. Kuriansky.

Evaluation/Procedure

The overall evaluation of the IAAP team was that the Camp was a huge success: the processes went smoothly, the team worked exceptionally well together, the facilities were excellent, and the girls were observed to enjoy the camp, benefit greatly, bond well together, and be enthusiastic about their future. It was most outstanding to note several positive but unexpected outcomes, that (1) the girls spontaneously mentioned that they would like to be coaches; (2) the girls also spontaneously said that they would like to spread the message and their lessons learned to others in their villages; and (3) the girls were receptive to testing for HIV/AIDS (Kuriansky and Berry, 2011a, 2011b; Kuriansky and Berry, 2012). Positive outcomes of the entrepreneurial elements of the camp have also been reported, for example, a 30 percentage point increase in the attendees' ratings of the amount they knew about income-generating activities, as measured at the start of the camp and again at the end (Berry et al., 2013).

Evaluation instruments were administered in group settings. Coaches (the word locally used to signify the trainers) circulated throughout the room while the girls were filling out the paper questionnaire protocol (with pencils provided each time) to check if any respondents needed assistance. Some questionnaires were in the native language of Sesotho, some in English only, and some in both languages. The reasons why not all of the instruments were translated included the short planning time immediately prior to the camp, the last-minute nature of some of the questionnaire development, and limited translation resources. In cases where questionnaires were in English only, coaches translated the questions aloud in Sesotho. It was announced that participants who could not understand could go outside the room with a coach (one of the OFL staff) for further clarification and guidance.

The Evaluation Protocol was administered to the camp participants at the beginning and at the end of the camp, in order to determine the impact of the camp and changes in certain key variables over the time of the experience (a few items, e.g., overall satisfaction with the camp, were asked post-camp only). While there had been some initial concern about the girls filling out questionnaires (including the subject matter and the length), the group seemed overall highly cooperative. Furthermore, it was pointed out that filling out forms of this nature can be considered a form of literacy promotion.

Outcomes based on the evaluation

Self-esteem ratings (Rosenberg Scale)

Overall, 25 of the 40 respondents (63%) showed improvement in self-esteem from the start of the camp to the end. Of the five respondents who scored "Low" on the scale (less than 15 points), all showed improvement (+5 to +10, a mean improvement score of +8 points).

Of the remaining 35 respondents, 20 showed improvement (+1 to +10 points, a mean improvement score of +4 points); 14 respondents showed declines (−1 to −8, a mean decline of −3 points); and one respondent showed no change. A paired t-test showed that the difference between scores at the start of the camp and at the end of the camp is statistically significant [$t(24) = -4.863$, $p < .001$]. The means and standard deviations for this result are shown in Table 5.1.

Depression

Ratings on the CES-D (Center for Epidemiologic Studies Depression Scale showed statistically significant improvement from the start of the Camp to the end of the Camp [$t(16) = 3.709$, $p < .01$], indicating reduced depression among the attendees. The means and standard deviations for this result are shown in Table 5.2.

Table 5.1 Self-Esteem Ratings – Pre–Post Means and Standard Deviations

	Mean	Standard deviation
Pre	18.84	4.634
Post	22.56	2.873

$p < .001$

Table 5.2   Depression Ratings – Pre–Post
Means and Standard Deviations

	Mean	Standard deviation
Pre	30.00	7.929
Post	22.76	9.769

$p < .01$

Myths

Common myths about HIV/AIDS and sexual behavior were presented in the protocol as a list of statements, for example, "If you get tested and find out you are positive, you will die very soon thereafter" "Having sex with a virgin will rid an HIV-positive person of the virus" and "If girls do not have sex, their blood will clot." The girls rated the statements as to whether they agreed with the mythical statement ("Yes") or they disagreed with it ("No") or they just did not know one way or another ("Don't Know"). There were significantly more correct answers at the end of the camp than at the start $[t(39) = -3.842(p < .001)]$, while there were significantly fewer "Don't Know" answers at the end of the camp than at the start $[t(39) = 2.596(p < .05)]$. The means and standard deviations for these results are shown in Table 5.3A and Table 5.3B.

Table 5.3A   Myths Ratings – Correct Answers –
Pre–Post Means and Standard Deviations

	Mean	Standard deviation
Pre	31.33	8.017
Post	35.53	8.262

$p < .001$

Table 5.3B   Myths Ratings – Don't Know Answers –
Pre–Post Means and Standard Deviations

	Mean	Standard deviation
Pre	6.15	6.196
Post	3.87	4.954

$p < .05$

Table 5.4 Income-Generating Activities Ratings –
Pre–Post Means and Standard Deviations

	Mean	Standard deviation
Pre	2.88	1.385
Post	3.84	1.079

$p < .01$

Both of these results demonstrate that the camp had a positive impact on the prevailing lack of knowledge about myths and "local legends" regarding sexual behavior and HIV/AIDS issues.

Overall satisfaction with the camp

In response to the question (asked only at the end of the camp), "Thinking of the Camp in general, how would you rate your overall satisfaction?," over 80% of the respondents said "Very Satisfied" (on a five-point scale), with a further 13% saying "Satisfied." These ratings are admirably high: not a single respondent rated themselves "Dissatisfied" with the camp overall.

Income-generating activities

On the quantitative item, "How would you rate your knowledge about income-generating activities (doing something that makes money for you)?," ratings improved significantly from 41% of the attendees responding "A Great Deal" or "A Lot," at the start of the Camp to 71% at the end of the Camp [$t(30) = -3.186$, $p < .01$] (Berry et al., 2013). The means and standard deviations for this result are shown in Table 5.4.

Overall, it was evident that the girls want to go back to school and get an education to achieve their dreams.

All the girls could come up with a long-term goal – a dream of what they want to become. The most common dreams were to become a nurse, teacher or accountant.

The vast majority – eight out of ten – were optimistic that they would achieve their dream, that is, they rated themselves as "very confident" that they could achieve their goals.

Immediately following the camp

Almost half of the Camp attendees (19 girls) also attended a subsequent two-week Income-Generating Activities Workshop conducted by the Lesotho Ministry for Gender, Youth, Sports, and Recreation (the same Ministry whose staff provided an introduction to such activities as part of the Camp program). On the last day of that Workshop, the girls were given the opportunity to be voluntarily tested for HIV/AIDS (confidential testing and counseling were provided by Population Services International (PSI), a prominent testing company in Lesotho); of the 19 attendees, 17 agreed to be tested, a very high proportion. This in itself is a vote of confidence in the efficacy of the Camp: the girls felt sufficiently empowered to take the crucial step of getting tested and knowing their HIV/AIDS status, a critical piece of information for their future health and well-being.

Conclusion

The evaluation showed that the GEP led to improvements on the dimensions expected and thus that the intervention was successful in achieving its goals. Over the course of just one week, substantial improvements were seen on most of the assessment measures used. Additional follow-up work is needed to demonstrate whether these improvements have been sustained.

The GEP serves as a model of collaborative multidisciplinary work in action involving psychologists from various perspectives. The skills of the three psychologists, while different, proved to be complementary: the whole was, as the saying goes, greater than the sum of its parts. Each contributed a wealth of separate though related experience, which strengthened the program and its evaluation. In addition, the collaboration shown by the various groups in Lesotho also enhanced the robust nature of the program and contributed to its success. Further, the various skills of the MDPT contributed to insuring the applicability of the intervention to the setting in Africa, and the collaboration between the international partners.

While conducted with a small number of individuals, this model is now poised to be replicated with larger groups in Lesotho as well as in other African countries. At international conferences/meetings where the camp has been presented and discussed, representatives from other African countries have shown great interest in having the GEP implemented in their nation. Ideally, the program would be institutionalized in a more permanent setting, for example, in the secondary school system. This would, of course, require the involvement of at least one additional stakeholder, namely, the national Ministry of Education. However, such a long-term arrangement would ensure the sustainable continuation of the program as an effective means to address a major global issue: the empowerment of women and girls in combating HIV/AIDS and securing a prosperous future for themselves and their communities.

The present model shows the viability, importance and usefulness of a collaboration of psychologists from various disciplines, to develop and evaluate an international intervention addressing a public health problem (e.g., HIV/AIDS infection) and a social development issue (entrepreneurship training). While this effort was focused on sexuality education and entrepreneurial training and skills-building in Africa, the possibilities of applying this approach in other target populations, goals, and countries is suggested.

References

Bamberger, M. (2000). The evaluation of international development programs: A view from the front. *American Journal of Evaluation*, 21(1), 95–102. Accessed September 30, 2013 from doi: 10.1177/109821400002100108.

Berry, M. O., Kuriansky, J., Lytle, M. C., Vistman, B., Mosisilli, M. S., Hlothoane, L., & Pebane, J. (2013) Entrepreneurial training for girls empowerment in Lesotho: A process evaluation of a model programme. *South African Journal of Psychology*, 43, 445–458. doi: 10.1177/0081246313504685.

Ebbutt, D. (1998). Evaluation of projects in the developing world: Some cultural and methodological issues. *International Journal of Educational Development*, 18(5), 415–424. Accessed September 30, 2013 from doi: 10.1016/S0738-0593(98)00038-8.

Housley, W. (2003). *Interaction in Multidisciplinary Teams*. Farnham, Surrey, UK: Ashgate Publishing, Ltd.

Kuriansky, J. (2009). Letters to Dear Francis and Sisi Aminata: Questions of African youth and innovative HIV/AIDS and sexuality education collaborations for answering them. In E. Schroeder, & J. Kuriansky (Eds.), *Sexuality Education: Past, Present and Future*. Westport, Connecticut: Praeger. (Vol 2, Chapter 10), pp. 133–150.

Kuriansky, J., & Berry, M. O. (2010). GLOBAL DIALOGUE supported by the United Nations foundation: 'Making the millennium development goals happen: executive summary of a camp conducted by the Office of the First Lady of Lesotho, April, 2010' Girls Empowerment Programme. Retrieved September 23, 2010, from http://mdg.devex.com/mdg3-topic1-promote-gender-equality-and-empower-women/#respondEmpower.

Kuriansky, J., & Berry. M. O. (2011a). Advancing the UN MDGs by a model program for girls empowerment, HIV/AIDS prevention and entrepreneurship: IAAP Project in Lesotho, Africa. Retrieved June 9, 2012, from http://www.new.iaapsy.org/uploads/newsletters/April2011.pdf, pp. 36–39.

Kuriansky, J., & Berry. M. O. (2011b). The Girls Empowerment Programme: A multistakeholder camp model in Africa addressing the United Nations Millennium Development Goals. *Centerpoint Now*. New York: The World Council for Peoples of the United Nations, 70–71.

Kuriansky, J., & Berry, M. O. (2012). Advancing empowerment and poverty eradication in Africa through the camp model: Discussions at the UN Commission for Social Development. *Bulletin of the International Association of Applied Psychology*, 24, 2–3. Retrieved July/October from http://www.iaapsy.org/uploads/file/newsletters/July2012.pdf.

Kuriansky, J., & Corsini Munt, S. (2009). Engaging multiple stakeholders for healthy teens sexuality: Model partnerships for education and HIV prevention. In E. Schroeder, & J. Kuriansky (Eds.), *Sexuality Education: Past, Present and Future*. Westport, CT: Praeger. (Vol 3, Chapter 14), pp. 311–334.

Kuriansky, J., & Jean-Charles, W. (2012). Haiti Rebati: Update on activities rebuilding Haiti through the Global Kids Connect Project. *Bulletin of the International Association of Applied Psychology*, 24, 2–3. Retrieved July/October from http://www.iaapsy.org/uploads/file/newsletters/July2012.pdf.

Kuriansky, J., Spencer, J. & Tatem, A. (2009a). The sexuality and youth project: delivering comprehensive sexuality education to teens in Sierra Leone. In E. Schroeder, & J. Kuriansky (Eds.) *Sexuality Education: Past, Present and Future*. Westport, Connecticut: Praeger. Vol 3, Chapter 11, pp 238–268.

Kuriansky, J., Simonson, H., Varney, D., & Arias, J. (2009b). Empower now: An innovative holistic workshop for empowerment in life skills and sexuality education for teens. In E. Schroeder, & J. Kuriansky (Eds.), *Sexuality Education: Past, Present and Future* (pp. 129–162). Westport, CT: Praeger. (Vol 3, Chapter 7).

Locke, B.Z. and Putnam, P. (1971). *Center for Epidemiologic Studies Scale*. Washington, DC: Epidemiology and Psychopathology Research Branch, Public Health Service, National Institute of Mental Health.

Mann, M., Hosman, C., M. H., Schaalma, H. P., & deVries, N. K. (2004). Self-esteem in a broad-spectrum approach for mental health promotion. *Health Education Research*, 19(4), 357–372. doi: 10.1093/her/cyg041. Retrieved September 20, 2013, from http://her.oxfordjournals.org/content/19/4/357.full.

McBride, A. (2009). The first ladies of Africa make history. Retrieved August 9, 2013, from http://www.thedailybeast.com/articles/2009/04/27/the-first-ladies-of-africa-make-history.html.

Mertens, D., & Wilson, A. (2012). *Program Evaluation Theory and Practice: A Comprehensive Guide*. New York, NY: Guilford Press.

Patkar, V., Acosta, D., Davidson, T., Jones, A., Fox, J., & Keshtgar, J. (2011). Cancer multidisciplinary team meetings: Evidence, challenges, and the role of clinical decision support technology. *International Journal of Breast Cancer*, Volume 2011, Article ID 831605, 7 pages Retrieved from http://dx.doi.org/10.4061/2011/831605.

Rosenberg, M. (1965). *Society and the Adolescent Self-Image*. Princeton, NJ: Princeton University Press.

Rychetnik, L., Frommer, M., Hawe, P., & Shiell, A. (2002). Criteria for evaluating evidence on public health interventions. *Journal of Epidemiology and Community Health*, 56,119–127. Retrieved September 20, 2013, from doi:10.1136/jech.56.2.119. http://jech.bmj.com/content/56/2/119.full.

Schmitt, D. P., & Allik, J. (2005). Simultaneous administration of the Rosenberg Self-Esteem Scale in 53 nations: Exploring the universal and culture-specific features of global self-esteem. *Journal of Personality and Social Psychology*, 89(4), 623–642.

UNAIDS (2012). Lesotho global AIDS response country progress report. Retrieved September 20, 2013, from http://www.unaids.org/en/dataanalysis/ knowyourresponse/countryprogressreports/2012countries/ce_LS_Narrative_ Report[1].pdf.

UN Millennium Project (2005). www.unmillenniumproject.org/documents/ Gender-frontmatter.pdf Washington University in St. Louis (March 15, 2013). Depression in kids linked to cardiac risks in teens. *Science Daily.* Retrieved September 9, 2013, from http://www.sciencedaily,com/releases/ 3013/03/130315202640.htm.

UNICEF. (2009). http://www.unicef.org/infobycountry/lesotho_51255.html.

6
Entrepreneurship Training in Developing Countries

Kim Marie Bischoff, Michael M. Gielnik, and Michael Frese

Introduction

There are more than a billion people who live in poverty (Collier, 2007; Reynolds, 2012). Twenty-one percent of the population in developing countries (1.22 billion people) can only spend $1.25 or below a day in the year 2010 (Olinto, Beegle, Sobrado, and Uematsu, 2013). In addition to poverty, a major problem for developing countries is the high rate of unemployment (The International Labor Office [ILO], 2013). Two thirds of the young population in developing countries was unemployed or worked in irregular employment in the year 2012 (ILO, 2013; UNDESA, 2013). What will aggravate the situation is that many more young people will enter the future job market. In least developed countries 40% of the population was younger than 15 years in 2012, and 20% were aged between 15 and 24 years (UNDESA, 2013). Consequently, many governmental and non-governmental bodies argue that solving the problem of unemployment and fostering employment creation in developing countries is of high importance (ILO, 2013; UNDESA, 2013). A possible approach to address the issue of unemployment is entrepreneurship since research shows that entrepreneurship supports employment creation (Acs, Desai, and Hessels, 2008; Gries and Naudé, 2010; Mead and Liedholm, 1998; Naudé, 2010, 2012; Naudé, Gries, Wood, and Meintjies, 2008). This implies that through promoting entrepreneurship it is possible to contribute to employment creation.

Recent research suggests that entrepreneurship can be effectively promoted by entrepreneurship trainings (Martin, McNally, and Kay, 2013; McKenzie and Woodruff, 2012). In this chapter, we seek to present an entrepreneurship training which we developed in order to foster entrepreneurship and employment creation. The training we developed is an action-oriented entrepreneurship training called Student Training for Entrepreneurial Promotion (STEP). STEP is based on action regulation theory (Frese, 2009; Frese and Zapf, 1994; Hacker, 1998). To provide a brief introduction, we first describe how entrepreneurship generally contributes to economic development (including employment creation). We then outline the STEP intervention, describe its effects on entrepreneurship, and report the experiences and professional development of two students who participated in STEP. We conclude by providing an outlook on future implementations and planned evaluation studies of STEP.

Entrepreneurship and economic development

Entrepreneurship is defined as the identification and exploitation of business opportunities for new products or services (Shane and Venkatamaran, 2000). Entrepreneurship is an important means for poverty alleviation in developing countries because it contributes to economic development (Acs and Armington, 2004; Acs et al., 2008; Audretsch and Keilbach, 2004; Carree and Thurik, 2003, 2008; Gries and Naudé, 2010; Mead and Liedholm, 1998; Naudé, 2010, 2012; Naudé et al., 2008; Thurik, Carree, van Stel, and Audretsch, 2008; van Praag and Versloot, 2007; van Stel and Storey, 2004). Economic development comprises economic growth (e.g., growth in GDP), productivity growth (e.g., higher efficiency in production), and employment creation (number of employment opportunities) (Beck and Demirguc-Kunt, 2008; van Praag and Versloot, 2007). It is important to note that some scholars state that entrepreneurship does not generally drive economic development (Naudé, 2012). The literature distinguishes between opportunity and necessity entrepreneurship. Opportunity entrepreneurs start businesses because they have identified business opportunities and wish to pursue them (Reynolds et al., 2005; Xavier et al., 2013). Necessity entrepreneurs start businesses because they have no better job alternatives (Reynolds et al., 2005; Xavier et al., 2013). Some scholars argue that whereas opportunity entrepreneurs are a driving force for economic development, necessity entrepreneurs do not contribute to economic development (Gries and Naudé, 2010; van Stel, Carree and Thurik, 2005; Xavier et al., 2013). This would mean that a large part of entrepreneurs does not contribute to a country's economic development because many entrepreneurs living in developing countries are necessity entrepreneurs (Xavier et al., 2013). Yet, it is important to note that many necessity entrepreneurs manage profitable businesses and because of the profitability these necessity entrepreneurs contribute to economic development (Reynolds, 2012). Given the contradictions in the literature, we cannot draw any definite conclusions and it is still unclear whether only opportunity entrepreneurship contributes to economic development. Therefore, in the following, we do not distinguish between opportunity and necessity entrepreneurship and discuss the effects of entrepreneurship on economic development in general.

The literature argues for a positive impact of entrepreneurship on economic development in terms of productivity growth and employment creation (Carree and Thurik, 2003, 2008; Fritsch, 2008; Mead and Liedholm, 1998; Thurik et al., 2008; van Praag and Versloot, 2007). Research has shown that entrepreneurial ventures contribute to productivity growth and employment creation to a higher extent than larger and established businesses (Thurik et al., 2008). Entrepreneurial ventures that survive in the market grow faster than larger and established businesses in terms of production (van Praag and Versloot, 2007). Their fast growth also leads to an expansion in terms of employment and, hence, contributes to employment creation.

Furthermore, entrepreneurial ventures are considered a "vehicle for innovation and change" (Carree and Thurik, 2003, p. 22). In comparison to large and established firms, entrepreneurial ventures have more innovations per employee, are quicker in implementing innovations, and have a higher share of sales as a result of these innovations (Czarnitzki and Kraft, 2004; Dechenaux, Goldfarb, Shane, and Thursby, 2003; Love and Ashcroft, 1999; van Praag and Versloot, 2007). With the introduction of innovative products and services, entrepreneurial ventures also affect the innovation and productivity of established businesses (Carree and Thurik, 2008; Fritsch, 2008). When entrepreneurial ventures enter the market, they launch new products and services which leads to enhanced competition (Carree and Thurik, 2008; Fritsch, 2008). Enhanced competition, in turn, affects the productivity of established businesses (Fritsch, 2008). The established businesses have to become more efficient and refine their products and services in order to remain in the market (Baumol, 1986; Fritsch, 2008). These aspects of innovation and enhanced competition also drive economic development (Carree and Thurik, 2008).

In addition to the positive effects of entrepreneurship on economic development, entrepreneurship has also a positive effect on people's personal development. For example, research provides evidence for a positive impact of entrepreneurship on people's life satisfaction (Andersson, 2008; Benz and Frey, 2008; Blanchflower, 2004; Blanchflower and

Oswald, 1998). Entrepreneurship is related to life satisfaction because entrepreneurship provides independence, autonomy, and a feeling of being in control of one's own life (Andersson, 2008; Blanchflower, 2004; Benz and Frey, 2004, 2008). In the context of developing countries, Stark and her colleagues (2013) show that entrepreneurship had long-term effects on life satisfaction. Those who started a business were more satisfied with their lives and this effect held over several measurement periods (Stark et al., 2013).

Promoting entrepreneurship in developing countries

Based on the research findings that entrepreneurship contributes to a country's economic development, scholars and practitioners developed different approaches to promote entrepreneurship in developing countries. For example, a common approach used by many governments is to establish an administrative and regulatory framework that facilitates starting and operating private enterprises. According the World Bank, 85% of the world's economies introduced regulatory reforms between 2005 and 2010 aimed at making it easier to do business; in the last year alone, 117 economies implemented 216 regulatory reforms to facilitate entrepreneurship (The World Bank, 2010).

However, only changing the administrative and regulatory framework may not be sufficient to enhance entrepreneurship. People may lack the necessary knowledge and skills to benefit from the favorable frameworks and engage in entrepreneurship. In fact, research shows that skills and knowledge are particularly important in developing countries for successful entrepreneurship (Unger, Rauch, Frese, and Rosenbusch, 2011). A further approach to promote entrepreneurship focuses on entrepreneurship education and training. The number and diversity of entrepreneurship courses and trainings aiming to produce more entrepreneurs have increased in recent years (Fiet, 2000; Kabongo and Okpara, 2010; Klandt, 2004; Solomon, 2007). In developing countries, there is a high amount of entrepreneurship trainings offered by governments, non-governmental organizations, universities, or microfinance organizations in developing countries (Glaub and Frese, 2012; Martin et al., 2013; McKenzie and Woodruff, 2012). These entrepreneurship trainings differ in length, content, and target group (Glaub and Frese, 2012; Martin et al., 2013; McKenzie and Woodruff, 2012). The various trainings target, for instance, nascent entrepreneurs, business owners, women, students, adolescents, school drop-outs, rural dwellers, or people living in urban areas (Glaub and

Frese, 2012; Martin et al., 2013; McKenzie and Woodruff, 2012).
Examples of entrepreneurship trainings are Start and Improve Your
Business (SIYB), Women's Entrepreneurship Development (WED) and
Know About Business (KAB) of the International Labor Organization
(ILO), Competency-Based Economies through Formation of Enterprise
(CEFE) of the Deutsche Gesellschaft für Internationale Zusammenarbeit
(GIZ, German Society for International Cooperation), Emprendedores
Technologia (EMPRETEC) of the United Nations Conference on Trade
and Development (UNCTAD), Entrepreneurship Development Pro-
gramme (EDP) of the United Nations Industrial Development Orga-
nization (UNIDO), SME Toolkit and Business Edge Training of the
International Finance Corporation (IFC), the business plan competi-
tions conducted by TechnoServe, the Goldman Sachs 10,000 Women
initiative, and the STEP developed by our research team.

There are impressive figures regarding the number of participants in
some of the entrepreneurship trainings: For instance, 4.5 million people
in over 100 countries participated in ILO's SIYB training between 2003
and 2010 (Lieshout, Sievers, and Aliyev, 2012) and 300,000 people in 34
developing countries took part in EMPRETEC (United Nations Conference on Trade and Development, 2012). Although a very high number
of people participated in the trainings, the literature and understanding
about the trainings' impact is limited. Most of the studies evaluating the
entrepreneurship trainings have methodological limitations with the
consequence that the studies do not provide meaningful results (Glaub
and Frese, 2012; Martin et al., 2013; McKenzie and Woodruff, 2012).
A major limitation of many evaluation studies is a lack of a randomized
control group. As a consequence, these studies do not control for effects
that occur because the trainees have a preexisting inclination toward
entrepreneurship (self-selection), the trainees may develop naturally
(maturation), the trainees learn how to correctly respond to the assessment (testing), or that economic and regulatory conditions become
more favorable for entrepreneurship (history) (Glaub and Frese, 2012;
McKenzie and Woodruff, 2012). Furthermore, another major limitation
is that only few studies assess long-term training effects (McKenzie and
Woodruff, 2012).

A design that follows highest scientific standards is the randomized control group design with pre- and post-testing that examines
both short- and long-term effects (Banerjee and Duflo, 2009; Duflo,
Glennerster, and Kremer, 2007). Such a design limits potential biases
and controls for effects of maturation, history, testing, and self-selection
(Cook, Campbell, and Peracchio, 1990). It allows the comparison of

training participants with participants of a control group who do not receive the training. A random selection of participants to a training group and a control group is important to ensure that both groups are equivalent before the training. The groups should not differ in any characteristics, such as cognitive ability, age, sex, education, existing entrepreneurial experience, participation in former business courses, or employment experience. Since a random selection ensures that the participants of the training and control group are equivalent before the training and live in the same contextual setting, it is possible to conclude that any differences after the training are due to the training and not caused by other factors (Banerjee and Duflo, 2009; Cook et al., 1990; Duflo et al., 2007). The study design should also imply several post-training measurements to assess short- and long-term training effects (Martin et al., 2013; McKenzie and Woodruff, 2012). Measuring both short- and long-term training effects is necessary because the impact of the training varies over time (McKenzie and Woodruff, 2012): Some effects occur shortly after the training whereas others will take more time to unfold McKenzie and Woodruff (2012).

Student training for entrepreneurial promotion (STEP)

In this section, we present the STEP training as an entrepreneurship training which was evaluated according to the highest scientific standards. STEP is a 12-week action-oriented entrepreneurship training that successfully trains participants in entrepreneurship (Gielnik et al., in press). STEP aims to provide a solution for the lack of employment opportunities, in particular for the youth, in developing countries. The main idea of STEP is to train entrepreneurial skills and knowledge for successful entrepreneurship and employment creation. In the following, we describe the training's methodological approach and the impact of STEP on entrepreneurship. We conclude with a description of how we implement STEP at our partner institutions in a sustainable manner.

The methodological approach: STEP as an action-orientated entrepreneurship training

Building on action regulation theory (Frese, 2009; Frese and Zapf, 1994; Hacker, 1998), STEP uses an action-oriented training approach to promote entrepreneurship (Gielnik et al., in press). Many scholars suggest that an action-oriented training approach is particularly useful to promote entrepreneurship (Barr et al., 2009; Fiet, 2000; Frese,

2009; Gielnik and Frese, 2013; Gielnik et al., in press; Johannisson et al., 1998; Pittaway and Cope, 2007; Rasmussen and Sørheim, 2006). An action-oriented training approach promotes entrepreneurship by providing skills and knowledge that facilitate entrepreneurial actions. Entrepreneurial actions are a key factor for entrepreneurship to occur because only through actions business opportunities are identified and successfully implemented (Baron, 2007a; Baum, Frese, Baron, and Katz, 2007; McMullen and Shepherd, 2006; Shane and Venkatamaran, 2000). An action-oriented training approach comprises various components that help training participants develop skills and knowledge. These components are teaching action principles, making use of learning through action, matching training tasks with job tasks, and providing feedback on participants' behavior (Frese, Beimel, and Schoenborn, 2003; Gielnik and Frese, 2013; Gielnik et al., in press; Glaub, Fischer, Klemm, and Frese, 2011; Keith and Frese, 2008). In the following, we describe how the components of an action-oriented training approach support the development of skills and knowledge and how these components were applied to STEP.

Action principles are theory- and research-based principles that teach practical knowledge (Frese, 2009; Frese et al., 2003; Gielnik et al., in press; Glaub et al., 2011). Action principles are heuristics or "rules of thumb" that facilitate taking action (Frese, 2009; Frese and Zapf, 1994). Action principles help participants to apply the knowledge and skills they learned in the training to real-life situations (Frese, 2009; Frese et al., 2003 Gielnik et al., in press; Glaub et al., 2011). Instead of abstract theoretical knowledge about entrepreneurship, action principles provide concrete guidelines about how to deal with the tasks of an entrepreneur. For STEP, we drew on scientific knowledge and theories about successful entrepreneurship to develop the action principles. We developed action principles for 12 modules from three different domains important for entrepreneurship: business administration, psychology and entrepreneurship (Baron, 2007b). The 12 modules are: identifying business opportunities, marketing, managing strategically, finding starting capital, managing finances, bookkeeping, planning and implementing plans, conducting leadership, overcoming barriers, networking, persuading, negotiating, writing a business plan and registering the business (legal framework). The following provides some examples for action principles taught in STEP: "Use your strength and talents to identify business opportunities"; "formulate concrete actions to achieve your goal, and write down the time you want to carry out the actions"; "determine signals that point to potential problems before they occur and develop back-up plans"; "set high and specific goals"; "collect all documents (receipts, invoices, etc.) for every transaction"; "divide a page into two and record all money coming into the business on the left side and all money going out of the business on the right side." The action principles help the participants to understand what they have to do in order to be successful in starting and managing a business.

Learning through action means that training participants actively perform the target behavior during the training (Frese, 2009; Frese et al., 2003; Gielnik et al., in press). The target behavior is performing entrepreneurial actions to successfully start and manage a business. Performing actions during the training leads to the development of action knowledge and to a smoother implementation of actions after the training (Frese, 2009; Frese and Zapf, 1994). Thus, performing entrepreneurial actions during STEP enhances the trainees' action knowledge about entrepreneurship and, consequently, facilitates implementing entrepreneurial actions after STEP (Gielnik and Frese, 2013; Gielnik et al., n.d.). In STEP, the trainees take entrepreneurial actions in the form of starting and managing a new venture within the time-frame of the training. Directly after the first session, the trainees form start-up teams of four to seven people and immediately start a business. To be able to immediately start a business every STEP start-up team receives about $100 starting capital. The starting capital has to be refunded at the end of the training. The start-up teams can use the starting capital to acquire the necessary equipment and resources to start their business. It is important for the learning process that the start-up teams start their business within the first week of the training. During the three months of training, the trainees should experience the whole entrepreneurial process including identifying a business opportunity, launching the business, and managing the business. STEP participants in Uganda, for instance, started businesses that sold fresh juices, fruits and vegetables, bakery products, books, or clothes. Other businesses offered laundry services, beauty services, consultancy services for computer programs, designed greeting cards, or produced bags or jewelry. There were also groups with more unique business ideas. For example, trainees in Kenya produced flavored sugar cubes which could be used to sweeten tea or other beverages. The sugar cubes were produced with easily accessible materials, for example, sugar as the basic material and ginger, cinnamon, or other spices for the flavors. Setting up and managing a business right at the start of the training also increases the trainees' transfer which is the application of the learned skills and knowledge to the working context (Baldwin and Ford, 1988). For the STEP trainees, transfer means to apply the entrepreneurial skills and knowledge learned in the training to the process of starting and running a business. Transfer can be facilitated if training tasks and job tasks match (Baldwin and Ford, 1988; Thorndike and Woodworth, 1901).

A further essential component of the action-oriented training approach is *providing feedback on participants' behavior*. Research shows that providing feedback about the participants' behavior during the training supports the learning process (Frese, 2009; Frese et al., 2003). Providing feedback is important because it helps trainees to modify their behavior and to correct their actions (Frese and Zapf, 1994; Frese et al., 2003; Friedrich, Glaub, Gramberg, and Frese, 2006; Keith and Frese, 2005, 2008; Martocchio and Dulebohn, 1994). Feedback allows trainees to compare their behavior with the action principles taught in the training and shows whether the behavior is in accordance with the action principles or whether it needs to be modified. Both negative and positive feedback provides trainees with useful information. Negative feedback signals that the trainees' behavior was not effective. It reveals gaps in trainees' skills and knowledge and helps trainees to understand which behavior they need to change and how they can improve their behavior (Frese, 2009; Frese and Zapf, 1994). Positive feedback ensures that the trainees are reinforced for effective behavior (Frese and Zapf, 1994).

In STEP, trainees receive positive and negative feedback on their behavior by both the trainer and by the other trainees. Within the weekly sessions the trainees conduct exercises that are geared toward their businesses. These exercises constitute typical entrepreneurial tasks, such as conducting a market analysis, a competitor analysis, or developing an operations plan for the businesses. After each exercise there is time for discussing the exercises. These discussions allow the trainer and the other trainees to provide feedback on trainees' behavior and how they deal with the exercises. The feedback is based on the action principles taught during the training. The action principles provide participants with concrete guidelines for completing the exercises and solving problems.

In addition, the discussions enable trainees to share experiences regarding failures and errors. Failure and errors are a form of negative feedback (Frese, 2009; Frese and Zapf, 1994; Heimbeck, Frese, Sonnentag, and Keith, 2003; Keith and Frese, 2005, 2008). Failures and errors are thus an important source for learning (Frese, 2009; Frese and Zapf, 1994; Heimbeck et al., 2003; Keith and Frese, 2005, 2008). Emphasizing that errors are a valuable form of feedback helps trainees to understand that they should be open toward errors and use the feedback they receive to further develop their skills and knowledge. During the training, the STEP trainers emphasize that errors are inevitable and should be seen as a chance to learn. If trainees do not fear errors and failure, but make use of them to improve their entrepreneurial skills, learning to deal with failures contributes to entrepreneurial success.

The impact of STEP on entrepreneurship

The main goal of STEP is to promote successful entrepreneurship among youths in developing countries by providing skills and knowledge about entrepreneurship. To achieve the main goal, STEP targets three sub goals: First, STEP aims at changing the mindset of the training participants such that self-employment becomes an attractive and feasible career option. Second, STEP is geared toward increasing the start-up rate, and, third, STEP intends to turn job seekers into job creators. In order to understand if STEP meets these three sub goals and, hence, contributes to successful entrepreneurship among the youth in developing countries, we are continuously conducting rigorous evaluation studies.

To assess the impact of STEP, we use a study design that meets the highest scientific standards (Gielnik et al., in press). All studies we carried out so far were longitudinal studies with several measurement waves over a period of up to 36 months to test for long-term training effects. The studies were randomized controlled field experiments. We randomly assigned applicants to a training group that received the training and to a control group that did not receive the training. Participants of the studies were randomly assigned to the training or control groups by lottery.

So far, we conducted evaluation studies with students of seven universities and with trainees from a vocational training institute. The university students were mainly undergraduates from different faculties, such as arts, natural science, social science, technology, education, law, and medicine. Up to 400 students participated in each evaluation study with up to 200 students in the training group and up to 200 students in the control group. We conducted the evaluation studies in five countries located in sub-Saharan Africa: Uganda, Kenya, Tanzania, Ruanda and Liberia. The evaluation studies revealed similar results across the countries suggesting that the positive impact of STEP is generalizable to different cohorts and contexts. In the following, we present the most important findings regarding the positive impact of STEP on entrepreneurship.

Performance of start-up teams during the training

We evaluated the performance of the start-up teams during the training on two dimensions: Repayment of the starting capital and profits made by the start-up teams with their businesses. The results of our studies show that STEP trainees were successfully repaying their starting capital. Across all evaluation studies the repayment rate of the starting capital was very high. On average 83% of the starting capital was refunded. More than half of all start-up teams returned the starting capital completely: The full amount of $100 was repaid by 63% of the start-up teams. If the start-up teams incur a loss, the trainees did not need to add own money to repay the full amount; rather, they gave back what was left of their starting capital. Only 7% of the start-up teams could not pay back any of the starting capital. Furthermore, the results reveal that most of the start-up teams' businesses were operating successfully. A profit was made by 78% of the start-up teams. The average profit of these businesses was $50.44 with a range from $1.70 to $221.00.

Scholars and practitioners may be concerned that the starting capital and the profit of the businesses give STEP trainees an advantage over participants of the control group and that this advantage influences the training outcomes. Their concern may be that STEP trainees have more money available after the training than participants of the control group, since STEP trainees receive starting capital and keep the businesses' profits they make during the training. We argue that the starting capital and the businesses' profits do not affect training outcomes. The STEP trainees have to repay the starting capital at the end of the training and the amount of money that students receive from the profits during the training is very small. To evaluate whether there is an advantage for the STEP trainees, we tested if the profit affects the training outcomes. The amount of profits made was not related to starting a business after the training. The profits are usually not very high per person. Of the 78% of start-up teams that made a profit, 95% generated an amount of less than $148 per team, that is, less than $30 per person. Half of the start-up teams that made profits obtained an even smaller amount ($37) per team. This implies that more than half of the trainees that make profits with their start-up teams generate an amount of less than $7.40 per person.

Long-term outcomes of STEP

The first evaluation study that measured long-term effects was done in Uganda. Gielnik et al. (in press) provide empirical evidence that STEP meets its goal to increase the start-up rate after the training. Students who took part in the training were significantly more likely to start businesses than students who did not take part in the training. In comparison to the control group, the training led to 50% more business start-ups within one year and 31% more business start-ups within 18 months. One year after the training 51% of the training participants owned a business. The number of business start-ups even increased over time: 18 months after the training 63% of the STEP trainees were business owners. In the control group, 35% were business owners after one year and 48% after 18 months. For each 100 participants, the STEP trainees started 17 more businesses than an equivalent control group within one year and 15 more businesses within 18 months. Examples of the businesses the Ugandan STEP trainees started after the training are hair and beauty salons, copy shops, restaurants, the production and sale of jewelry or African crafts, repair, maintenance of computers, farming businesses such as poultry farms, pig farms or seed planting, and various consultancy services.

Our evaluation study in Uganda also reveals that STEP meets its goal to turn job seekers into job creators. Besides creating their own employment, the STEP trainees created employment for others. Compared to the control group, the STEP trainees created 47% more jobs one year after the training and 38% more jobs after 18 months. STEP supported the creation of 88 additional jobs in a year's time for each 100 participants trained. Within one year, 100 students of the control group created employment for 60 people. The number of created jobs rose to 134 for STEP participants and to 96 for control participants after 18 months. Thus, 100 STEP trainees created 28 more jobs within one year's time and 38 more jobs within 18 months than an equivalent control group. Hence, the STEP trainees' businesses produced more jobs than the businesses normally started by students in these countries.

Regarding owners' salary, revenue, and growth rate, the long-term evaluation shows that the STEP trainees' businesses were the equivalent to the businesses of the control group. We did not find significant differences between the STEP trainees' businesses and the businesses of the students of the control group in terms of revenue, growth rate and in the salary the owners pay themselves. This means that the businesses started by STEP trainees were of the same value than the control group's businesses. The average revenue of the STEP participants' businesses is approximately $395 per month. The business owners of the training group pay themselves an average monthly salary of almost $75. The businesses of the students in the control group make monthly sales of about $370 on average, and they earn an average salary from their own businesses of around $80 per month. The businesses of the control group grow in profit, sales and investments, on average, by 16% within one year. The average growth rate of the STEP trainees' businesses within one year was 19%. These similarities between the training group and the control group imply that the businesses that emerge from STEP were not of lower quality than businesses students usually started in their countries.

The second evaluation study was done in Liberia and shows that STEP helped students to become portfolio and serial entrepreneurs. Portfolio and serial entrepreneurs are people who own more than one business at the same time, while these businesses are independent from each other or who have owned at least one business before their present business (Westhead, Ucbasaran, and Wright, 2005). Eighteen months after the training, every STEP participants owned on average 13% more businesses at the same time than each student of the control group. When we include the additional businesses in our analyses, the monthly revenue of businesses started by STEP trainees' was 71% higher than the monthly revenue of the businesses started by students of the control group. Whereas the businesses of the control group made monthly sales of $242 per business, the monthly revenue of the training group was $414 per business. In conclusion, these findings show that STEP led to portfolio and serial entrepreneurship. Students who became portfolio or serial entrepreneurs were more successful in terms of generated revenues. This is in line with the current research literature arguing that portfolio and serial entrepreneurship in developing countries leads to more business success in the long run (Rosa, 2013).

Mediators between STEP and long-term outcomes

In this section, we report mediators of the effect of STEP on entrepreneurship. A mediator is the mechanism underlying the relationship between a cause and effect; a mediator thus provides an explanation for why a cause leads to an effect (Baron and Kenny, 1986; Preacher and Hayes, 2004). With regard to the evaluation of STEP this means that these underlying mechanisms account for the relationship between STEP and the long-term outcomes. We have seen that STEP has valuable long-term effects: It successfully increases business start-ups, creates employment, and leads to business success. An important question is why and how these effects emerge. To answer this question, Gielnik and his colleagues (in press) investigated the underlying mechanisms mediating the effect of the training on business start-ups. They found that STEP had a significant impact on entrepreneurial action and business opportunity identification and these factors predicted business start-up (Gielnik et al., in press).

STEP positively affected business opportunity identification (Gielnik et al., in press), which is the identification, evaluation, and exploitation of opportunities for new products and services (Shane and Venkatamaran, 2000). Business opportunity identification is of high importance as it is the starting point for new venture creation (Baron, 2007b; Shane, 2000; Shane and Venkatamaran, 2000). The evaluation study in Uganda shows that the STEP training group significantly improved in business opportunity identification (Gielnik et al., in press). After the training, STEP participants identified 20% more business opportunities than the control group. STEP trainees identified on average 1.78 business opportunities per person after the training, whereas every student of the control group only identified 1.48 business opportunities on average. Assuming 100 students participate in STEP, they identify 30 more business opportunities in total than the same number of students who do not take part in the training.

In addition, STEP influenced students in their entrepreneurial actions (Gielnik et al., in press). Entrepreneurial actions are start-up activities that help the entrepreneur to successfully pursue business opportunities and, hence, contribute to the successful creation of a new venture (Davidsson and Honig, 2003; Dimov, 2007; Frese, 2009; Gartner, 1985; Gielnik and Frese, 2013; Reynolds, 2007). Examples for such start-up activities are (1) discussing a business idea with business men, advisors, potential investors, family or friends; (2) identifying target customers; (3) saving money for starting a business; and (4) gathering resources to purchase or rent equipment, raw materials, or other facilities (Dimov, 2007; Davidsson and Honig, 2003). Within one year, the Ugandan students participating in STEP performed 36% more entrepreneurial actions than the students of the control group. Entrepreneurial actions remained higher in the training group than in the control group even 18 months after the training. It is particularly striking that the effects of STEP on entrepreneurial action hold in the long-run. In one of our studies in Liberia we compared the business owners of the training group with owners of the control group. We find that 18 months after the training, business owners of the training group performed 37% more entrepreneurial actions than business owners of the control group. This means that business owners of the training group remained entrepreneurially active in the long run. They did not only start a business, but continued to be entrepreneurial.

A further reason why and how STEP leads to an increase in business start-ups is that the training successfully influences antecedents of entrepreneurial action (Gielnik et al., in press). The training improves participants' action knowledge, action planning, entrepreneurial self-efficacy and entrepreneurial goal intentions (Gielnik et al., in press). In the context of entrepreneurship, action knowledge means knowledge about entrepreneurial actions (Frese, 2009). Action planning means performing mental simulations of entrepreneurial actions that specify how to reach one's goals, for example, to start a business (Frese, 2009; Frese and Zapf, 1994). Entrepreneurial self-efficacy is the belief in one's own abilities regarding successfully starting a business (Bandura, 1986; Boyd and Vozikis, 1994; Chen, Greene, and Crick, 1998; McGee, Peterson, Mueller, and Sequeira, 2009; Zhao, Seibert, and Hills, 2005). Goal intentions imply what people want to achieve (Gollwitzer, 1999; Gollwitzer and Brandstätter, 1997). Action knowledge, action planning, entrepreneurial self-efficacy, and entrepreneurial goal intentions are action-regulatory factors. The action-regulatory factors mediated the effect of the training on entrepreneurial action and are, therefore, relevant for the process of starting a business (Gielnik et al., in press). STEP enhanced participants' action knowledge (Gielnik et al., in press). In comparison to the control group, the STEP trainees had 32% more action knowledge directly after they participated in the training. Furthermore, the training increased participants' action planning (Gielnik et al., in press). They showed 30% more action planning directly after the training than the control group. STEP also had positive effects on participants' entrepreneurial self-efficacy (Gielnik et al., in press). Directly after the training, STEP participants showed 6% higher entrepreneurial self-efficacy than students of the control group. This means that training participants believed more strongly in their capabilities to start a new venture than the control group did. In addition, STEP successfully affected trainees' entrepreneurial goal intentions (Gielnik et al., in press). The training group showed 23% stronger goal intentions than the control group directly after the training. This implies that STEP trainees had a stronger intent to start their own businesses than participants of the control group have. These results show that STEP is able to enhance important antecedents of entrepreneurial action which, in turn, promotes the establishment of new businesses and creation of new jobs.

Cases

Two cases show the dynamics of the students' entrepreneurial action and illustrate the positive effects of STEP on students' entrepreneurial actions through affecting antecedents of entrepreneurial action. The first student, Jane (name has been changed for reason of anonymizing) was typical of many students in Uganda. Before the training, she had not been involved in any entrepreneurial ventures, and she had not attended any prior entrepreneurship courses. Jane knew that the job market conditions were poor for her even with a university degree, but she did not consider becoming an entrepreneur as an attractive and feasible career option for her. She was afraid of the challenges entrepreneurs face. According to her report, starting and running a business in the training was a "totally new experience." The experience that it is possible to overcome the challenges of entrepreneurship and to successfully operate a business "opened her eyes," as she said. Jane elaborated that the training was a turning point in her life which changed her belief that entrepreneurship is an insurmountable series of tasks. She also explained that she learned to reflect after failures, learned from errors, and that she learned to start anew despite unfavorable circumstances. Thus, she developed a "never-give-up" attitude and learned to use errors and failures as a valuable source of feedback for her development. After the training, Jane started a poultry farm and managed to supply retail shops and hotels in Uganda's capital city Kampala with eggs and chickens. One year after the training, she employed five full-time employees, and she intended to use the profits from the poultry farm to set up a fish farm. She had conducted market research and had found an appropriate location for her business. In addition, Jane generated the idea of growing rice. However, after some time of research, she came to the conclusion that farming fish and growing rice required too much capital; therefore, she rather expanded the poultry farm. The poultry farm was located in a village some hours away from Kampala, where she lived with her husband. Commuting between the village where her farm was located and Kampala was demanding; at the same point she decided to sell the farm and start another business that would allow her to stay in Kampala. To achieve her goal, she came up with the idea of starting an event management business, which she had successfully set up when we talked to her 18 months after the training. The business offered support in planning events such as weddings. It provided decorations and equipment and organized the preparations necessary for successfully hosting an event. She paid herself a monthly salary of about $590 from that business and employed three persons. At that time, Jane was also employed as assistant sales administrator at a broadband company. Her tasks were bookkeeping, reports on customers, and the coordination of other departments. Her salary from the employment was around

$315. Thus, Jane made more money with her business than with her employment, excluding the profit from selling the poultry farm.

When we met her again 24 months after the training, her employment situation had changed further. She was still employed at the same company, but now held the position of a network engineer who worked on trouble-shooting networks, installing software, and maintaining software and hardware, with a monthly salary of about $705. In addition, she had closed the event management business and, instead, had started an information technology consultancy that developed computer software, designed Web pages for companies and private persons, and set up and installed networks for offices and homes. Similar to the salary from her former business, she paid herself a monthly salary of about $590 from the information technology consultancy. Comparing the event management business with the information technology consultancy, we found out that the event management business had slightly higher average sales per month (around $1,370) but also required a high amount of investments (around $2,745). The consultancy's average monthly sales were about $795, but required less investment (around $470) than the event management business. Jane started the information technology consultancy because she had acquired a good knowledge of the field after studying computer science at the university. Thus, Jane successfully put her skills and knowledge gained in her studies at the university and at work into practice. It is interesting to observe that she had started out with a business of low complexity, and in the course of time she opened up a business in her field of study. When we met Jane again around four years after the training, she informed us that she still owned the information technology consultancy. Furthermore, she had started an additional business by launching an ice cream parlor in the city center of Kampala. According to Ugandan experts, this is a unique business idea, because there are very few places in Kampala where ice cream is made and can be purchased. Most of these places are supermarkets or rather expensive restaurants and coffeehouses with wealthy customers. There was nearly no ice cream parlor for the youth and young adults. Thus, Jane's ice cream parlor was a good business idea with potential market success.

In conclusion, through STEP Jane has formed and pursued different entrepreneurial goals; she has changed from a non-entrepreneurial student to a successful portfolio and serial entrepreneur. This case illustrates how the training facilitated a mastery experience of entrepreneurship which increased the student's entrepreneurial self-efficacy, how the training led to a more persistent and positive attitude toward entrepreneurship, and how the student used her actions as a source of learning to improve their action knowledge after the training. Jane's entrepreneurial progress also demonstrates that students start multiple businesses they successfully pursue after the training. They are also confronted with a lot of barriers and failure. In the training the participants learn that errors and failures are part of the entrepreneurial process. Jane explained to us that acknowledging errors and failures and learning to deal with them was one of the most important learning experiences in STEP. She mentioned that through the training she understood that some things will not work out the way she wants them to, but that this is not a reason to give up; just the opposite, it is a reason to stay active and change processes in the business or start anew.

The second student, Richard (name has been changed for reasons of anonymity) had been employed before. He had worked for eight months as a field manager at a telecommunications company and as a sales person at a bank. He was not employed during the training. Richard told us that he had been thinking about becoming an entrepreneur because he could not imagine being employed for his whole life and being satisfied with the goal of becoming "the employee of the month." However, he had never tried to become self-employed before the training, since he lacked the practical skills. He explained that he had some knowledge in entrepreneurship before the training but did not know how to put it into practice and, hence, never started a business. Asked about the most important learning experiences, Richard said that the training taught him how to plan and execute the start-up of a business in general, how to develop financial plans, and how to manage finances. After the training, Richard recognized several opportunities to enter the gastronomy industry. He started a restaurant in a town near Uganda's capital, recognizing a lack of restaurants in the local market. In his restaurant he served lunch up to 4 p.m.; drinks, including freshly squeezed juices, were still available after 4 p.m. Since the restaurant was equipped with a TV, customers came to the restaurant to watch soccer. His target group was students of a university. Richard identified the business idea of a restaurant during STEP, where he sold fresh juice together with his colleagues of the start-up team. He wanted to move on with his idea of starting a restaurant and opened the restaurant about eight months after the training. When we met him 18 months after the training, he managed his restaurant successfully and made about $380 sales per month. He paid himself a monthly salary of about $195, employed five persons, two full-time employees, and three part-time employees, and he invested about $195 in this business within a period of ten months.

Two years after the training, we again talked to him about his restaurant. He explained that his monthly sales had decreased. On average his revenue was around $255 per month. He paid himself a salary of about $160 and had invested about $470 within the last 12 months. Richard still employed five people in the restaurant. He increased the number of full-time employees from two to three and decreased the number of part-time employees from three to two.

The restaurant is not the only business that Richard successfully started after the training. About 15 months after the training, he also started a boutique that sold clothes and shoes for women and children. The business was located in his parents' home village some hours away from Kampala. Richard's boutique made average sales of about $235 per month 18 months after the training. He paid himself a salary of around $80 per month and invested $235 in the business within the last few months. One full-time employee was working in the boutique. When we met him again 24 months after the training, he mentioned that his revenue had decreased and that he sold clothes for about $100 on average per month. He explained that within the last 12 months, he invested $235 into the business and that he still employed one full-time employee in the boutique.

Richard also identified the opportunity to start a construction material supply company that sells building materials such as bricks or cement. Whenever we met him, he had this business idea in mind and wanted to pursue it. He had already done some start-up activities; however, he was not able to successfully launch this venture because this kind of business requires a high amount of capital that he had not secured yet. Richard mentioned that despite the high amount of starting capital, he will not give up on that business opportunity but for now will concentrate on businesses that do not require such high amounts.

Twenty-four months after the training, Richard told us that he wanted to start a piggery project in Masaka, a town in Uganda. He had already bought eight pigs, had constructed the shelter, and was currently in the process of identifying the best market. He thought the best market for this business was outside the country, and he intended to export to nearby countries. Richard had already planned his next steps: He planned to buy more pigs, to construct more shelters, and to improve the fertility rate of his pigs, which he could do with special animal feeds and treatment. He had, furthermore, established contacts to a market in southern Sudan.

After some time Richard faced sudden setbacks and difficult challenges. We met Richard again four years after the training, and he mentioned that in the meantime he had also opened up a small hotel. His workload from managing several businesses at the same time had been very high, so he had decided to employ his girlfriend to manage the hotel. However, the hotel incurred losses because she had taken money from the business to use it for her private expenses and had not taken proper care of the customers and their needs. He told us that therefore, he had lost a high amount of money. Because he put all his effort into trying to save the hotel, he did not have much time for his restaurant, and its sales declined. He decided to close down the hotel to be able to put more effort into the restaurant, which became successful again due to his increased efforts.

Despite the fact that he had diligently planned the different steps to start and run the businesses, he stated that he experienced numerous challenges and setbacks in the start-up phase of his businesses. He explained that the training was a crucial factor in deciding to continue with entrepreneurship because STEP gave him the determination and courage to do so. After the training, his most important principle became not to give up. This determination and persistence resulted in new businesses and in employment he created for himself and others. Again, STEP led Richard toward portfolio and serial entrepreneurship. Richard faced severe setbacks; however, these setbacks did not lead to complete bankruptcy. He had to close one business but was able to continue running his other businesses and had not lost his entire income. He wanted to use the profit of this business to invest into the start-up of yet another business. During and after STEP, Richard explained, he had learned to reinvest the profit and had experienced that a business can start small and grow over time.

The sustainable implementation process

In this section, we describe how we implement STEP at a partner institution. The implementation process of STEP is geared toward sustainability. We aim to ensure that STEP will be continued at the institutions where it is implemented. We have already implemented STEP at seven universities plus a vocational-training institute in five African countries. The implementation of STEP at an institution is the starting point for a regular and sustainable application of the training. We make use of the following strategies to ensure a sustainable implementation of STEP: We cooperate with local lecturers from the respective institutions, we fade out our support in preparing and organizing the training, and we keep the cost of the training low.

We cooperate with the local lecturers at the institutions where STEP is implemented. To best support the trainees' learning process, it is important that the training is conducted by local lecturers. The trainers have to be aware of their trainees' level of knowledge and know the context of their participants. This context knowledge facilitates the learning process and increases the transfer of learned skills to real-life situations. Local lecturers often understand the knowledge level of their trainees better than lecturers who are unfamiliar with the contextual setting of the country. In addition, local lecturers have much greater knowledge of their own cultural context and the real-life situations of entrepreneurs in their countries. In the implementation process of STEP, we make sure that local lecturers deliver the training at each participating institution.

To prepare the local lecturers and to make them familiar with the methodological approach of STEP, we conduct a three-day train-the-trainer workshop with the local lecturers. The train-the-trainer workshops enable the local lecturers to understand and apply STEP. The workshops introduce the action-oriented training approach of STEP, teach how this approach can be applied, provide knowledge about the training content, and teach how to make use of the training material. The process of training local trainers in conducting STEP also allows us to hand over the organization and preparation of STEP to them. In the long run, the lecturers thus become able to implement STEP without any external support. To ensure that the trainers are well prepared in conducting STEP without external support, we fade out our support. During the first implementation, the core team of German project coordinators is very much involved in organizing and preparing STEP at the respective institution. During the second implementation, at least one local STEP trainer of the institution takes over the organization and coordination of the training, and the German project coordinators provide less support than in the first implementation. The subsequent implementations are fully conducted by the STEP trainers of the local institution, which ensures a sustainable implementation.

Discussion and outlook

To summarize, entrepreneurial ventures are an important driver for a country's economic development, because they have a positive impact on innovation, employment creation, productivity growth, and economic growth. Thus, entrepreneurship can be seen as an effective means for contributing to economic development and reducing poverty in developing countries.

A useful approach to promote entrepreneurship in developing countries is to provide entrepreneurship trainings. We developed and evaluated an action-oriented entrepreneurship training (Student Training on Entrepreneurial Promotion – STEP) that builds on theories from the field of industrial and organizational psychology, for example, action regulation theory (Frese, 2009; Frese and Zapf, 1994; Hacker, 1998). In contrast to many other training evaluations, we conducted rigorous studies that meet the highest scientific standards in order to evaluate STEP. Our evaluation studies show that STEP achieved its objectives in successfully providing trainees with skills and knowledge in entrepreneurship. STEP increased the business start-ups (Gielnik et al., in press) and it turned job seekers into job creators who successfully created employment for themselves and for others. STEP also had a positive impact on business opportunity identification (Gielnik et al., in press) and entrepreneurial action. STEP trainees also stayed entrepreneurially active over the long-term. STEP increased entrepreneurial actions by improving trainees' action regulations, specifically influencing goal intentions, action knowledge, action planning and self-efficacy (Gielnik et al., in press). Finally, STEP successfully promoted portfolio and serial entrepreneurship and led to long-term business success. By promoting portfolio and serial entrepreneurship STEP supports the continuous creation of future businesses. Research shows that portfolio and serial entrepreneurs are more interested in engaging in future ventures than non-portfolio entrepreneurs (Westhead et al., 2005).

The effects of STEP on entrepreneurship is particularly valuable for countries that have an adverse labor market and lack employment opportunities for the youth, as most developing countries do (Reynolds, 2012). Since STEP successfully promotes business start-ups, it provides the youth with an opportunity to create their own employment instead of looking for jobs and failing to find employment. Furthermore, STEP is valuable for developing countries, because the implementation of STEP requires only minimal costs. If an institution continues to deliver STEP, the costs the institution faces comprise the trainers' fees, starting capital for the start-up teams, and costs for printing training material. The starting capital is $100 for each start-up team. It is important to note that some of the start-up teams may not be able to repay the starting capital. The institutions have to take this loss into consideration when they plan for a sustainable and ongoing implementation of STEP. In our experience, the costs for the delivery of STEP are manageable for the institutions in developing countries. A fruitful strategy to raise money that covers the costs of STEP is incorporating STEP in the yearly budget of the institutions (e.g., in the yearly university budgets) and integrating STEP into the curricula of the institutions.

In the future, we want to investigate whether STEP has similar effects in different populations, such as secondary school students or school drop-outs, and in other cultural contexts. In addition, we aim to evaluate the sustainable implementation process that enables the institutions to continuously run STEP without external support. An important part of the implementation process is the train-the-trainer workshop for STEP trainers, which aims to provide trainers with the necessary knowledge on how to conduct the training. To investigate whether these workshops are effective, we are conducting evaluation studies on these train-the-trainer workshops. These studies seek to establish a causal chain from the workshop over the trainers to the students in the STEP training. We examine the effects of the workshop's effects on trainers' entrepreneurial and teaching skills and how this translates into the successful training of STEP students. Such an evaluation approach provides comprehensive insights into the process of developing an entrepreneurship training and the widespread implementation of the training at many different institutions through local partners.

References

Acs, Z., & Armington, C. (2004). Employment growth and entrepreneurial activity in cities. *Regional Studies*, 38(8), 911–927.

Acs, Z. J., Desai, S., & Hessels, J. (2008). Entrepreneurship, economic development and institutions. *Small Business Economics*, 31(3), 219–234.

Andersson, P. (2008). Happiness and health: Well-being among the self-employed. *The Journal of Socio-Economics*, 37(1), 213–236.

Audretsch, D. B., & Keilbach, M. (2004). Entrepreneurship capital and economic performance. *Regional Studies*, 38(8), 949–959.

Baldwin, T. T., & Ford, K. J. (1988). Transfer of training?: A review and directions for future research. *Personnel Psychology*, 41, 63–105.

Bandura, A. (1986). *Social Foundations of Thought and Action: A Social Cognitive Theory*. Englewood Cliffs, NJ: Prentice Hall.

Banerjee, A. V., & Duflo, E. (2009). The experimental approach to development economics. *Annual Review of Economics*, 1, 151–178.

Baron, R. A. (2007a). Behavioral and cognitive factors in entrepreneurship: Entrepreneurs as the active element in new venture creation. *Strategic Entrepreneurship Journal*, 1(1–2), 167–182.

Baron, R. A. (2007b). Entrepreneurship: A process perspective. In J. Baum, M. Frese, & R. A. Baron (Eds.), *The Psychology of Entrepreneurship* (pp. 19–39). Mahwah, NJ: Lawrence Erlbaum.

Baron, R. M., & Kenny, D. A. (1986). The moderator-mediator variable distinction in social psychological research: conceptual, strategic, and statistical considerations. *Journal of Personality and Social Psychology*, 51(6), 1173–1182.

Barr, S. H., Baker, T., Markham, S. K., & Kingon, A. I. (2009). Bridging the valley of death?: Lessons learned from 14 years of commercialization of technology education. *Academy of Management Learning & Education*, 8(3), 370–388.

Baum, J. R., Frese, M., Baron, R. A., & Katz, J. A. (2007). Entrepreneurship as an area of psychology study: An introduction. In J. R. Baum, M. Frese, & R. A. Baron (Eds.), *The Psychology of Entrepreneurship* (pp. 1–18). Mahwah, NJ: Lawrence Erlbaum.

Baumol, W. J. (1986). Entrepreneurship in Economic Theory. *American Economic Review*, 58(2), 64–71.

Beck, T., & Demirguc-Kunt, A. (2008). Access to finance: An unfinished agenda. *The World Bank Economic Review*, 22(3), 383–396.

Benz, M., & Frey, B. S. (2004). Being independent raises happiness at work. *Swedish Economic Policy Review*, 11, 95–134.

Benz, M., & Frey, B. S. (2008). Being independent is a great thing: Subjective evaluations of self-employment and hierarchy. *Economica*, 75, 362–383.

Blanchflower, D. G. (2004). Self-employment?: More may not be better. *Swedish Economic Policy Review*, 11(2), 15–73.

Blanchflower, D. G., & Oswald, A. J. (1998). What makes an entrepreneur? *Journal of Labor Economics*, 16(1), 26–60.

Boyd, N. G., & Vozikis, G. S. (1994). The influence of self-efficacy on the development of entrepreneurial intentions and actions. *Entrepreneurship Theory and Practice*, 18, 63–77.

Brinckmann, J., Grichnik, D., & Kapsa, D. (2010). Should entrepreneurs plan or just storm the castle? A meta-analysis on contextual factors impacting the business planning–performance relationship in small firms. *Journal of Business Venturing*, 25(1), 24–40.

Carree, M. A., & Thurik, A. R. (2003). The impact of entrepreneurship on economic growth. In Z. J. Acs, & D. B. Audretsch (Eds.), *Handbook of Entrepreneurship Research* (pp. 437–471). Boston/Dordrecht: Kluwer Academic Publishers.

Carree, M. A., & Thurik, A. R. (2008). The lag structure of the impact of business ownership on economic performance in OECD countries. *Small Business Economics*, 30, 101–110.

Chen, C. C., Greene, P. G., & Crick, A. (1998). Does entrepreneurial self-efficacy distinguish entrepreneurs from managers? *Journal of Business Venturing*, 13(4), 295–316.

Collier, P. (2007). *The Bottom Billion*. Oxford: Oxford University Press.

Cook, T. D., Campbell, D. T., & Peracchio, L. (1990). Quasi experimentation. In M. D. Dunnette, & L. M. Hough (Eds.), *Handbook of Industrial and Organizational Psychology* (Vol 1, 2nd Edition. pp. 491–576). Palo Alto, CA: Consulting Psychologists Press.

Czarnitzki, D., & Kraft, K. (2004). Firm leadership and innovative performance: Evidence from seven EU countries. *Small Business Economics*, 22(5), 325–332.

Davidsson, P., & Honig, B. (2003). The role of social and human capital among nascent entrepreneurs. *Journal of Business Venturing*, 18(3), 301–331.

Dechenaux, E., Goldfarb, B., Shane, S. A., & Thursby, M. C. (2003). *Appropriability and the timing of innovation: Evidence from MIT inventions* (No. w9735). National Bureau of Economic Research.

Dimov, D. (2007). Beyond the single-person, single-insight attribution in understanding entrepreneurial opportunities. *Entrepreneurship Theory and Practice*, 31(5), 713–731.

Duflo, E., Glennerster, R., & Kremer, M. (2007). Using randomization in development economics research: A toolkit. *Handbook of Development Economics*, 4, 3895–3962.

Fiet, J. O. (2000). The pedagogical side of entrepreneurship theory. *Journal of Business Venturing*, 16, 101–117.

Frese, M. (2009). Towards a psychology of entrepreneurship: An action theory perspective. *Foundations and Trends®in Entrepreneurship*, 5(6), 437–496.

Frese, M., Beimel, S., & Schoenborn, S. (2003). Action training for charismatic leadership: Two evaluations of studies of a commercial training module on inspirational communication of a vision. *Personnel Psychology*, 56(3), 671–698.

Frese, M., & Zapf, D. (1994). Action as the core of work psychology. In H. C. Triandis, M. D. Dunnette, & L. M. Hough (Eds.), *Handbook of Industrial and Organizational Psychology* (Vol 4, pp. 271–340). Palo Alto, CA: Consulting Psychologists Press.

Friedrich, C., Glaub, M., Gramberg, C., & Frese, M. (2006). Does training improve business performance of small-scale entrepreneurs? An evaluative study. *Industry and Higher Education Journal*, 20, 75–84.

Fritsch, M. (2008). How does new business formation affect regional development? Introduction to the special issue. *Small Business Economics*, 30(1), 1–14.

Gartner, W. B. (1985). A conceptual framework for describing the phenomenon of new venture creation. *Journal of Management Review*, 10(4), 696–706.

Gielnik, M. M., & Frese, M. (2013). Entrepreneurship and poverty reduction: Applying I-O psychology to microbusiness and entrepreneurship in developing countries. In J. B. Olson-Buchanan, L. L. Koppes Bryan, & L. Foster Thompson (Eds.), *Using I-O Psychology for the Greater Good: Helping Those Who Help Others* (pp. 394–438). New York: Routledge.

Gielnik, M. M., Frese, M., Kahara-Kawuki, A., Katono, I. W., Kyejjusa, S., Munene, J.,...Dlugosch, T. J. (in press). Action and Action-Regulation in Entrepreneurship: Evaluating a Student Training for Promoting Entrepreneurship. *Academy of Management Learning & Education*. doi: 10.5465/amle.2012.0107.

Glaub, M., Fischer, S., Klemm, M., & Frese, M. (2011). A theory-based controlled randomized field intervention: Increasing proactive behavior (personal initiative) in small business owners leads to entrepreneurial success. National University of Singapore: Manuscript.

Glaub, M., & Frese, M. (2012). A critical review of the effects of entrepreneurship training in developing countries. *Enterprise Development and Microfinance*, 22(4), 335–353.

Gollwitzer, P. M. (1999). Implementation intentions: Strong effects of simple plans. *American Psychologist*, 54(7), 493–503.

Gollwitzer, P. M., & Brandstätter, V. (1997). Implementation intentions and effective goal pursuit. *Journal of Personality and Social Psychology*, 73(1), 186–199.

Gries, T., & Naudé, W. (2010). Entrepreneurship and structural economic transformation. *Small Business Economics*, 34(1), 13–29.

Hacker, W. (1998). *Allgemeine Arbeitspsychologie. Psychische Regulation von Arbeitstätigkeiten.* Bern: Huber.

Heimbeck, D., Frese, M., Sonnentag, S., & Keith, N. (2003). Integrating errors into the training process: The function of error management instructions and the role of goal orientation. *Personnel Psychology,* 56(2), 333–361.

International Labour Organization (2013). *Global Employment Trends for Youth: A Generation at Risk.* Geneva: International Labour Office.

Johannisson, B., Landstrom, H., & Rosenberg, J. (1998). University training for entrepreneurship – An action frame of reference. *European Journal of Engineering Education,* 23(4), 477–496.

Kabongo, J. D., & Okpara, J. O. (2010). Entrepreneurship education in sub-Saharan African universities. *International Journal of Entrepreneurial Behaviour & Research,* 16(4), 296–308.

Keith, N., & Frese, M. (2005). Self-regulation in error management training: emotion control and metacognition as mediators of performance effects. *The Journal of Applied Psychology,* 90(4), 677–691.

Keith, N., & Frese, M. (2008). Effectiveness of error management training: A Meta-Analysis. *The Journal of Applied Psychology,* 93(1), 59–69.

Klandt, H. (2004). Entrepreneurship education and research in German-speaking Europe. *Academy of Management Learning & Education,* 3(3), 293–301.

Lieshout, S. Van, Sievers, M., & Aliyev, M. (2012). *Start and Improve Your Business Global Tracer Study 2011: ILO's Business Management Training Programme.* Geneva: ILO.

Love, J. H., & Ashcroft, B. (1999). Market versus corporate structure in plant-level innovation performance. *Small Business Economics,* 13, 97–109.

Martin, B. C., McNally, J. J., & Kay, M. J. (2013). Examining the formation of human capital in entrepreneurship: A meta-analysis of entrepreneurship education outcomes. *Journal of Business Venturing,* 28(2), 211–224.

Martocchio, J. J., & Dulebohn, J. (1994). Performance feedback effects in training: the role of perceived controllability. *Personnel Psychology,* 47(2), 357–373.

McGee, J. E., Peterson, M., Mueller, S. L., & Sequeira, J. M. (2009). Entrepreneurial self-efficacy: Refining the measure. *Entrepreneurship Theory and Practice,* 33(4), 965–988.

McKenzie, D., & Woodruff, C. (2012). What are we learning from business training and entrepreneurship evaluations around the developing world?? Working Paper. Washington, DC: The World Bank.

McMullen, J. S., & Shepherd, D. A. (2006). Entrepreneurial action and the role of uncertainty in the theory of the entrepreneur. *Academy of Management Review,* 31(1), 132–152.

Mead, D. C., & Liedholm, C. (1998). The dynamics of micro and small enterprises in developing countries. *World Development,* 26(1), 61–74.

Naudé, W. (2010). Entrepreneurship, developing countries, and development economics: new approaches and insights. *Small Business Economics,* 34(1), 1–12.

Naudé, W. (2012). Entrepreneurship and Economic Development: Theory, Evidence and Policy. Working Paper. Maastricht, NL: United Nations University.

Naudé, W., Gries, T., Wood, E., & Meintjies, A. (2008). Regional determinants of entrepreneurial start-ups in a developing country. *Entrepreneurship & Regional Development,* 20(2), 111–124.

Olinto, P., Beegle, K., Sobrado, C., & Uematsu, H. (2013). The State of the Poor?: Where Are The Poor, Where Is Extreme Poverty Harder to End, and What Is the Current Profile of the World's Poor? *Economic Premise*, 125, 1–8.

Pittaway, L., & Cope, J. (2007). Entrepreneurship education: A systematic review of the evidence. *International Small Business Journal*, 25(5), 479–510.

Preacher, K. J., & Hayes, A. F. (2004). SPSS and SAS procedures for estimating indirect effects in simple mediation models. *Behavior Research Methods, Instruments, & Computers*, 36(4), 717–731.

Rasmussen, E. A., & Sørheim, R. (2006). Action-based entrepreneurship education. *Technovation*, 26(2), 185–194.

Reynolds, P. D. (2007). New firm creation in the United States: A PSED I overview. *Foundations and Trends®in Entrepreneurship*, 3(1), 1–149.

Reynolds, P. D. (2012). Entrepreneurship in developing economies: The bottom billions and business creation. *Foundations and Trends®in Entrepreneurship*, 8(3), 141–277.

Reynolds, P. D., Bosma, N., Autio, E., Hunt, S., De Bono, N., Servais, I., & Chin, N. (2005). Global entrepreneurship monitor: Data collection design and implementation 1998–2003. *Small Business Economics*, 24(3), 205–231.

Rosa, P. (2013). *The Concept of the Entrepreneurial Career Ladder and its Implications for Supporting Entrepreneurship Education and Training in sub-Saharan Africa*, Working Paper, Centre for Entrepreneurship Research, University of Edinburgh.

Shane, S. (2000). Prior knowledge and the discovery of entrepreneurial opportunities. *Organization Science*, 11(4), 448–469.

Shane, S., & Venkatamaran, S. (2000). The promise of entrepreneurship as a field of research. *Academy of Management Review*, 25(1), 217–226.

Solomon, G. (2007). An examination of entrepreneurship education in the United States. *Journal of Small Business and Enterprise Development*, 14(2), 168–182.

Stark, M., Gielnik, M. M., Frese, M., & Bischoff, K. M. (2013). *Entrepreneurship Training Makes Happy: Examining the Short- and Long-Term Effects of an Entrepreneurship Training on Life Satisfaction*. Leuphana University of Luneburg, Germany unpublished manuscript.

The World Bank (2010). *Doing Business 2011: Making a Difference for Entrepreneurs*. Washington DC.

Thorndike, E. L., & Woodworth, R. S. (1901). The influence of improvement in mental function upon the efficiency of other functions: functions involving attention, observation and discrimination. *The Psychological Review*, 8, 553–564.

Thurik, A. R., Carree, M. A., van Stel, A., & Audretsch, D. B. (2008). Does self-employment reduce unemployment? *Journal of Business Venturing*, 23(6), 673–686.

Unger, J. M., Rauch, A., Frese, M., & Rosenbusch, N. (2011). Human capital and entrepreneurial success?: A meta-analytical review. *Journal of Business Venturing*, 26(3), 341–358.

United Nations Conference on Trade and Development (2012). *Empretec Annual Report*. New York, NY: United Nations.

United Nations Conference on Trade and Development (2012). Trade and Development Report 2012 UNCTAO/TDQ/2012. Sales number E.12.11.D-6

United Nations (2013) World Population Projects: The 2012 Revision. Extended data set in Excel and SSC II formats. Sales No. E.13.XIII.IO.

Van Praag, C. M., & Versloot, P. H. (2007). What is the value of entrepreneurship? A review of recent research. *Small Business Economics*, 29(4), 351–382.

Van Stel, A., Carree, M. A., & Thurik, R. (2005). The effect of entrepreneurial activity on national economic growth. *Small Business Economics*, 24(3), 311–321.

Van Stel, A., & Storey, D. J. (2004). The link between firm births and job creation: Is there a upas tree effect? *Regional Studies*, 38(8), 893–909.

Westhead, P., Ucbasaran, D., & Wright, M. (2005). Decisions, actions, and performance: Do novice, serial, and portfolio entrepreneurs differ? *Journal of Small Business Management*, 43(4), 393–417.

Xavier, S. R., Kelley, D., Kew, J., Herrington, M., & Vorderwülbecke, A. (2013). *Global Entrepreneurship Monitor: 2012 Global Report*. Babson Park, MA: Babson College.

The World Bank (2010). *Doing Business 2011: Making a Difference for Entrepreneurs*. Washington, DC: The World Bank.

Zhao, H., Seibert, S. E., & Hills, G. E. (2005). The mediating role of self-efficacy in the development of entrepreneurial intentions. *Journal of Applied Psychology*, 90(6), 1265–1272.

7
Dual Salary and Workers' Well-being in Papua New Guinea

Leo Marai

Introduction

This chapter discusses the experiences of workers, including myself, who work under a dual salary system in Papua New Guinea (PNG), as well as how the disparities in remuneration affect many of us in various ways, including our well-being. Based on my own industrial-organizational psychological understanding of the effects of remuneration on work motivation, attitudes, performance, and occupational well-being, I draw from relevant research and theories that link the practice of dual salary to our qualitative work experiences. I try to show that being involved in the *process* of challenging the adverse impacts of dual salary is a "living reality" for anyone who works in a dual contract environment. I start by taking an historical look at the introduction of the dual salary system in PNG, which serves as a springboard for us to understand the impact of the *continuous* practice of this type of remuneration package in this low-income economy. I discuss the link between dual salary and work attitudes and well-being, as well as the implications for workers and organizations in PNG and elsewhere. Finally, I also discuss what can be done about dual salary by offering examples of research and advocacy roles involved in addressing this issue (Marai, 2013; Marai et al., 2010).

History of the dual salary system in PNG

The definition of the "dual salary system" is as follows: the dual salary policy stipulates two types of salaries or contracts – one for the expatriate worker (usually a foreigner from another country and not a PNG citizen) and the other for the local worker (PNG citizen). The expatriate worker is usually paid higher than the local worker for doing the same or similar job. Why is this so? The original rationale for dual salary (Payani, 2000; Ritako, 2012) was that salaries and benefits (remuneration) should reflect the level of "development" in a country and its respective workforce (Ila'ava, 1999). Because "developing" countries like PNG and their labor forces were less "developed" (less educated elites, etc.) than those from "developed" economies, where expatriate labor originated, it was presumed that compensation should reflect that gap (Ritako, 2012).

To understand the introduction and continuous practice of dual salary in PNG, a brief historical review is necessary. The dual salary system in PNG was a by-product of colonialism under Australian administration (PNG was formerly a territory of Australia and administered directly from Australia), and it continues to be practiced by the PNG government from the establishment of political independence in 1975 to the present time. It was first introduced in September 1964 by the Australian colonial administration (Ritako, 2012). One of the first early highly educated Papua New Guineans during the colonial time, in his recent autobiography, provided an historical account of dual salary system in a critical vein, arguing that

> [t]he instigator of the two salary ranges, the Public Service Commissioner, Mr. Neil Thompson [an Australian], as I understand it, worked in isolation and in conjunction with Canberra [the capital city of Australia] and pushed through the two salary structures in the one stream Public Service. It appeared he starved the government of essential information and avoided the Administrator [in Papua New Guinea] when finalizing details with the Department of Territories in Canberra [government capital city of Australia] prior to the official announcement of the salary differentiation.
>
> (Ritako, 2012, pp. 106–107)

The manner in which the dual salary system was introduced is arguably a breach of *procedural justice* (Greenberg, 1988). Procedural justice is the way through which procedures such as awarding salaries to workers are implemented. In particular, the way of distributing the remunerations between expatriates and locals was flawed and did not follow government protocols (Ritako, 2012). The Australian government, led by Neil Thompson, orchestrated the dual salary policy in PNG, and, surprisingly, the policy has not been changed up to the present time. The maintenance of a dual salary system is seen as a "justified pay structure" by the government with the argument that expatriates come from differently paid economies and therefore have to be compensated differently (usually higher) than locally remunerated colleagues.

The after-effect of the decision to establish a dual salary system was a marked difference in the distribution of salary between expatriates and local workers. A comparison of the distributive nature of salary levels between these two groups provides statistical evidence for such inequity in salary:

> For example, in 1973, expatriate earnings were calculated to be 9.6 times those of nationals, whereas in 1982 the difference had fallen to approximately 5.5 times.
>
> (Turner, 1990, p. 76)

This significant difference continues to be an issue of contention, especially among local workers. What was pointed out by two Pacific scholars three decades ago could equally have been written today:

> The conditions of employment enjoyed by many expatriates exceed that of Papua New Guineans, and the mere fact they are for-eigners gives them that right to live well. The majority of Papua New Guineans just manage to live day-to-day existence in their own country. The presence of expatriates doing the same job as Papua New Guineans but with an obvious higher standard of living adds to the high occurrence of industrial disputes and disruptions. The expatriates set the terms whether intentionally or not, and as Papua New Guineans become aware of this they began to place heavy demands on the political system to accommodate their interests.
>
> (Crocombe and Ali, 1982, p. 53)

The rationale behind the dual salary system stems from the fact that the expatriates are highly qualified, skilful, and come from a more "developed" economy than Papua New Guinean workers. That may have been so in the years preceding and immediately after independence. However, there are now more highly educated and qualified Papua New Guineans. Ila'ava (1999) has proposed the abolition of this policy calling it "economic apartheid," and argued that every worker should be paid the same for doing the same job despite their country (and economy) of origin (p. 65).

My personal journey in dual salary

It was during my early twenties that I first came to realize that the practice of dual salary exists in PNG, after entering the University of Papua New Guinea (UPNG) in 1987 to undertake an undergraduate degree program in psychology. Since the establishment of the UPNG in 1966 and up to the present time, expatriate academics are paid higher than local academics for doing identical jobs, with similar human capital and experiences. The differences in remuneration among expatriates and their local academic counterparts had led to various protests and negotiations.

The concept of a dual salary system was contested by the *National Academic Staff Association* (NASA) at UPNG, an organization formed primarily by PNG national academics to tackle the issue. At one time during those years, which I still remember vividly, there was a work strike organized by NASA at the UPNG main campus, and I saw some national academic staff walking around the campus wearing white sleeveless shirts with thick black words in capital letters printed on the backs of the shirts that read: "EQUAL WORK FOR EQUAL PAY." During that strike, lectures were canceled for a week. At that time, the majority of the academics were foreign expatriates and a few were locals who taught at UPNG. From that moment, my journey of being consciously aware of the dual salary system began to take shape. There were various protests organized by NASA both before and after that particular strike, most of these activities focused on dual salary. However, nothing has been done by the government to abolish the system, although salaries for local/national academics were raised in 2009 and implemented in 2010. Recently, NASA made a call again for the abolition of the dual salary system, and a threat of possible work strike was put before the UPNG's administration if nothing was done about it (The National, July 4, 2010, p. 3). In 1997, I joined the Psychology Department as a teaching assistant at the UPNG, which practices dual salary to this day. As a "victim" (a local academic) in a dual salary system, I began to question the "wisdom" of dual contracts. I compared myself to other expatriate academic colleagues and wondered why they were paid more than me even though we did the same jobs and our curriculum vitae looked alike (see Adams, 1963, 1965; Festinger, 1954). The expatriate academic colleagues came from Australia, England, United States, Asia, and Africa, and all were paid higher than us (local academics) although we held the same positions and had similar human capital and work in the same university. I could not see any *justification* for a dual salary and felt *under-valued* in the institution I worked for. A worker in an organization feels valued when that organization recognizes and rewards him or her appropriately (Latham and Pinder, 2005).

I also developed a sense of anger and frustration about the practice of dual salary. Similar feelings were observed in Carr, Chipande, and MacLachlan (1998) organizational survey at The National University of Malawi, where they found that local academics felt frustrated and angry for being paid comparatively lower than similar-skilled, higher-paid expatriate counterparts.

Research findings: The psychology of remuneration

Industrial-organizational psychology has a number of theories in support of pay's motivating factor, which includes classical utility/behaviorist models that stress the instrumentality aspects of rewards like money and wages (e.g., Latham and Pinder, 2005). In particular, there are links between remuneration and work behavior (Carr, 2004; Carr et al., 2012). For instance, financial incentives have been found to increase affective and cognitive motivation, for example, respectively, enhanced mood and job interest (Eisenberger, Rhoades, and Camerron, 1999). There is evidence in the literature that low pay has a negative effect on the performance of workers (e.g., Kingma, 2001, 2007) and is a core factor in worker de-motivation (Willis-Shattrick et al., 2008). Moreover, there are experiments (e.g., Carr, McLoughlin, Hodgson, and MacLachlan, 1996, Study I) and work evidence that show that inequitable pay de-motivates both the higher- and lower-paid groups (Carr et al., 1996, Study II; Carr et al., 1998) – a "double de-motivation" (see MacLachlan and Carr, 2005).

The dual salary system and its link with work attitude and workers' well-being

Work attitudes

In advocating for decent salary for workers in PNG, there were a number of research projects in which I was involved, which directly explore the links between dual salary and workers' work attitudes, including occupational well-being and work distance (propinquity) among differently remunerated workers. Propinquity is defined as proximity in physical and thereby psychological space, which creates the opportunity for one to meet another person (Vaughan and Hogg, 2005).

First, turning to the ADDUP (Are Development Discrepancies Undermining Performance?) project (a six-country international project including PNG; for details, see Carr, McWha, MacLachlan, and Furnham, 2010), we found that across those six countries pay ratio thresholds between locals and international workers were unacceptable to locally remunerated workers, and that dual salary was seen as unjust and stimulated feelings of de-motivation and fuelled turnover and mobility intentions among locally paid workers. Interestingly, the researchers from low-, middle-, and high-income countries involved in the ADDUP study were paid on one international rate (New Zealand dollars), pegged with their respective positions for each country (see Carr et al., 2013).

Second, in my own doctoral research (Marai, 2013) based on the PNG–ADDUP study (Marai et al., 2010), with the same participants ($N = 200$), the results showed that less remuneration was linked to negative occupational mental health among the workers. Moreover, less remuneration was also linked to less occupational propinquity among workers, which may undermine *local capacity building* (Eyben, 2005) in a "low-income/high-cost" economy like PNG. All these responses were directly linked to *inequality* in remuneration in the dual salary system in PNG.

Well-being

Remuneration injustice at work can create a strain on workers' well-being, as can inequality (Judge and Colquitt, 2004). Following VandenBos (2007), well-being is the general physical, behavioral, and mental psychological comfort of any individual – in this case, workers in organizations.

The finding of the link between dual salary and well-being extends the work from my earlier research in Indonesia (Marai 2002/2003). This field survey study investigated the links between double de-motivation and mental well-being. A sample of 188 English teachers (expatriates and locals) within an educational setting in Indonesia voluntarily responded to questions relating to remuneration type, job satisfaction, and mental well-being. Mental well-being was measured by anxiety, depression, and hopelessness (on the Beck Anxiety Inventory, the Beck Depression Inventory, and the Beck Hopelessness Scale). Higher-paid expatriates and lower-paid local teachers compared to equitably paid teachers were not only de-motivated (regarding job satisfaction and/or double de-motivation) but, to a significant extent, experienced comparatively poor mental well-being.

The link between remuneration and workers' well-being can also be viewed from the perspective of effort and reward imbalance. The effort–reward imbalance model claims that failed reciprocity in terms of high efforts and low rewards received in turn is likely to elicit recurrent negative emotions and sustained stress responses in exposed people. Conversely, positive emotions produced by appropriate rewards promote well-being, health, and survival (Siegrist, 1996). In the case of dual salary, the effort–reward imbalance applies to locally remunerated workers who are paid comparatively less than internationally remunerated counterparts although they perform identical jobs. Hence, the lower-paid workers are likely to be negatively affected. In PNG, there is scarcity of research in the link between dual salary and well-being except one recent study (Marai, 2013). In this study, it was found that dual salary was linked directly to more negative mental health of the workers across the organizations in the study.

This finding reinforces those of other earlier studies, which have shown the effort–reward imbalance link to well-being (e.g., Kivimäki et al., 2007; Siegrist, 2008; Stansfeld, Fuhrer, Shipley, and Marmot, 1999). In a survey in Europe, Kivimäki et al. (2007) investigated effort–reward imbalance and justice among public sector employees and found that high effort–reward imbalance and high organizational injustice were both independently associated with negative health. In another study, Siegrist (2008) found that effort–reward imbalance was linked to negative emotions such as depression, and a combination of high effort–reward imbalance and high organizational injustice was related to poorer health. A study conducted by Stansfeld et al. (1999) found that low social support, low decision authority, high job demands, and effort–reward imbalance among workers were associated with increased risk of psychiatric disorder as assessed by the General Health Questionnaire (GHQ), adjusting for age, employment level, and baseline GHQ score. These findings imply that workers' feelings of being under-rewarded (especially those locally remunerated workers in dual salary systems) may lead them to experience emotions such as not feeling positive about their salaries.

Dual salary linked to well-being (Marai, 2013) have implications for both workers and organizations. The decline in workers' well-being affects their performance at work. Lower well-being has been found to be related to reduced job performance of workers in organizations (Miller, Lipsedge, and Litchfield, 2002). Moreover, when workers' well-being is adversely affected and they perform poorly on the job, then the organizations they work for are likely to suffer from declines in productivity.

What can be done about the practice of dual salary in Papua New Guinea? *Research-Advocacy*

As a way forward through my experiences in dual salary, I have taken the challenge to conduct research on dual salary and advocate for the *alignment* (Accra, 2008) of dual salary so that local workers in PNG can have decent salaries. I consider myself to be playing the role of *research-advocacy* in dual salary (see Carr, 2013). The International Labour Organization calls for "Decent Work" practice, as captured in United Nation's Millennium Development Goal 1.B (MDG-1.B), which states that "decent work" practice includes better remuneration for workers. The practice of dual salary in PNG cannot be seen as decent because workers in general suffer from what is termed as "zero balance" in that country context, meaning a weekly shortfall in one's bank savings account until the next salary arrives (Marai, 2013). PNG is classified as a collectivist society (Bleus and Frewer, 1991; Triandis et al., 1986), where one works not only for oneself but for the extended family and friends as well. This means that a worker's salary is part and parcel of one's in-group survival needs, just as Social Identity theory suggests that in-group identity and needs are of crucial importance for a concerned individual in a defined group (Tajfel, 1978). At present, however, the dual salary system does not provide an acceptable level of living for local workers (Marai, 2013), and a collectivist consideration also adds more to this financial inadequacy. The dual salary system makes life harder for locally remunerated workers to meet everyday needs.

I have disseminated the research findings on dual salary system to stakeholders in the ADDUP project in 2009 and 2010 (Marai, 2013; Marai et al., 2010). I continue to make emerging research findings available to the senior management team in my institution. Since 2009, these findings have also been communicated to NASA and will shape the submission to be made to the government in PNG for a review of dual salaries in our country. In October 2013, I was invited to be part of the review team (which I accepted) to review the practice of dual salary in universities in PNG by the PNG Commission of Higher Education. This appointment came about as a result of my research on dual salary and advocacy for a review and alignment of dual salary.

Conclusion

The dual salary system has been found to link to perceptions of remuneration injustice, de-motivation, and mobility intentions among workers across both for-profit and non-profit organizations (Carr et al., 2010; Marai et al., 2010). Moreover, the practice of dual salary predicts double de-motivation and negative well-being among workers (Marai, 2002/2003; Marai, 2013).

The dual salary system in PNG is at odds with the global labor policy. The global labor policy (International Labour Organization, Equal Remuneration Covention, 1951 (No. 100)) stipulates "equal work for equal pay," not based on gender, religion, ethnicity, or country from which a worker originates. The dual salary system contradicts the principles of both *alignment* and *harmonization* of remuneration among workers *within* organizations (expatriate versus local), and *between* organizations (e.g., local versus international NGOs), which clearly show equal work for *unequal* pay. In particular, salary differences between organizations and between expatriate versus local workers are often considerable, particularly when organizations are based out of different countries (even if the staff are working in the same country site). Such differences often exist by virtue of the remuneration norms and expectations of different countries, rather than on the basis of performance of the workers (Ila'ava, 1999).

In the PNG–ADDUP organizational survey, conducted following their workshop, the participants consensually suggested the abolishment of dual salary practice in PNG (Marai et al., 2010). Moreover, they argued for a single-line system that is based on performance. However, from the survey, most expatriates declined to offer their suggestions on improvements to dual salary system, and their responses may be attributed to the *sensitivity* and the *taboo* surrounding dual salary. Future research should aim at breaking that taboo and exploring more fully the perspectives of diverse participants about dual salary. Future projects exploring the factors that reinforce the practice of dual salary and links to well-being are required.

Dual salary systems are a *negative recipe* for workers' work-related attitudes and well-being in organizations and therefore remain an *obstacle* to *decent work* practice (MDG-1b). One possible way forward is to disseminate research findings on the impact of dual salary to concerned authorities and advocate for a review and alignment of the dual salary system to make salaries *decent* for local workers, which will have a positive impact on mental health and well-being in the workplace.

References

Accra Agenda for Action (2008). *Third High-Level Forum on Aid Effectiveness.* OECD: Accra, Ghana. September 2–4.

Adams, J. S. (1963). Towards an understanding of inequity. *Journal of Abnormal and Normal Social Psychology*, 67, 422–436.

Adams, J. S. (1965). The equity in social exchange. *Advances in Experimental Social Psychology*, 2, 267–299.

Carr, S. C. (2004). *Globalization and Culture at Work: Exploring their Combined Locality*. Boston: Kluwer Academic Press.

Carr, S. C. (2013). *Anti-Poverty Psychology*. New York: Springer.

Carr, S. C., Chipande, R., & MacLachlan, M. (1998). Expatriate aid salaries in Malawi? A doubly de- motivating influence? *International Journal of Educational Development*, 18(2), 133–143.

Carr, S. C., de Guzman, J., Eltyeb, S. M., Furnham, A., MacLachlan, M., Marai, L., & McAuliffe, E. (2012). An introduction to humanitarian work psychology. In S. C. Carr, M. MacLachlan, & A. Furnham (Eds.), *Humanitarian Work Psychology* (pp. 3–33). Basingstoke, UK: Palgrave Macmillan.

Carr, S. C., Eltayeb, S., MacLachlan, M., Marai, L., McAuliffe, E., & McWha, I. (2013). Aiding international development: Some fresh perspectives from industrial and organizational psychology. In J. Olson-Buchanan, L. K. Bryan, & L. F. Thompson (Eds.), *Using Industrial-Organizational Psychology for the Greater Good: Helping Those Who Help Others* (pp. 490–528). New York: Routledge Academic.

Carr, S. C., McLoughlin, D., Hodgson, M., & MacLachlan, M. (1996). Effects of unreasonable pay discrepancies for under and overpayment on double de-motivation. *Genetic, Social, and General Psychology Monographs*, 122, 475–494.

Carr, S. C., McWha, I, MacLachlan, M., & Furnham, A. (2010). International-local remuneration differences across six countries: Do they undermine poverty reduction work? *International Journal of Psychology*, 45(5), 321–340.

Crocombe, R., & Ali, A. (1982). *Politics in Melanesia*. Suva: Institute of Pacific Studies.

Eisenberger, R., Rhoades, L., & Camerron, J. (1999). Does pay for performance increase or decrease perceived self-determination and intrinsic motivation? *Journal of Personality and Social Psychology*, 77, 1026–1040.

Eyben, R. (2005). Donor's learning difficulties and responsibilities. *IDS Bulletin*, 36(3), 98–107.

Festinger, L. (1954). A theory of social comparison processes. *Human Relations*, 7, 117–140.

Frewer, L., & Bleus, A. V. (1991). Personality assessment in a collectivist culture. *South Pacific Journal of Psychology*, 4, 1–5.

Greenberg, J. (1988). Equity and workplace status: A field experiment. *Journal of Applied Psychology*, 73, 606–613.

Ila'ava, Vele Pat (1999). The dual salary policy: An obstacle to real human and national development. *Development Bulletin*, 50, 65–66.

Judge, T. A., & Colquitt, J. A. (2004). Organizational justice and stress: The mediating role of work-family conflict. *Journal of Applied Psychology*, 89(3), 395–404.

Kingma, M. (2001). Nursing migration: Global treasure hunt or disaster in making. *Nursing Inquiry*, 8, 205–212.

Kingma, M. (2007). Nurses on the move: A global review. *Health Service Research*, 42, 1281–1298.

Kivimäki, M., Lawlor, D. A., Smith, G. D., Kouvonen, A., Virtanen, M., Elavaino, M., & Vahtera, J. (2007). Socioeconomic position, co-occurence of behavioural-related risk factors, and coronary heart disease: The Finnish public sector study. *American Journal of Public Health*, 97(5), 874–879.

Latham, G. P., & Pinder, C. C. (2005). Work motivation theory and research at the dawn of the twenty-first century. *Annual Review of Psychology*, 56, 485–516.

MacLachlan, M. & Carr, S.C. (2005). The human dynamics of aid. OECD Policy Insights, 10, www.oecd.org/dev/insights.

Marai, L. (2002/2003). Double de-motivation and negative social affect among teachers in Indonesia. *South Pacific Journal of Psychology*, 14, 1–7.

Marai, L. (2013). *Dual Salaries in Papua New Guinea: Links to their Perceived Justice, Motivation and Well-being*. Unpublished PhD Thesis Submitted to the School of Business Administration. Port Moresby, Papua New Guinea: University of Papua New Guinea.

Marai, L. Kewibu, V., Kinkin, E., Peniop, P., Salini, C., & Kofana, G. (2010). Remuneration disparities in Oceania: Papua New Guinea and Solomon Islands. *International Journal of Psychology*, 45(5), 350–359.

Miller, D. M., Lipsedge, M., & Litchfield, P. (Eds.) (2002). *Work and Mental Health: An Employer's Guide*. London: Gaskell.

Payani, H. (2000). Selected problems in Papua New Guinean Public Service. *Asian Journal of Public Administration*, 22(2), 135–160.

Ritako, T. (2012). *An Autobiography of Thomas Ritako*. Wagani: UPNG Press.

Siegrist, J. (1996). Adverse health effects of high effort–low reward conditions at work. *Journal of Occupational Health Psychology*, 1, 27–43.

Siegrist, J. (2008). Chronic psychosocial stress at work and risk of depression: Evidence from prospective studies. *European Archives of Psychiatry and Clinical Neuroscience*, 258, 115–119.

Stansfeld, S. A., Fuhrer, R., Shipley, M. J., & Marmot, M. G. (1999). Work characteristics predict psychiatric disorder: Prospective results from the Whitehall II study. *Occupational and Environmental Medicine*, 56, 302–307.

Tajfel, H. (1978). *Differentiation between Social Groups: Studies in the Social Psychology of Intergroup Relations*. London: Academic Press.

Triandis, H. C., Bontempo, R., Betancourt, H., Bond, M., Leung, K., Brenes, A., Georgas, J., Hui, H., Marin, G., Setidadi, B., Sinha, J., Verma, J., Spangenberg, J., Touzard, H., & Montmollin, G. (1986). The measurement of etic aspects of individualism and collectivism across cultures. *Australian Journal of Psychology*, 38, 257–267.

Turner, M. (1990). *Papua New Guinea: The Challenge of Independence*. Melbourne: Penguin.

VandenBos, G. R. (Ed.) (2007). *APA Dictionary of Psychology*. Washington, DC: American Psychological Association.

Vaughan, G. M., & Hogg, M. A. (2005). *Introduction to Social Psychology*. 4th Edition. Frenchs Forest, NSW: Pearson Education Australia.

Willis-Shattrick, M., Bidwell, P., Thomas, S., Wynes, L., Blauuw, D., & Ditlopo, P. (2008). Motivation and retention of health workers in developing countries: A systematic review. *BMC Health Service Research*, 8, 247.

8
Exploring Haiti from an Organizational Psychology Perspective: Lessons Learned along the Way

Jeffrey Godbout

Introduction

There is an increasing awareness, and often outspoken disgust, that international aid is failing those it seeks to "help." Academics and practitioners from a variety of disciplines are challenging the aid community to identify new and more effective approaches to humanitarian assistance that will be more aligned with the needs of the communities they serve (Easterly, 2006; Easterly, and Pfutze, 2008; MacLachlan, Carr, and McAuliffe, 2010). While spending three months in Haiti exploring the relationship between humanitarian aid organizations' intent (i.e., mission, vision, goals) and their actual impact on the community members, I was able to experience firsthand how aid and development work was perceived as having both a positive and negative outcome on communities. Although there were certainly examples of the positive impact of aid, based on my conversations with Haitians' and aid workers, the brutal realities of inadequacies that aid and development work was having on the communities often overshadowed these positive outcomes. It quickly became apparent that a socially responsible mission (e.g., reduce poverty by providing housing/food/shelter/education) did not necessarily equate to socially responsible organizations (e.g.,

---

I dedicate this chapter to Jeff Rogers – the friend that introduced Haiti to me and me to Haiti. And I want to thank everyone I met along the way for the hospitality, friendship, stories, and insights shared with me during my time in Haiti.

organizations doing what is in the best interest of the communities and taking into account the needs of community members) and that the old paternalistic "we know what is best for you" methods of aid work would be more effective if adjusted to new approaches that are more inclusive and community driven.

With organizations often working as a mediator between donors, partner organizations, aid workers, and local communities, this alarming lack of social responsibility must be addressed. It was during my time in Haiti, while discussing the delivery of aid and the associated attitudes, perceptions and beliefs of those living and working in the communities that I began to identify some possible causes of this lack of social responsibility. From an industrial organizational (I-O) perspective, some of these issues may be understood as internal organizational problems around staffing and leadership, external glitches in the supply chain of services, and a basic overall lack of capacity and/or desire to understand local community needs to name a few. As a means to address these challenges, it is recommended that directors of nongovernmental organizations (NGOs) work with managers and spend more time focusing internally on organizational structure and employee relations. Furthermore, it is recommended that managers also evaluate external perspectives, especially community expectations, as these were often overlooked.

2011: A year on the road

I had high hopes for the year 2011. My goal for the year was to build a deeper understanding of how I-O psychology could be applied to humanitarian assistance in general and aid and development work in particular. I was also trying to increase exposure and capacity of humanitarian work psychology (HWP) through presentations at universities, conferences, and organizations around the world. I wanted to do what I could to contribute to the humanitarian assistance process while identifying ways to bridge the gap that seemed to exist between local community needs and the distribution of international aid. Specifically, I wanted to spend my time with international and local relief organizations to help them collaborate with communities and governments to ensure that the most important needs were prioritized.

The lead up to 2011 was just as important to my professional development and understanding of aid and development work than what would come of my experiences throughout the year. It was very early on in my transition from a young property manager with a Bachelor's degree in Market to a globally cultured I-O psychologist that I would be fortunate enough to learn about the work of Stuart Carr, Mac MacLachlan and other psychologists with a vision of applying I-O to humanitarian assistance. I was first introduced to Stuart's work and vision in 2008. I had just started graduate school when I came across an article he wrote about I-O and poverty reduction (see Carr, 2007) and responded to a request at the end of the article to contact him with comments. We talked, and soon there after I found myself sitting with Stuart, Mac, and a group of like-minded individuals at a meeting in London in 2009. Following the London meeting I traveled to New Zealand to intern with Stuart Carr and the Poverty Research Group at Massey University. The focus was on summarizing the thoughts and opinions shared during the London meeting, drafting a paper to define HWP, and proposing a way forward as a formal organization. My time in NZ would also be spent starting the HWP Network which consisted of a website to stand as a hub of information on HWP, a Facebook and Linked-In page, and listserve group which Stuart Carr had previously created. The next year and a half would be a busy time for me as I would coordinator the growth of the Task Force for the Global Organisation for Humanitarian Work Psychology and continue promoting the development of HWP, mostly through outreach efforts such as university presentations, symposiums on HWP at profession conferences and events, and pretty much talking about HWP to anyone that would listen.

I would see, do, and learn a lot in 2011! My goal to travel the world and learn about humanitarian assistance and how to apply I-O psychology was to commence in Haiti and end on a plane ride to New Zealand where I would begin my PhD – a thesis motivated by both previous experiences and all that I would learn along the way in 2011. During 2011 I had the opportunity to travel throughout Haiti, Dominican Republic, Jamaica, Nicaragua, and across the United States exploring the approach humanitarian aid and development organizations utilize when trying to align with local community needs, and the resulting impact on community members. I would also spend time in England, Paris, Netherlands, and the United States at conferences and other professional events to learn about and discuss economics, aid and development, and of course I-O psychology. Among all of my experiences over the year, the first three months in Haiti had the most profound and lasting effect. Not only was I able to learn about the potential of I-O in Haiti, but I also fell in love with a country and culture that was unlike anything I had ever seen.

Exploring Haiti

I chose to go to Haiti exactly one year after the 2010 earthquake that killed over 200,000 people and devastated the infrastructure of several major cities within the country. The news in America was continually reporting on all the money going into the country and the limited results this money was having for the people of Haiti. The reports peeked my interest in traveling to Haiti because I immediately knew that the I-O psychology disciplines' focus on people, systems and organizations had the potential to positively impact the rebuilding process. The only problem was that I had no idea what needed to be done, what to focus on, or even where to start. I just knew that I wanted to learn more about whether the reports were true, and if so, how I-O psychology could help address the lack of effectiveness by organizations in particular and the reconstruction process in general.

My plan was to take a flight to Haiti and just start traveling around the country to look, listen, and learn from the people living and working in the country. My only agenda was to keep my approach informal and ask a lot of questions while keeping my ears and eyes open to what was going on around me. My informal research approach was designed to offer an unobtrusive method of learning about the lives of Haitians and aid workers in general and the gap between local communities needs and distribution of humanitarian assistance in particular. This ground-up community focused approach would quickly prove to be a great vantage point to learn about the complexity of aid and development work in Haiti.

I would spend most of my three months in Haiti visiting communities and organizations throughout the country to conduct formal and informal focus groups as well as structured and semi-structured interviews. I would meet with aid and development organizations to discuss their internal organizational structure and common issues, external pressures, stakeholder expectation, and the supply chain of services. My meetings with leaders and members of the most populous and remote communities in the country would include discussion on such topics as the pros and cons of aid and development projects taking place around the country and in their community. Similar conversations took place outside of community groups and with human rights activist like Charlotte

Charles, and other Haitians doing good work like Djaloki, who works to insure aid and business projects are imported with as much of a Haitian-centered philosophy as possible. Additionally, I was able to hear about life in Haiti during the wildly interesting discussions about everything Haitian on the variety of different public transport vehicles I used while in Haiti (buses, motorcycles, pickup trucks, coal trucks, airplanes, boats, and tap taps).

After each interview, focus group or conversation I felt like I gained a better understanding of the realities of life and work in Haiti. Although I will certainly never fully understand the realities of life in Haiti I did begin to find a newfound appreciation for the role I-O psychology could have in the humanitarian sector with both for and not-for profit companies, and ultimately learned the importance of taking time to learn about and from the people and environment where I want to be of assistance.

Along my journey I recorded the conversations when possible but mostly relied on taking notes during meetings or more often than not immediately after. During down time the last two weeks in the country (and several months after I left Haiti) I would rely on Thematic Analysis to extract themes from these recordings and notes. I chose to focus on the areas that community members stressed when describing their experiences with aid organizations. I would then use this information to help my own understanding of how to best work in these environments in the future, as well as identify the avenues I-O psychology could best be utilized.

The following are just a few of the themes with related quotes that reflect stories and opinions from community members and aid workers in Haiti. The quotes are chosen to provide the read with a glimpse into the complexity of aid and development work in Haiti.

Theme I. Community–Aid organization divide

For Us – By Us – With Us
>   (Community Leaders in Cite Soleil)

We would like to abolish the word – GIVE!
>   (Jacmel Community Member)

These two quotes reflect the way many Haitians I spoke with said they would prefer aid and development work to be done. The first quote was shared during a focus group organized to discuss ways the international community could be more effective with delivering aid. The group consisted of nine local community leaders in Cite Soleil and the feeling that humanitarian assistance both short and long term should be done in a manner that is "For Haitians" "By Haitians" and "With Haitians" was agreed upon by everyone in the group.

The second quote from a local community member and aid worker in Jacmel was shared following an interview question asking what barriers he thought were present between aid organization processes and their impact. Similar to the first quote he would go on to explain that he felt the word "Give" was inappropriately dividing the aid work between an international group that was doing "for" but not "with" another group – Haitians. These two quotes reflect the importance of organizations to involve local communities and local leaders in their aid and development efforts. I-O psychology can play an important role in helping organizations develop practices that better connect with community members be it through helping with selection of local workers, outreach training, or assessments of local perceptions.

Theme II. Organizational Justice

> Treat me as if I was an overseas employee
> (Haitian Employee for international NGO)

> Learn about Ayiti – our history is rich … Our people and communities have a lot to offer – NGO's seem to always forget that
> (Guerda – Manages a Haitian NGO)

The two quotes were representative of what was commonly shared by Haitians I interviewed who were currently working or had worked for an international NGO. The common organizational issues mentioned reflected the potential organizational injustices taking place. Haitian workers were expressing their discomfort with the differences between how they felt international workers were being treated and how local workers were being treated. In particular international workers were given special treatment in areas such as security, housing, holiday time, and pay. The international workers also reported noticing this difference and feeling uncomfortable with it. The second quote reflects feelings that international organizations do not respect the capacity of local communities and constantly focus on looking internationally for employees. I-O psychology can help overcome this barrier by working with organizations on selection and training of local employees or working directly with community members on building occupational skills that could help with employability.

Theme III. External pressures

> I have deadlines and budgets to focus on...a community needs assessment is just not on the agenda
>
> (International NGO manager in Jacmel)

> They (international NGOs) are doing so many similar projects in our community so why do we have to find them instead of them talking to us?
>
> (Community leaders in Cite Soleil)

The first quote is a reflection of what was shared by many NGO managers, both local and international. The managers felt that they were forced to focus more on the demands of the donors, because they were supplying the money for the projects, than on the exact needs of the community. The second quote is an example of the relationship that can exist between local and international groups. The local governing bodies and organizations can feel bullied by international aid organizations that often have more resources and power. When the international organizations begin to work in communities and do not consult with local groups, even if this is inadvertent, it can undermine the relationship between the two groups before they even meet. I-O psychology can play an important role in mediating these relationships with our skill set in organizational development, training, and mediation between groups.

Theme IV. Transparency and trust

> I would like to know who is driving that fancy car with the big NGO sticker on the side...why are you here?
>
> (Community Leader in Petigove)

> The same project by another organization with the same results – results we in the community don't want
>
> (Tap Tap conversation)

> They (NGOs) over promise and under deliver...we don't know what is the truth anymore
>
> (Jane – Community Leader in Kenscoff)

With such a long history of aid and development work taking place in Haiti the average Haitian has been exposed to a large number of NGOs or other development organization, often on a daily basis. The over saturation of NGOs and other organizations doing similar and at times repetitive work across the country has made some Haitians wary of these groups. The three quotes are concrete examples of the lack of confidence and trust Haitians can feel toward these organizations and how this may be due to the limited amount of organizational transparency. I-O psychologists can work with organizations to help them more effectively share their mission and values with communities. This can be done by organizational change techniques that promote the inclusion of community members in decision making and puts meeting community expectations at the center of organizational goals and performance appraisals.

I-O, Haiti, and humanitarian assistance

Although my goal was to use the time in Haiti to focus on learning, I was able to do some consulting during formal and informal meetings with aid organizations. My work consisted mostly of sharing what I heard and learned while in Haiti in a manner that would build awareness for employees and managers, as well as relate to organizational outcomes such as performance and goals. For example, I would discuss challenges the organization was facing, relate that to common issues expressed by local community members and aid workers from my experiences, and then discuss how this information could be used to specifically help the organization. I would always be sure to also offer advice on ways to move forward with projects that would promote a more community-driven approach and address the importance of human factors of aid (e.g., dominance, justice and identity – for an overview see MacLachlan et al., 2010). Building awareness within aid and development organizations by discussing what I heard and relating it to organizational outcomes is just the tip of the iceberg when it comes to how to effectively apply the discipline of I-O to humanitarian assistance in Haiti. The following section discusses other areas that I-O can be utilized in Haiti and in other areas where humanitarian assistance take place.

I believe that an I-O psychologist can have a very significant positive impact in Haiti. The amount of work that could be done with local communities as well as local and international organizations is seemingly limitless. There are also important lessons that our discipline can learn when applying our research and applied techniques to conditions like those in Haiti.

Haiti has a unique dynamic between local communities and international communities. This is due to the substantial number of NGOs (estimates range from 5,000 to 15,000) in the country and fact that most foreigners are working for an NGO or other international organizations. Few are there just to be there. What I found is that when I explained that I did not work for an NGO or was just traveling around to visit friends, Haitians found it strange. This would ultimately impact how we interacted and when it came time for me to set up interviews or meetings in 2011 I had to take time to reflect on the interview methods that would work best in these types of environments.

I found that an open and less formal approach was far more effective at getting people to open up about their experiences than the traditional formal structured interview. In fact I often relied on the informal discussions and environments such as tap taps or dinners to gather important information. It is not that I would try and use these places to gather information all the time but instead I would make sure that I paid close attention to what was said and shared during these conversation, and when appropriate ask follow up questions that I thought were both relevant and important – later taking notes on what was said. I would also always make it clear what my intentions were before, if possible, but always after the interactions. This approach to data collection is a good example of how our discipline can adapt and train for specific methods of collecting data in similar environments. In other words always keep your ears and eyes open but do so in a respectful and genuine manner.

The diverse groups and relationships that form in Haiti due to the large number of international organizations and whole host of other factors lay a solid foundation to learn about the human dynamics involved in aid and development. Every area of I-O psychology has a place in this type of environment, with some areas seeming more pressing than others. For example, I sat in on two cholera training and leadership building sessions. These were hosted by different organizations but for the same audience, Haitian community leaders, who were to take the information they learned back to their respective communities and train others – meaning the effectiveness of training delivery could have life or death consequences.

The training approach taken by one organization stood out over the other mainly because of the way culturally based learning strategies (e.g., group activities, including dancing and acting) were respectfully incorporated into the meeting. The community leaders were much more receptive to the training and seemed to have a much stronger understanding of the information, thus showing the opportunity for effective training and development methods. This type of an approach is what the UN calls "alignment" of aid (with local needs, values, aspirations, etc.). In other words, what I observed was a macro-level policy principle being enacted at a local, workplace, and organizational level. Alignment made perfect organizational psychology sense to me.

Other specific areas where an I-O psychologist could make a difference in Haiti include working with aid organization on selection and management of local workers and volunteers and working with Haitian-owned organizations to identify avenues that build a voice in the international community and where policy development occurs (e.g., helping local organizations gain a voice at the weekly UN cluster meetings). Above all, I think, I-O psychologists – local or international – can play a key role in helping organizations more effectively work with local communities, and communities with organizations. A culturally competent local or expatriate I-O psychologist might stand as a kind of mediating link between international aid organizations and Haitian people by evaluating the approaches taken by aid organizations and how that approach is perceived and ultimately accepted or dismissed by local communities. Process skills like these might be part of what have been described before as "new diplomacies" (Osicki, 2010; see also, Saner, 2010). The I-O psychologist can then assist organizations, if they are needed in the community, in learning how to more effectively align desired outcomes with local needs by assessing and listening to what the community itself wants and needs. After all, Haitian communities know what Haitians want, so why not start asking instead of telling?

I know there are I-O psychologists working with a few aid organizations across Haiti, and likely even some working with large unilateral organizations such as the UN. While in Haiti, I continually looked for opportunities to meet other I-O psychologists. I only came across a few names, and I never actually had the chance to meet any others working in the country. This apparent lack of connectivity illustrates a role for organizations like the Global Organisation for Humanitarian Work Psychology, for example, through its online network and website (see www.gohwp.org). Such networks help I-O professionals connect with others in the profession to provide support and advice whenever needed. These types of organizations and networks will help build capacity of I-O in humanitarian assistance as well as help reduce the isolation that often comes with being an I-O psychologists in the aid and development arena.

Conclusion

When it comes to Haiti, I have found that there is "what everyone tells you" about the country (e.g., Haiti is a dangerous place and nothing good is happening); What no one tells you" (e.g., Haiti is an absolutely beautiful country that will welcome you warmly if you respect the culture and people); and "what I-O needs to know" (e.g., Haiti is full of very similar issues that traditional I-O can address but offers our discipline opportunities to learn from this complex environment). I think I-O psychology as a profession has an important role to play not only in Haiti but across the international aid arena. By utilizing our understanding of individuals, groups, and organizations, we can work together to help reassess aid approaches to include more organizational perspectives in general and organizational psychology in particular. There are undoubtedly flaws in the system that can be reappraised. Understanding the role that human relationships, both in and between organizations and the community, play in the process will be pivotal to the development of more effective aid, relief, and reconstruction effort(s).

If I can offer nothing else from my time in Haiti to fellow I-O psychologists, please know this:

> Take your time and learn about and from the people you strive to support. I-O psychology can, as many other disciplines have, do more harm than good if not utilized correctly. Forget any preconceived notions about a population or group of people. Start your I-O work from the ground up, as you will then be equipped to conceivably make a positive impact.

References

Carr, S. C. (2007). I/O psychology and poverty reduction: Past, present and future? *The Industrial-Organisational Psychologist*, 48(1), 111–114.

Easterly, W. (2006). *The White Man's Burden: Why the West's Effort to Aid the Rest have Done So Much Ill and So Little Good*. London: Penguin Books.

Easterly, W., & Pfutze, T. (2008). Where does the money go? Best and worst practices in foreign aid. *Journal of Economic Perspectives*, 22(2), 29–52.

MacLachlan, M., Carr, S. C., & McAuliffe, E. (2010). *The Aid Triangle: Recognizing the Human Dynamics of Dominance, Justice and Identity.* Canada: Fernwood Publishing Ltd.

Osicki, M. (2010). New diplomacies in corporate social responsibility. *The Industrial-Organizational Psychologist,* 48(1), 111–114.

Saner, R. (2010). The new diplomacies. *The Industrial-Organizational Psychologist,* 47(4), 121–125.

9
Servants of Empowerment

Stuart C. Carr, Eilish McAuliffe, and Malcolm MacLachlan

Summary

The United Nations defines poverty as poverties of opportunity, including being denied access to good health, education, and decent work. Freedoms like these imply good health and educational services, staffed by motivated workers, and industries that are socially responsible toward their employees and the communities in which they operate. A psychology that is anti-poverty must therefore by definition include the empowerment of individuals in work, for health and in education. It must also connect with policy-makers and communities – contributing to the science of implementation. This chapter articulates a Humanitarian work psychology of empowerment. Research must speak "truth to power," naming, shaming, and issuing challenges to extant development inequities: A continuing "economic apartheid" in aid workers' wages; "brain waste" through employment discrimination against skilled (and relatively unskilled) migrants; transforming corporate social responsibility from image management to community empowerment; "task-shifting" health-care delivery from ensconced imported health professionals to local mid-level cadres; and influencing policy development and planning on social inclusion, for people living with disability. These cross-contextual cases also show how organizations can be more effective "capacitors" for human development. Taking empowerment seriously requires that industrial-organizational (I-O) psychology, just like organizations themselves, become a servant of empowerment.

Introduction

"Empowerment" is more than just hackneyed buzzword in poverty reduction. It has become ever more central to stated goals and processes in contemporary aid and development. Across the United Nations (UN) Millennium Development Goals, or MDGs (Annan, 2000), poverty is defined not just in monetary terms, but also as poverties of opportunity. These deprivations of opportunity are perpetuated by structures and entrenched practices: They include access not only to basic health and education but also to decent work (World Bank, 2012). The UN has proposed a set of moral processes for how to achieve the MDGs. Their pursuit is meant to be guided by principles like local "ownership, alignment, and international "accountability" (Paris Declaration on Aid Effectiveness, 2004).

Averring like this depends on organizations and employees (in health clinics, schools, factories, and aid agencies) doing their jobs; and doing them well (World Bank, 2012). These vital organizational and human dynamics not withstanding however, the UN and Paris Declaration "grand plan" has yet to be translated into everyday workplace practices (Easterly, 2006). This yawning hiatus places a blatant moral obligation on industrial and organizational (I-O) psychology, which has so far been relatively silent on poverty reduction (Berry et al., 2011). Now more than ever before is a time for I-O psychology to step up to the global moral, social, and economic challenge of poverty reduction, and show "how" empowerment can be instantiated "at" work; and for communities "through" work performance (Carr, 2013).

This chapter drills down into the human dynamics of empowering people and organizations against poverties of opportunity in the workplace, in aid and global development. Specifically, we show "how" organizations can become metaphorical "capacitors" for human development in practical everyday life (Carr, MacLachlan, and Furnham, 2012). In the physical world, capacitors are devices for storing a charge of electrical energy. Metaphorically then, we envisage ways in which organizational structures and people can be brought together to release human potential, and reach their inherent "capability" (Sen, 1999).

In the past, I-O psychology has been criticized for being too much a "servant of power" (Baritz, 1960; Brief, 2000); usually referring to their relationships with large for-profit corporate organizations. However these dangers also exist for humanitarian organizations, so evocatively captured in the title of Hancock's (1989) classic *"Lords of Poverty: The Power, Prestige, and Corruption of the International Aid Business,"* and more recently echoed in Moyo (2009). An effective Humanitarian work psychology must not only be aware of this, but demonstrate understanding, reflexivity, and measures to counter it. Social dominance theory (Sidanius and Pratto, 1999) warns that even "hierarchy-attenuating" organizations – prototypically perhaps, aid agencies – will implicitly resist putting themselves "out of business" by empowering others *too much* (LeMieux and Pratto, 2003). An authentic work psychology of empowerment therefore has the potential, and a duty, to (1) cast fresh light on poverty reduction efforts, while (2) carving out a more transformative role for the (I-O) profession itself (Lefkowitz, 2012).

Perhaps we should stress here that we do not feel that there is necessarily anything wrong with organizational psychologists making more money for, for example, a major multinational that is already prospering commercially for its shareholders, and that many of them will already probably do it in a humanitarian way – at least from the workers' point of view. Thus we do not wish to alienate corporate psychologists – quite the contrary in fact, as we shall see under corporate social responsibility (below), empowerment work psychology needs their support just as they may benefit from taking a wider perspective on life at work.

Empowerment operationalized

At an everyday level, empowerment at work has at least four major facets (Thomas and Velthouse, 1990): "Competence" means having a sense of efficacy at work; "Meaning" at work entails having valued goals; "Self-determination" is having the autonomy to pursue the goals; and "Impact" is a resultant sense of making a difference at work, that is, *achieving* one's or the group's meaningful goals (Spreitzer, 1995). These facets of empowerment at work are logically intertwined and interrelated. Empirically, they have been replicated across a variety of workplace sectors and settings (Spreitzer, 2008). Crucially for us in this chapter, these contexts have recently been extended to include humanitarian work and poverty reduction – specifically through "Technical Assistance" work from expatriate aid (Smith, 2012).

From a local worker perspective, to be empowering, we have observed that expatriate aid workers should be aware of and prevent a pernicious triangle of human factors: Dominance; Justice; and Identity (MacLachlan, Carr, and McAuliffe, 2010). In Smith's (2012) direct empirical test of this triangle, perceived expatriate dominance was most closely linked (negatively) to the capacitation of competence; justice (expatriate fairness) was most closely linked to the capacitation of meaningful self-determination; and identity (keeping one's own identify, in Smith's study as a Filipino person) was linked most closely to capacitating a sense of impact ("I can make a difference round here").

Smith's (2012) study focused on expatriate aid in one particular context, The Philippines. This chapter aims to explore whether and to what extent the linkages found in that particular study might extend to other contexts and sectors within international aid and development. To do so we consider a number of cross-contextual case studies – narrative accounts of recurring situations issues (SIOP, 2013).

A key for I-O psychology to become anti-poverty, we argue, is that work psychologists become servants of empowerment.

Challenging dual salaries

This is a "researchers" story about dual salaries, a widespread practice in aid work in which expatriates are paid more than their local counterparts doing a similar job, even though they may have the same, or very similar, qualifications, and experience. The practice has been in place since "international development" (aid to low-income countries) began (Harrod, 1974). Aid rationale at the time was that local capacity was in short supply, having to be capacitated by "international experts" who would work themselves out of a job – technical assistants who would mentor and empower local mentees. In order to attract these "international experts" to work in poor resource settings, the argument was that these technical assistants would have to be paid high-income country rates. Decades later, technical assistance remains firmly in place and to that extent, unsuccessful (Manning, 2006), appearing to imitate – at least in the eyes of some – the privileges of entitlements more congruent with the colonial-era.

"Working for the UN means a good life, but you can get caught up in it. I get about US $100,000 a year, tax-free. Why should I ever look for another job?" (Fechter, 2012, p. 1484). Comments like this, quoted verbatim from an international aid worker/technical assistant, imply that dual salaries may have something to do with the stasis in technical assistance *work*, and that empowerment is part of the (poverties-of-everyday-opportunity) problem, not its solution.

Granted a highly paid worker may not have high "Western-style" bills to pay, such as school loans, for example. It might also be pointed out that the locals will have access to a network of family and friends who serve as a support system an expatriate will never have. The local employee will also have the benefit of familiarity with the culture and knowledge of how local systems work, both formal and informal. The expatriate might also be viewed as a rich "Westerner" and charged deluxe prices for basic services. All of these factors mean that in some senses, the international worker is dependent on the goodwill of local people, and local colleagues; and that there may be some room, in their minds, for a loading of some sort. The question then becomes how much of a loading would be both practical and equitable for living costs, as well as for social justice.

We first began researching dual salaries some 25 years ago, after being challenged to do so by a perspicacious colleague at the National University of Malawi. At the time, and despite a few expatriates (like ourselves) being employed on local contracts, local wages in the organization were anywhere between 5% and 10% of the international packages (depending on aid agency) paid to lecturers who were on international contracts sponsored by aid agencies under the rationale of "technical assistance." Today there remain substantial variations in the gap between local and expatriate salaries, ranging from ratios of 2:1 to 10:1 (Carr, McWha, MacLachlan, and Furnham, 2010), between and within countries (Munthali, Matagi, and Tumwebaze, 2010; Zhou et al., 2010). While in some cases the ratio may have diminished, the symbolic and practical differences in living conditions remain extant and in many cases, substantial. This may be seen as an "economic apartheid" between local and international remuneration (Marai et al., 2010). This disparity splits not only wages and benefits but also extends to a "dual standard" in work conditions more generally (Carr, 2013).

Dual salaries are an institution of disempowerment; of unequal privileges; and thwarted capability.

To the best of our knowledge, no research has shown beneficial effects, from dual salaries, on human relations in aid and development work. Instead they fuel feelings of work injustice, motivate brain drain and early return, and exacerbate culture shock for expatriates (Carr et al., 2010; for a full academic and applied review, MacLachlan et al., 2010). In short, in our view dual salaries are a major impediment to the mutual respect and workplace cooperation on which capacitation depends (McWha and MacLachlan, 2011).

How can research speak truth to this continuing power? In our experience, researchers are in a privileged position to do so – they are not employed directly by the aid agencies although their research may be funded, at least in part, from such sources. The impact of research is, in real world terms, through its utilization in policy and practice – a moral as well as professional obligation (Usuramo, 2009). Finding a pathway to these sorts of impacts is the real (main) obstacle to developing a genuinely humanitarian work psychology of decent wages.

This in turn is a question of implementation science.

How might aid organizations reconfigure their incentives and incentive systems toward empowerment rather than economic apartheid? Here we turn to consider each of the major facets of empowerment.

Enabling competency, and self-efficacy, begins with recruitment and selection. Aid organizations can utilize local rather than international subject matter experts when defining the job specification (Manson and Carr, 2011). This is meta-competency. It entails trusting the competencies of local experts to define the competencies required to work successfully with people in the context of their own community. One of the most destructive practices that we have witnessed with respect to recruitment and selection, one that has been widely reported from settings as far apart as Tanzania and the Solomon Islands (MacLachlan et al., 2010, *The Aid Triangle*), is the fact that local people often do not even get to see the job notice, or apply for it. "Tied aid" like this not only disempowers the local applicant pool, internal or external to the aid project, but also makes the new job more difficult and more likely to result in an early return, for the expatriate hire (Toh and Denisi, 2007).

Enabling meaning, namely through the facilitation of valued goals, requires that the employing aid organization implements an equitable performance management and personnel development system. According to our researcher experience with dual salaries, performance appraisals are often an exception rather than the rule. As a result, dual salary systems create a metaphorical "concrete ceiling" (meaning palpable, visible, and seemingly unbreakable barrier above one's head, MacLachlan et al., *The Aid Triangle*, 2010) for local aid workers. Again the solution to capacitating workforce relations, though technically complex and threatening the privileges enjoyed by the dominant group, lies in designing and implementing a performance appraisal system based on agreed and valued goals that is equitable (and safe) for all aid workers (Marai et al., 2010).

Enabling autonomy to pursue valued goals means increasing the decision-making latitude entrusted to local workers. A potential problem with the aid system (as it has been practiced since the 1960s) is that dual standards have become almost normalized into aspects of "aid culture" (Fechter, 2012; Harrod, 1974). They and what they represent inside the aid architecture itself may have helped to provoke, even cultivate reactance, that is, opposition to the system in an attempt to exert one's own freedom (MacLachlan et al., 2010). A common expression of this is in expectations of reciprocity, including payment for "participation" in aid projects themselves, even by those who are deemed to be the "recipients" of aid (Ridde, 2010). These seeming "pay me" reactions actually often reflect a backlash to perceived double standards in aid, a way of rebalancing perceived power discrepancy (Carr, MacLachlan, Zimba, and Bowa, 1995): Resistance rather than Capacitance. Such entrenched reactions create a distrust of the local population amongst aid agencies, resulting in intransigence on their part. Curing systemic "perdiemitis" (the widespread expectation of receiving a daily allowance for partaking in development workshops/activities away from one's main place of work) requires courage, collaboration and patience (Ridde, 2010). Any temptation among donor aid agencies to keep "control" of a project may, in our view, be partly driving preferences for project aid (directly funding particular projects) over centralized budget support (providing funding for low-income governments to allocate according to their own priorities). We would suggest that the circumvention of government should be resisted, not just to break the cycle of mistrust – disempowerment – mistrust but also because stand-alone projects have limited impact unless they can be sustained. Thus the system needs to be strengthened and capacitated; it provides the context for development, be it in industry, education, or health.

Finally, we come to enabling workers to strive for impact; make a difference. Dependent on continuity of employment, sustained performance in aid is frequently short-circuited by disempowering salary structures: Experienced local staff members learn that their reward package is much less than their equally (in fact in many cases substantially less) experienced international colleague's remuneration, leading them to quit the organization and/or emigrate (e.g., Peters, 2013). In that sense, capacitation depends on enabling competency, meaning and autonomy, as outlined above. But the knowledge that local people often leave also compels us to ask another question: What happens *next* in their trajectories of mobility?

Challenging brain waste

Since the advent of the MDGs, human mobility has been touted as a means of development out of poverty, rather than its predecessor, "brain drain" (Carr, Inkson, and Thorn, 2005). According to a "migration-development nexus," in global policy circles, expatriating from a lower-income setting into a higher-income economy, and labor market, can mean increased job and career prospects, higher earnings, and remittances for extended families "back home," This line of thinking applies equally to any kind of worker who migrates for a better life in another country. An implicit assumption in this line of reasoning is that the emigrating person has access to decent employment opportunities. A problem for this rationale though is that in many higher-income settings, they do not. The evidence increasingly has shown that immigrants from lower-income countries, even when they are highly skilled, seldom get the opportunity to work at the same level in their new country even when they do manage to secure employment (UNDP, 2009). What is less clear however is why? Unless this "theory" question can be answered, with reliable, valid and readily implementable evidence, there will be no migration-empowerment nexus.

Transnational south-south mobility has in the past been proposed as a part-solution to dual salaries (Dore, 1994). Dore's argument was that relocating between low-income countries, rather than from low- to higher-income ones, would both save resources (because workers would accept local, or near-local wages) and enable smoother transfer of workplace capabilities (people from low-income settings have on-the-ground experience already; although this does of course neglect often important cultural and contextual differences). These considerations are certainly not financially insignificant – salary budgets for technical assistants from donor countries, or tied aid, can tie up as much as 50% of an entire aid project's funding (Marai et al., 2010). Thus "south-south" mobility could, in principle, meet the learning and development objectives of many migrant workers and in the process potentially substantiate a south-south migration-development-nexus.

Unfortunately, the pathway to such opportunities, for individual and project alike, is not always so smooth. A couple of vignettes illustrate. Job applications from neighboring low-income settings, despite being strong and in principle cost-efficient, were unofficially dumped from the applicant pool even before initial screening began, in favor of expatriate applicants from high-income countries. This is a clear instance of access bias. In a case of treatment bias, an expatriate employee from a neighboring low-income island was employed on a local contract rather than an international one, unlike his colleagues from a neighboring high-income country.

Anecdotes like ours above suggest that prejudice and discrimination constitute barriers to empowerment through regional mobility, leading to exclusion and demotivation, termed "brain waste" (Mahroum, 2000). In addition, the resistance to a south–south migration development nexus may have something to do with perceived power and status between "developed" and "developing" countries and the presumed capabilities of their peoples (MacLachlan et al., 2010, *The Aid Triangle*). According to this logic, appearing to have a similar background and experience to the country in which a job is advertised may actually resonate negatively with job selectors and appraisers, an "inverse resonance" (Carr, Ehiobuche, Rugimbana, and Munro, 1996).

An initial test of inverse resonance was conducted in Tanzania (Carr, Rugimbana, Walkom, and Bolitho, 2001). Across a range of jobs and sectors, local subject-matter experts clearly predicted that equally skilled and experienced candidates from within the same region, even the same trade bloc in which labor movement was supposedly free, would be rejected in favor of expatriates from wealthier economies. Other research has found that the bias can extend to treatment bias, in this case of workers from the People's Republic of China compared to Western countries-of-origin, who were employed in the relatively high-income economy of Singapore (Lim and Ward, 2003).

Evidently inverse resonance has the potential to block employment opportunities in higher- as well as lower-income settings.

One study unpacks some of its contributing motivation (Coates and Carr, 2005). Subject-matter experts with on average ten years observing job selection practices in New Zealand organizations, reported that candidates from lower-income countries of origin, regardless of their qualifications and experience, would normally experience significant job access disadvantages, all else (including costs of employment) being equal.

Crucially, the *extent* to which a candidate was disadvantaged (bumped down the list) co-varied significantly and simultaneously not only with cultural similarity (perceived and measured in cross-cultural archives of the time). Disadvantage also co-varied significantly with social dominance, with candidates whose country-of-origin was classified as "developing" in the UN Human Development Index of the time experiencing greater brain waste. As one respondent succinctly remarked, even when candidates are objectively equal to the task, "HR and Line managers feel that people who come from a *standard of living* most *similar* to New Zealand will fit into the environment more easily" (Coates and Carr, 2005, p. 590, emphasis and parenthesis added).

Knowing the reasons for people's resistance to diversity (socio-economic and cultural) is itself potentially empowering. It can enable us to mount more effective challenges to brain waste.

First, the dynamics of brain waste – as the quotation above implies – are likely quite implicit, not fully recognized as discriminatory. Recognizing the denial would be part of a solution to it. Research evidence itself has the potential to make the implicit explicit – by acting as a mirror to people's own decision-making processes. We suggest that research findings on the reasons for brain waste, including social dominance as we have just seen, be more widely disseminated, at management training courses and professional development seminars for HR managers involved in recruitment and performance appraisal. Training interventions like these have reportedly proved successful (Evers and van der Flier, 1998). Information is not only power, it can be empowerment. This would be a case of empowering efficacy, and competency, *for the selectors* – and hence for migrants themselves.

Valued goals, and meaning, for immigrants, would include finding decent work. The motivational deficit is likely, again, to be on the organization's side. As I-O psychologists, we already know the most effective way to reduce human biases in job selection and promotion is by *structuring selection processes* (Carr, 2010). Basing the selection on job analysis, using situational interviews, critical incidents for performance scales, and so on, are already proven ways that I-O psychology can be applied to reduce selection-related bias. Persuading selectors and appraisers to adopt these practices is where the challenge really lies in our experience, partly because many organizations still rely on unstructured methods. Changing that practice will require evidence-based advocacy on the merits of having a diverse workforce, for example the potential for increased workplace innovation (Carr, 2010).

Autonomy to pursue one's goals through and at work would seem to be predominantly a question of speaking out against treatment rather than access bias. Short of challenging the system itself from inside an organization, a promising way to enable empowerment, for new settlers at work, would be through training in political skill, or "PQ," for example based on critical incidents (MacLachlan et al., 2010, *The Aid Triangle*). PQ has been found to be more predictive of career progress within organizations than either Intelligence Quotient (IQ) or Emotional Intelligence (EQ) (Blickle et al., 2011), although as far as we know its applications have not yet been extended to empowering disadvantaged minorities per se.

Finally we come to impact, and to making a difference. In our view this can best be achieved in at least two major ways: First is top down in direction, by drawing the attention of organizations to human rights legislation in the relevant countries, around employment discrimination. Evidence linking social dominance to employment decisions is a case in point, since the decision is not based on capability alone. Second is bottom up in direction. This would include government and NGO-sponsored, evidence-based empowerment training for immigrants themselves, not just on cross-cultural and language skills, but also on the human dynamics of power at work, including how to constructively respond to experiences of social dominance at work (Evers and van der Flier, 1998; Mace, Atkins, Fletcher and Carr, 2005).

Challenging organizational responsibility

A wider ambit for removing barriers to equitable employment opportunities would be Corporate Social Responsibility (or "CSR"). A major impediment to CSR being taken seriously by many people is captured in the cynic's definition of corporations – that they are "an ingenious device for obtaining individual profit without individual responsibility" (Bierce, 1999). Overcoming that particular psychological barrier (to taking CSR seriously, and supporting further CSR) requires that organizations visibly, but not ostentatiously, go beyond apologizing and cleaning up, and then doing some more polluting or resource-destruction (Idemudia, 2009). Corporations must find ways to actually benefit the community, in this case, as we argue by being anti-poverty, that is, enabling prosperity (Carr, 2013).

Unfortunately when we look at the research on CSR, there are tell-tale signs that Ambrose Bierce might have been right all along: CSR can enhance company reputation (Godfrey, 2005); boosts recruitment (Turban and Greening, 1996); and enhances profit (Waddock and Graves, 1997). Systematic reviews show that on average CSR "pays off" (Orlitzky, Schmidt, and Rynes, 2003). Of course the problem here is that reputation, recruitment, profit, and paying off are all gains accrued by the *corporation*! As Bierce might have guessed, and predicted, there is no real research, at least that we are aware of, which focuses systematically, or even partially, on benefits to the *community* (Ingram et al., 2013). Thus all the available research initiatives to do with CSR have so far been for CORPORATE social responsibility (Csr) rather than corporate SOCIAL responsibility (cSr).

Research has been doing the corporations' bidding: A servant of power.

Speaking truth to corporate power will require applying the empowerment model from workplaces *to* the community. An example would be IBM's Corporate Citizenry Project to supply rural health clinics with medical records, and record-keeping capacity (Osicki, 2010). This project, which to the best of our knowledge has not been deliberately publicized for commercial gain enables: Competency and efficacy by training local workers to staff the system, and by pledging to maintain the hardware; meaning and valued goals by creating decent jobs; autonomy to pursue the goals by entrusting local people to run the record-keeping system; and impact to make a difference by enabling people from the community to save lives in their community. Of course such projects may also eventually secure future markets for IBM products – a genuine joint win.

What is lacking in the research domain is a systematic evaluation of the configurations of organizational policies that make a difference to poverty, in cSr initiatives across health, education, and decent work in general.

Challenging resistance to task-shifting

As we have just seen, combating any reliance on overseas experts, in health education or business depends on building capacity *locally* (Carr, 2010). Building capacity locally is also a more sustainable, and desirable way of speaking truth to the power of dual salaries than the alternative of migration, separation, and the like. Task-shifting is a relatively new, and arguably radically localized (at least in terms of scale) solution to shortages in health care and to a lesser extent perhaps education, in many low-income settings. There, the effectiveness of the health system is limited by a range of resource constraints, but most particularly, human resource constraints (McAuliffe et al., 2010; MacLachlan, 2012). The Global Health Workforce Alliance has estimated that Africa alone needs 1.5 million new health workers to be trained to address shortfalls in its health systems (World Health Organization, 2008). The need is particularly acute in community rehabilitation: Thus according to The World Report on Disability (2011), 0.04–0.6 psychologists per 100,000 of population are required in low- and middle-income countries (World Health Organization, 2011).

Task-shifting means that specific tasks are reallocated, from professionals with longer training to professionals with shorter training (Callaghan, Ford, and Schneider, 2010). For instance, Clinical Officers, who may train for three years, are able to substitute for obstetricians whose training can take more than ten years, and of whom there are very few in most low-income countries. In Mozambique, registered nurses have been trained to perform caesarean sections – a procedure that would normally be undertaken by an obstetrician in high-income countries.

Research in emergency obstetric care provides strong evidence for the clinical efficacy (Chilopora, Pereira, and Kamwendo, 2007; McCord, Pereira, Nzabuhakwa, and Bergstrom, 2009) and economic value (Kruk et al., 2007) of these "so-called" mid-level cadres. A recent systematic review of lay community health workers trained in the prevention of mother and child illness confirmed the effectiveness of this cadre (Gilmore and McAuliffe, 2013). The research thus indicates that people trained for shorter periods on specific tasks are equally effective as conventionally trained health professionals (obstetricians) with much longer training. Indeed, compared to conventional solutions like reliance on expatriate workforces, local workforce capacitation like this may render health care more accessible, cost-effective, and efficient (Buse et al., 2008).

Some key systems challenges for these mid-level, or alternative cadres are their motivation, support, supervision, and management. A major challenge to such innovations (we believe) are on the socio-political side, specifically they come from the power dynamics of professional status. Having trained a cohort of mid-level cadres, how will they become integrated into the wider healthcare system? Humanitarian work psychology has made particular contributions here (McAuliffe et al., 2009; McAuliffe, et al., 2010; McAuliffe et al., 2013). However, more can and needs to be done by applying the skills of organizational psychology to Job Analysis, skill set specification, training and supervision within "task-shifting" paradigms (MacLachlan, Mannan, and McAuliffe, 2010; Mannan et al., 2012; McAuliffe et al., 2013).

In the case of task-shifting, the empowerment of one group may indeed increase access to health care for the community, but may be perceived to be linked to the disempowerment of another group – in the case of obstetric care, physicians. The challenges of addressing social dominance may for instance be seen in the preference to refer to mid-level cadre collectively not as "clinicians," but rather as "non-physician clinicians" so that the distinction between them and "doctors" is maintained, regardless of their effectiveness. Improving access to health care will require the cooperation of other health professionals. Furthermore, evidence on its own will likely not be enough. Empowerment opportunities such as continuing professional development (competency and efficacy), meaning (respecting valued goals among mid-level cadres themselves), autonomy (to pursue those goals), and room for impact (making more of a difference) will in all probability need to be *advocated* (Carr, 2013).

Challenging policy development

Advocacy is not restricted to workforce segments. It also includes community segments. We have already seen the disability sector needs community rehabilitation workers, and the empowerment of mid-level cadres. However the end-goal in this sector, as in others concerned with enablement of opportunity, is empowerment of people *in the community*. With this goal of social inclusion in mind, we would like to close with an evidence-based-advocacy focused case.

Policy documents indicate how resources should be distributed – who should get what – and to that extent are inherently political. In low-income contexts, it becomes increasingly important that resources are equitably distributed, yet this is rarely the case. Social dominance theory (LeMieux and Pratto 2003) has been a stimulus for developing a policy analysis tool which evaluates the extent to which different vulnerable groups are included in health polices, and whether they are conferred with core concepts of human rights in service provision. Developed by a multidisciplinary team, including psychologists from Sudan, South Africa and Ireland, our policy analysis tool – "EquiFrame" (Amin et al., 2011) – has been used to analyze over 70 national, regional and international polices. Jefferson stated that "there is nothing more unequal, than the equal treatment of unequal people"; alluding to the idea that if one wants equality as an outcome then it requires equity in the processes to achieve it – resources have to be distributed equitably (according to need and addressing barriers) to achieve equivalent outcomes. In many policies – across high, medium and low-income countries – resource allocation privileges some groups over others.

EquiFrame was developed through lengthy consultation with stakeholders across the four target countries that Project EquitAble (www.Equitableproject.org) focused on: Sudan, Malawi, Namibia, and South Africa. Literature searches and discussions helped to identify key themes around human rights, the right to health and vulnerability, which were of relevance across a variety of health, delivery contexts, and particular health equity challenges. The Draft Framework was presented at consultation workshops conducted in each country and attended by over one hundred participants drawn from relevant clinicians and practitioners, civil servants, elected government representatives, non-governmental organizations (NGOs), independent consultants, researchers, and academics, including members of different vulnerable groups. Feedback was incorporated into a revised Framework. The final EquiFrame tool (which can have elements added to it or removed from it) comprises 21 "Core Concepts of Human Rights" (including, for instance, non-discrimination, capability-based services, and coordination of services) and covers 12 "Vulnerable Groups" (including, for instance, people with disabilities, displaced populations, and ethnic minorities). Effectively EquiFrame creates evidence, by measuring the extent to which policies explicitly commit to addressing the distinctive needs of different vulnerable groups to access health care of the same quality and it has found that many policies dramatically privilege some groups over others (MacLachlan et al., 2012).

EquiFrame challenges the psychology of social dominance and helps policymakers think through the development of more inclusive policies, through which scarce resources can be more equitably distributed. EquiFrame has now been used to write the first ever National Health Policy for Malawi (Amin et al., 2011) and has been adopted to guide the development and revision of all future health policies in Sudan. It has also been used to train staff working across six African and Asian countries in the International Labor Organization's PROPEL (Promoting Rights and Opportunities for People with Disabilities in Employment through Legislation) Project; as well as to train United Nations, government, and civil society staff, working across ten South American, European, African, and Asian countries as part of the United Nations Partnership for the Rights of Persons with Disabilities; in projects ranging from employment, to health, education, and social protection. EquiFrame (Amin et al., 2011) is an open access resource, with freely downloadable manuals (Mannan et al., 2013).

Our work has gone beyond examining "policy on the books" and also includes applying psychological data collection techniques to exploring the process of developing and revising policies; essentially a process of social persuasion, of engaging with and encouraging stakeholders to embrace a particular agenda (Chataika et al, under review). Our work on policy analysis and revision has contributed to recently convening a WHO-funded consortium charged with the task of developing guidelines for the future rehabilitation workforce, globally. We expect that through the policy issues and the rehabilitation workforce, humanitarian work psychology will have much to contribute to promoting greater access and social inclusion in health care, and in community empowerment and development.

Conclusions

Humanitarian work psychology can contribute to helping workers, organizations, systems, and government "being good at doing good"; good in the sense of providing decent work which empowers individuals and communities and good in the sense of contributing to poverty reduction and social development. Humanitarian work psychology can contribute to task outcomes as well as to relational aspects of the process of achieving such outcomes; and it can contribute to advocacy processes and influence their outcome through developing more inclusive policy, monitoring, and evaluating its implementation. We have illustrated these facets of Humanitarian work psychology through a particular, anti-dominance prism. Through a metaphor in which organizations can be capacitors, we have used specific examples from our own experience, aware that there must be very many other demonstrations of each of these facets in different areas of the world, where psychologists and others are working as servants of empowerment.

The approach we have adopted in this chapter is probably more "research" than "practice." Nonetheless we are firmly of the belief that good research has applications, and should be empowering itself to key stakeholders. Evidence, in the form of narrative and number, qualitative and quantitative, can help to make the case for change; for improvement; for development that is aligned, accountable, and locally owned. In that spirit of collaboration with the community, including communities of research practice and policy-makers, a new online research incubator has recently been set up, designed to facilitate the exchange of ideas, and collaborative links, on empowerment-related issues and opportunities. Project INCUBATE (INternational Collaborations between Universities By Aligning Their Expertise, 2013) is designed to share ideas for research on poverty reduction across a global commons.

INCUBATE's rationale is that many great ideas for relevant and responsive research projects simply don't see the light of day for lack of time, opportunity, or resources to conduct them. This risk is especially salient for research aligned with poverty reduction and the empowerment of opportunity, and capability. Graduate thesis students, scholars, policy-makers, and citizens from all walks of life are hereby invited to scan and contribute to and draw from the ongoing list of ideas, which can be found listed at:

http://www.massey.ac.nz/massey/learning/departments/school-of-psychology/research/poverty/princubate/princubate_home.cfm.

References

Amin, M., MacLachlan, M., Mannan, H., El Tayeb, S., El Khatim, A., Swartz, L., & Schneider, M. (2011). EquiFrame: A framework for analysis of the inclusion of human rights and vulnerable groups in health policies. *Health and Human Rights*, 13(2), 1–20.

Annan, K. A. (2000). *We the Peoples: The Role of the United Nations in the 21st Century.* New York: United Nations (UN).

Baritz, L. (1960). *The Servants of Power: A History of the Use of Social Science in American Industry.* Middletown, CT: Wesleyan University Press.

Berry, M., Reichman, W., MacLachlan, M., Klobas, J., Hui, H. C. C., & Carr, S. C. (2011). Humanitarian work psychology: The contributions of organizational psychology to poverty reduction. *Journal of Economic Psychology*, 32, 240–247.

Bierce, A. (1999). *The Devil's Dictionary.* New York: Oxford University Press.

Blickle, G., Kramer, J., Schneider, P. B., Meurs, J. A., Ferris, G. R., Mierke, J., Witzki, A. H., & Momm, T. D. (2011). Role of political skill in job performance prediction beyond general mental ability and personality in cross-sectional and predictive studies. *Journal of Applied Social Psychology*, 41, 488–514. doi: 10.1111/j.1559-1816.2010.00723.x.

Brief, A. P. (2000). Still servants of power. *Journal of Management Inquiry*, 9, 342–351.

Buse, K., Ludi, E., & Vigneri, M. (2008). Can project-funded investments in rural development be scaled up? Lessons from the millennium villages project. *Natural Resource Perspectives*, 118, 1–6.

Callaghan, M., Ford, N., & Schneider, A. (2010). A systematic review of task-shifting for HIV treatment and care in Africa. *Human Resources for Health.* Retrieved January 2, 2012, from http://www.biomedcentral.com/content/pdf/1478-4491-8-8.pdf.

Carr, S. C. (2010). Global mobility, local economy: It's work psychology, Stupid! In S. C. Carr (Ed.), *The Psychology of Global Mobility* (pp. 125–150). New York: Springer.

Carr, S. C. (2013). *Anti-Poverty Psychology.* New York: Springer.

Carr, S. C., Ehiobuche, I., Rugimbana, R. O., & Munro, D. (1996). Expatriate's ethnicity and their effectiveness: "Similarity attraction" or "inverse resonance"? *Psychology and Developing Societies*, 8, 265–282.

Carr, S. C., Inkson, K., & Thorn, K. J. (2005). From global careers to talent flow: Re-interpreting brain drain. *Journal of World Business*, 40, 386–398.

Carr, S. C., MacLachlan, M., & Furnham, A. (2012). *Humanitarian Work Psychology.* Basingstoke: Palgrave-Macmillan.

Carr, S. C., MacLachlan, M., Zimba, C., & Bowa, M. (1995). Community aid abroad: A Malawian perspective. *Journal of Social Psychology*, 135(6), 781–783.

Carr, S. C., McWha, I., MacLachlan, M., & Furnham, A. (2010). International-local remuneration differences across six countries: Do they undermine poverty reduction work? *International Journal of Psychology*, 45(5), 321–340. Global special issue on psychology and poverty reduction. Retrieved from http://poverty.massey.ac.nz/#global_issue.

Carr, S. C., Rugimbana, R. O., Walkom, E. H., & Bolitho, F. H. (2001). Selecting expatriates in developing areas: "Country-of-origin" effects in Tanzana. *International Journal of Intercultural Relations*, 25, 441–457.

Chataika, T., Wazakili, M., Mji, G., MacLachlan, M., Dube, A. K., Mulumba, M., Massah, B. O., Wakene, D., Kallon, F., & Maughan, M. (under review). *Facilitating Disability Inclusion in Poverty Reduction Processes: Group Consensus Perspectives from Disability Stakeholders in Uganda, Malawi, Ethiopia, and Sierra Leone*.

Chilopora G., Pereira C., & Kamwendo F. (2007). Postoperative outcome of caesarean sections and other major emergency obstetric surgery by clinical officers and medical officers in Malawi. *Human Resource Health*, 5, 17.

Coates, K., & Carr, S. C. (2005). Skilled immigrants and selection bias: A theory-based field study from New Zealand. *International Journal of Intercultural Relations*, 29, 577–599.

Dore, R. (1994). Why visiting sociologists fail. *World Development*, 22, 1425–1436.

Easterly, W. (2006). *The White Man's Burden: Why the West's Efforts to Aid the Rest have Done So Much Ill and So Little Good*. London: Penguin Books.

Evers, A., & van der Flier, H. (1998). Ethnic minorities in the labour market. In P. J. D. Drenth, H., & J. de Wolff (Eds.), *Handbook of Work and Organizational Psychology* (2nd Edition, pp. 229–259). Hove, UK: Psychology Press.

Fechter, A. M. (2012). "Living well" whilst "doing good? Missing debates on altruism and professionalism in aid work. *Third World Quarterly*, 33, 1475–1491.

Gilmore, B., & McAuliffe, E. (2013). Effectiveness of community health workers delivering preventative interventions for maternal and child health in low- and middle-income countries: A systematic review. *BMC Public Health*, In press.

Godfrey, P. C. (2005). The relationship between corporate philanthropy and shareholder wealth: A risk management perspective. *Academy of Management Review*, 30, 777–798.

Hancock, G. (1989). *Lords of Poverty: The Power, Prestige, and Corruption of the International Aid Business*. New York: Atlantic Monthly Press.

Harrod, J. (1974). Problems of the United Nations specialized agencies at the quarter century. In G. W. Keeton, G. Schwarzenberger, & G. Burnham (Eds.), *The Year Book of World Affairs* (vol. 28). Westport, CT: Praeger 187–203.

Idemudia, U. (2009). Oil extraction and poverty reduction in the Niger Delta: A critical examination of partnership initiatives. *Journal of Business Ethics*, 90, 91–116.

Ingram, V., de Grip, K., de Ruyter de Wildt, M., Ton, G., Douma, M., Boone, K., & van Hoeven, H. (2013). *Corporate Social Responsibility: The Role of Public Policy. A Systematic Literature Review of the Effects of Government Supported Interventions on the Corporate Social Responsibility (CSR) Behaviour of Enterprises in Developing Countries*. The Hague: Ministry of Foreign Affairs of the Netherlands.

Kruk ME, Pereira C, Vaz F, Bergström M., & Galea S. (2007). Economic evaluation of surgically trained assistant medical officers in performing major obstetric surgery in Mozambique. *BJOG*, 114, 1253–1260.

Lefkowitz, J. (2012). From humanitarian to humanistic work psychology: The morality of business. In S. C. Carr, M. MacLachlan, & A. Furnham (Eds.), *Humanitarian Work Psychology* (pp. 103–128). Basingstoke, UK: Palgrave-Macmillan.

LeMieux, A. F., & Pratto, F. (2003). Poverty and prejudice. In S. C. Carr, & T. S. Sloan (Eds.), *Poverty and Psychology: From Global Perspective to Local Practice* (pp. 147–162). New York: Springer.

Lim, A., & Ward, C. (2003). The effects of nationality, length of residence, and occupational demand on the perceptions of "foreign talent" in

Singapore. In K. S. Yank, & K. Hwang (Eds.), *Progress in Asian Social Psychology* (pp. 247–259). Westport, CT: Praeger.

Mace, K. A., Atkins, S. G., Fletcher, R. B., & Carr, S. C. (2005). Immigrant job-hunting, labor market experiences, and feelings about occupational life in New Zealand: An exploratory study. *New Zealand Journal of Psychology*, 34, 97–109.

MacLachlan, M. (2012). Rehabilitation psychology and global health. In P. Kennedy (Ed.), *Oxford Handbook of Rehabilitation Psychology*. Oxford: Oxford University Press 554–573.

MacLachlan, M., Amin, M., Mannan, H. El Tayeb, S. El Khatim, A. Swartz, L. Munthal, A., & Van Rooy, G. (2012). Inclusion and human rights in African health policies: Using equiframe for comparative and benchmarking analysis of 51 policies from Malawi, Sudan, South Africa & Namibia. *PLoS One*, 7(5), e35864. doi:10.1371/journal.pone.0035864.

MacLachlan, M., Carr, S. C., & McAuliffe, E. (2010). *The Aid Triangle: Recognizing the Human Dynamics of Dominance, Justice and Identity*. London: Zed Books.

MacLachlan, M., Mannan, H., & McAuliffe, E. (2010). Staff skills not staff types for community based rehabilitation. *Lancet*, 399, 1988–1989.

Mahroum, S. (2000). High skilled globetrotters: Mapping the international migration of human capital. *R & D Management*, 23, 30–32.

Mannan, H., Amin, M., MacLachlan, M., & The EquitAble Consortium (2013). *The EquiFrame Manual: A Tool for Evaluating and Promoting the Inclusion of Vulnerable Groups and Core Concepts of Human Rights in Health Policy Documents*. 2nd Edition. Dublin: Global Health Press.

Mannan, H., Boostrom, C., MacLachlan, M., McAuliffe, E., Khasnabis, C., & Gupta, N. (2012). A systematic review of the effectiveness of alternative cadres in community based rehabilitation. *Human Resources for Health*, 10, 20.

Manning, R. (2006). Technical cooperation. *Development Assistance Committee Journal*, 7, 111–138.

Manson, J. M. C., & Carr, S. C. (2011). Improving job fit for mission workers by including expatriate and local job experts in job specification. *Journal of Managerial Psychology*, 26, 643–663. Global special issue on psychology and poverty reduction. Retrieved from http://poverty.massey.ac.nz/#global_issue.

Marai, L., Keribu, V., Kinkin, E., Peniop, J. P., Saline, C., & Kofana, G. (2010). Remuneration disparities in Oceania: Papua New Guinea and the Solomon Islands. *International Journal of Psychology*, 45, 350–359. Global special issue on psychology and poverty reduction. Retrieved from http://poverty.massey.ac.nz/#global_issue.

McAuliffe, E., Manafa, O., Maseko, F., Bowie, C., & White, E. (2009). Understanding job satisfaction amongst mid-level cadres in Malawi: The contribution of organizational justice. *Reproductive Health Matters*, 17, 80–90.

McAuliffe, E., Bowie, C., Hevey, D., Makoae, L., Manafa, O., Maseko, F., & Moleli-Habi, M. (2010). Managing and motivating: Pragmatic solutions to the brain drain in human resources in healthcare. In S. Kabene (Ed.), *Human Resources in Healthcare, Health Informatics and Health Systems*. IGI Global, online publication. Retrieved August 6, 2011, from http://www.irma-international.org/chapter/managing-motivating-pragmatic-solutions-brain/43265/.

McAuliffe E., Daly M., Kamwendo F., Masanja H., Sidat M. (2013). The critical role of supervision in retaining staff in obstetric services: A three country study. *PLoS ONE*, 8(3), e58415. doi:10.1371/journal.pone.0058415.

McCord, G. M., Pereira, C., Nzabuhakwa, C., & Bergstrom, S. (2009). The quality of emergency obstetrical surgery by assistant medical officers in Tanzanian district hospitals. *Health Affairs*, 28(5), w876–w885.

McWha, I., & MacLachlan, M. (2011). Measuring relationships between workers in poverty-focused groups. *Journal of Managerial Psychology*, 26, 485–499. Global special issue on psychology and poverty reduction. Retrieved from http://poverty.massey.ac.nz/#global_issue.

Moyo, D. (2009). *Dead Aid: Why Aid Is Not Working and How There Is Another Way for Africa*. London: Allen Lane.

Munthali, A., Matagi, L., & Tumwebaze, C. (2010). Remuneration discrepancies in the landlocked economies of Malawi and Uganda. *International Journal of Psychology*, 45, 341–349. Global special issue on psychology and poverty reduction. Retrieved from http://poverty.massey.ac.nz/#global_issue.

Orlitzky, M., Schmidt, F. L., & Rynes, S. L. (2003). Corporate social and financial performance: A meta-analysis. *Organization Studies*, 24, 403–441.

Osicki, M. (2010). New diplomacies in corporate social responsibility: Pro-Social I/O – Quo Vadis? *The Industrial-Organizational Psychologist*, 48, 111–114.

Paris Declaration on Aid Effectiveness. (2004). *Paris Declaration on Aid Effectiveness*. Paris: United Nations (UN).

Peters, R. W. (2013). Development mobilities: Identity and authority in an Angolan development programme. *Journal of Ethnic and Migration Studies*, 39, 277–293.

Ridde, V. (2010). Per diems undermine health interventions, systems and research in Africa: Burying our heads in the sand. *Tropical Medicine and International Health*, doi: 10.1111/j.1365-3156.2010.02607.x.

Sen, A. (1999). *Development as Freedom*. Oxford: Oxford University Press (OUP).

Sidanius, J., & Pratto, F. (1999). *Social Dominance: An Inter-Group Theory of Social Hierarchy and Oppression*. Cambridge, MA: Cambridge University Press (CUP).

SIOP [Society for Industrial and Organizational Psychology] (2013). *Humanitarian Work Psychology: Concepts to Contributions*. Washington, DC: SIOP International White Papers.

Smith, N. V. (2012). Equality, justice and identity in an expatriate/local setting: Which human factors enable empowerment of Filipino aid workers? *Journal of Pacific Rim Psychology*, 6, 57–74.

Spreitzer, G. M. (1995). Psychological empowerment in the workplace: Dimensions, measurement, and validation. *Academy of Management Journal*, 38, 1442–1465.

Spreitzer, G. M. (2008). Taking stock: A review of more than twenty years of research on empowerment at work. In C. Cooper, & J. Barling (Eds.), *The Handbook of Organizational Behaviour* (pp. 54–72). London: Sage.

Thomas, K. W., & Velthouse, B. A. (1990). Cognitive elements of empowerment: An "interpretative" model of intrinsic task motivation. *The Academy of Management Review*, 15, 666–681.

Toh, S. M., & DeNisi, A. S. (2007). Host country nationals as socializing agents: A social identity approach. *Journal of Organizational Behavior*, 28, 281–301.

Turban, D. B., & Greening, D. W. (1996). Corporate social performance and organizational attractiveness to prospective employees. *Academy of Management Journal*, 40, 658–672.

UNDP [United Nations Development Programme] (2009). *Human Development Report 2009 – Overcoming Barriers: Human Mobility and Development.* New York: UNDP.

Usuramo, J. (2009). *Opening Address: Workshop on Dual Salaries.* Honiara, Solomon Islands: University of the South Pacific.

Waddock, S. A., & Graves, S. B. (1997). The corporate social performance-financial performance link. *Strategic Management Journal,* 18, 303–319.

World Bank (2012). *World Development Report 2012: Jobs.* Washington, DC: World Bank.

World Health Organization (2008). *The World Health Report 2006: Working Together for Health.* Geneva: WHO.

World Health Organization (2011). *World Report on Disability.* Geneva: WHO.

Zhou, E., Lu, Z., Li, X., Li, T., Papola, T. S., Pais, J., & Sahu, P. P. (2010). Remuneration differences in the emerging economies of China and India. *International Journal of Psychology,* 45, 360–370. Global special issue on psychology and poverty reduction. Retrieved from http://poverty.massey.ac.nz/#global_issue.

10
Designing Learning Systems for Poverty Reduction in Least Developed Countries

Raymond Saner and Lichia Yiu

> Poverty could be understood as a form of "structural violence" through systemic discrimination and exclusion of a country's poor. It is a form of denying human rights to its citizens living in deprivation and poverty.
>
> (Yiu and Saner, 2003)

Background

Both authors are co-founders of the Centre of Socio-Eco-Nomic Development (CSEND), a research and development NGO (non-governmental organization) founded in 1993 and registered in Geneva. The reason for establishing CSEND was based on the two co-founders commitments to sustainable development, including ecological, social, and economic sustainability within a context of equitable development at national, regional, and international levels. Under the auspices of CSEND, both authors designed and implemented large system development and change projects in China (1985–1996), Slovenia (1990–1996), Russia (1993–1996), and Bolivia (1999–2001).[1] Having also conducted consulting projects for international organizations (IOs) in the 1980s and early 1990s and having followed closely the difficult survival of so many people living in the Least Developed Countries (LDCs), both authors took the initiative to propose a project for the International Labor Organization (ILO) to support their efforts in alleviating poverty in the LDCs through employment creation in the context of the poverty reduction strategy instruments developed and managed by the International Finance Institutions (the International Monetary Fund and World Bank). The PRSP instrument as well as the CSEND, PRPSP, ILO project is described further below in the project section of this chapter

The authors' academic background is organizational psychology, industrial sociology, and development economics. They have spent a large part of the last 20 years of practice in LDCs and low-income developing countries characterized by malignant poverty, political instability, and underperforming economies. Having designed and implemented organization, development, and change (ODC) projects previously in the private sector and mostly at intra-organizational level in the 1980s, the authors were used to apply traditional ODC theory and methods. However, the situation of LDCs demanded solutions which went beyond a private sector/single organization framework. They hence had to re-visit the ODC literature and look for alternative sources of knowledge that could provide insights and know-how for large-scale development and change projects. Some sources were useful, but overall the situation was novel and demanded innovation and stretching of intellectual capacity. The search for appropriate and adequate large system change theory and methods are described below in the theory section. The discussion and closure sections consist of discussions of lessons learned, further theoretical and methodological considerations and end with an outlook for future application in the related field of Humanitarian Work Psychology.

Poverty in Least Developed Countries

The great majority of low-income countries (48 countries) have a GNI per capita of less than $992, and are expected to reach 950 million people in 2015.[2] Economic activities of these countries are mostly informal, which means that 60–70% of its population is captives of precarious living conditions with no real gainful employment, other than trying ones luck as street vendor or involving in semi-legitimate activities like recycling of stolen goods and contraband. Often when such transient jobs are harder to come by and environmental catastrophes re-occur (inundations, droughts), the affected population embarks on clandestine migration to other countries. Large influx of illegal migrants tends to exacerbate socioeconomic conditions in the host countries, leading to tensions and sometimes to outbreaks of violence.

To address social exclusion, the ILO promotes the right to inclusion, in the sense of participation, protection, access to decent jobs, and decent incomes, through the development of economic and social capability (Rodgers, 1995). It puts the responsibility on the government and international communities to ensure that "the attainment of the conditions on which this shall be possible must constitute the central aim of national and International policy" (The Philadelphia Declaration, 1944). Therefore, for the ILO, employment creation has to be an economic priority to achieve poverty eradication.[3]

Poverty and poverty reduction strategy papers in least developed countries

In anticipation of the UN Millennium Summit, the Boards of the World Bank and the IMF approved the Poverty Reduction Strategy Papers approach to reduce poverty in low-income countries in December 1999. Since then, a PRSP has become the prerequisite for debt relief and concessional lending. Major donor agencies are expected to endorse the participatory process prescribed by the poverty reduction strategy (PRS) process and the PRSP as a precondition for international financial support. In other words, a PRSP is now supposed to be the basis for all donor and creditor relationships with a low-income country.

The PRSP idea was first conceived as an operational plan linked to the country-level Comprehensive Development Framework (CDF) that was designed and implemented by the World Bank. The new IFI approach has linked PRSPs to debt relief under the enhanced HIPC initiative. Countries are now expected to have developed a poverty reduction strategy, reflected in a PRSP, to show how they would use the funds released by debt relief to alleviate poverty in their countries.

The key point of departure from the previous structural adjustment programs and other pre-PRSP development instruments is that PRSPs embrace a high level of civil society participation along with a stronger national ownership. The civil society sector includes "non-governmental and not-for-profit organizations that have a presence in public life, expressing the interests and values of their members or others, based on ethical, cultural, political, scientific, religious or philanthropic considerations" (World Bank, 2013).

Core principles of PRSPs

Six core principles of PRSPs are to be adhered to (IMF, 2002):

- *Country-driven*: promoting national ownership by involving broad-based participation of civil society (country ownership of a poverty reduction strategy is paramount)

- *Result-oriented*: setting goals for poverty reduction which are tangible and monitorable outcomes, for instance, universal primary education (links between public actions and poverty outcome)
- *Comprehensive*: stressing the need for integrating macroeconomic, structural, sectoral, and social elements, and that policies in these areas must be consistent with the goal of poverty reduction
- *Participatory*: requiring that all stakeholders in the country participate actively in the process of choosing poverty reduction strategies in a transparent manner
- *Partnership-oriented*: involving coordinated participation of development partners such as the beneficiary government, the domestic stakeholders, and external donors
- *Long-term perspective*: reforming institutions and building capacity are understood to be put into a long-term perspective

According to the ILO Governing Body Report in 2002 (ILO, 2002a), 71 countries have been identified to qualify for a PRSP. Nearly 50 have produced interim PRSPs (I-PRSPs), and nearly 20 have produced full PRSPs.[4]

The missing element in PRSPs from the ILO's point of view: Employment!

The ILO believed that the fight against poverty and for social justice lies at the heart of the ILO's concerns and that high quality employment is the most effective means to reduce poverty in a sustainable manner. Historically, the ILO initiated many rights-based approaches to poverty, basic needs, and social exclusion. It has also identified other approaches to governance and empowerment, sustainable livelihoods, income/consumption, and participatory approaches. It noted that poverty is multidimensional and that it is essential that responses to poverty are integrated and multi-sectoral.

The ILO (2002b) also reviewed selected PRSPs, focusing on the employment and Decent Work concerns in PRSPs and drew from its experience from countries where it was engaged in their preparation, that is, Mali, Tanzania, Honduras, Cambodia, and Nepal. Its findings were confirmed when reviewing other PRSPs. The overarching issues seen from the ILO's perspective are four (ILO, 2002c):

- PRSPs need to include a more thorough analysis of employment and other aspects of Decent Work: At the moment, sound employment policies are often missing in the I-PRSPs or PRSPs.

- *Employers' organizations, workers' organizations and labor ministries need to be more systematically integrated into the participatory process underpinning the design and implementation of PRSPs.* In quite a few cases, ILO constituents were either sidestepped or marginalized in the process.

- *More attention is needed in PRSPs on policies that maximize the impact of sustainable growth on poverty:* Various macroeconomic policies geared to market liberalization, privatization, and labor market flexibility have failed to take the social impact on various vulnerable groups into account.

- In their *funding priorities, donor countries must include issues related to employment and enterprise creation, social protection, rights, representation and dialogue, promotion of tripartism* (i.e., government, trade unions, and employers' organizations) *and other poverty reduction policies* on which the ILO has expertise.

The strategic choice made by the ILO in order to achieve progress on the above points was one of constructive engagement, based on the conviction that the PRSP process constitutes a vehicle through which the voice of the ILO and its constituents can be heard at the level of national planning and budgeting.

This initiative was based essentially on preparing, in collaboration with the national authorities, an analysis of the role of employment and of the various elements comprising Decent Work in poverty alleviation, and organizing tripartite meetings in the countries to discuss the Poverty Reduction Strategy Papers. The ILO tripartite structure of

> "government, employer, and worker representatives" creates "a unique forum in which the governments and the social partners of the economy of its Member States can freely and openly debate and elaborate labour standards and policies."
>
> (ILO, 2013)

Additionally, there was an increasing need to build the capacity of the social partners to become actively involved in monitoring the implementation of PRSPs and to make the most of the opportunity to engage in PRSP dialogue.

Figure 10.1 depicts the core actors within the context of a PRSP process in a LDC, namely, ministry of finance and ministry of planning. They are the counterparts of the IMF and the World Bank within the country. Together, these four actors control and manage the PRSP process. Other

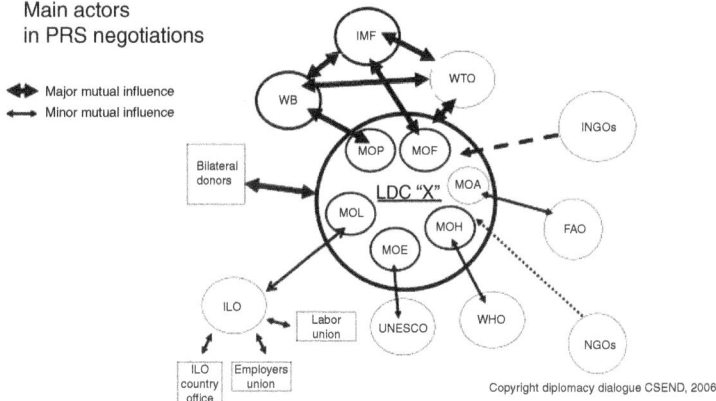

Figure 10.1 Main Actors in PRS Negotiation[5]

government ministries are often completely excluded from participating such as ministries of labor, manpower, youth, and rural development.

The ministry of labor is rarely invited to participate nor are its constituent partners, namely, labor unions and employer's associations. In other words, from an ILO and NGO perspective, the requirement of social dialogue and inclusion of national stakeholders was not confirmed by the evidence emerging from country reports.

CSEND's objective: Support ILO and add advocacy component through educational methods, large system analysis and advocacy measures

The Decent Work Agenda (DWA) of the ILO proposed a new approach to eradicate poverty and deprivation. The ILO Framework on the Measurement of Decent Work corresponds to the four key elements of the DWA: "Full and productive employment, rights at work, social protection and the promotion of social dialogue" (ILO, 2012).

Implementing the DWA gives back dignity and, to a varying extent, security and spending power to the poor. The DWA offered a theoretical understanding of poverty and practical solutions, which are different from neo-liberal macroeconomics in thinking.

In light of the reports from the field which indicated insufficient inclusion of employment in the PRSPs, the CSEND team considered important that a comprehensive and inclusive intervention be designed which would support the ILO's goal of using the social dialogue process to support the LDCs stakeholders in getting more involved in the PRSP negotiation process.

Building on already existing professional relations with the ILO, the CSEND team proposed an intervention consisting of education (writing of manual), training in PRSP negotiations and team building in the LDCs involving key stakeholders of the PRSP process. The ILO's department in charge of RPSPs and employment responded favorable and gave the CSEND team the green light to develop the agreed intervention tools and products.

The underlying concept consisted of identifying means to support participation and inclusion of national stakeholders in the PRSP process. The intervention's concept was based on Development Diplomacy and Advocacy – concepts which CSEND has developed and used in most of its large system change projects that included capacity building and institution development (Saner, 2005).

The CSEND Development Diplomacy and Advocacy approach for the ILO

Development Diplomacy (DD) describes the non-technical aspect of the development work of the IOs and the development worker. The onus of development diplomacy is on advocacy, influencing, networking, and negotiations. While advocacy has all the implications of "going public" with one's assertion and declared solutions, other aspects of DD consist of more discrete interventions in restricted spaces and are strongly focused on the relationships among individuals.

The aim of Advocacy and Development Diplomacy (ADD) is to build bridges between economic, social and ecological development policy objectives. In other words, ADD aims at bringing about reconciliation of different interests and communities. Ultimately, the goal of Development Diplomacy is to trigger a socioeconomic development process to arrest the vicious cycle of underdevelopment and to help countries progressively achieve sustainable development.

Advocacy and influencing are about changing the perception of what is right and appropriate; negotiation is about reaching agreement on what should be done and how to do it. All ADD-oriented actions are essential to accelerate the rate of adoption of the DWA by national authorities. Such actions are needed to foster consistency between words and actions within the international financial institutions (IFIs) and donor communities, which consist of the member countries of the Development Assistance Committee and provide aid to developing countries.

Competencies required to ensure successful advocacy campaigns

Identifying competencies on an organizational and individual basis provides a means for pinpointing the most critical competencies for a DWA-DD campaign. Organizational and individual competencies consist for instance of strengthening political will and vision, the availability of large system and organizational knowledge, the quality of the human resources involved in such a DD campaign, and resources to support Advocacy and Development Diplomacy.

In carrying out effective Advocacy and Development Diplomacy, the CSEND team considered the following competencies essential, namely:

- environmental scanning capacity;
- capacity in labor and macroeconomic research and policy analysis, including gender analysis of policies;
- capacity to plan, manage and monitor advocacy work;
- capacity to mobilize members of the public and targeted trend-setting organizations (e.g., information pamphlet, Internet, publications, public education events, demonstrations, direct actions);
- capacity to influence the policy makers through lobbying;
- capacity to manage the media and conduct development communication;
- capacity to conduct public relation campaigns at the grass-roots, national, and international level;
- capacity to network and coalition build;
- capacity for bilateral and multilateral negotiations.

Figure 10.2 depicts some of the advocacy and diplomatic activities which the CSEND team considered important and which needed to be developed and supported in the LDC countries involved in negotiating a PRSP against the IFIs (IMF and World Bank) and bilateral donors (called the "Bilaterals") in order to build momentum to influence the PRSP process in favor of inclusion of employment and Decent Work (Yiu and Saner, 2005; Saner and Yiu, 2012).

Affecting change in support of ILO's employment: PRSP strategy

The CSEND team hence proposed to strengthen ILO's goal of eradicating poverty and deprivation through inclusion of employment in the PRSP agreements. Implementing the DWA within a PRSP context was seen

Multiple means of advocacy

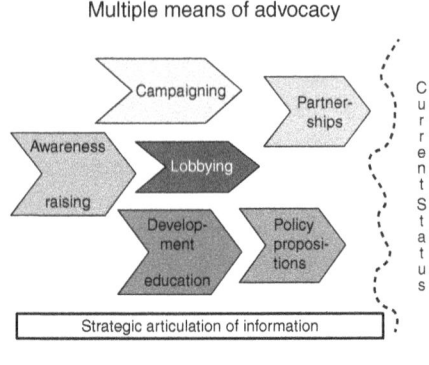

© CSEND 2003

Figure 10.2   Multiple Means of Advocacy[6]

as giving back dignity and, to a varying extent, security and spending power to the poor, the often silent majority of the LDCs. The DWA was seen as offering a theoretical understanding of poverty and practical solutions, which is different from neo-liberal macroeconomics in thinking. The ILO DWA had to reach a critical mass that could influence the public debate and the actual PRSP process in order to reach the bifurcation or tipping point where inclusion of DAW in the PRSP could become possible.

All ADD-oriented actions were seen as essential to accelerate the rate of adoption of the DWA by national authorities. Such actions were considered needed to foster consistency between words (helping the poor) and actions (including employment in the PRSPS) within the international financial institutions (IFIs) and donor communities.

CSEND's Advocacy and Development Diplomacy task list to ensure inclusion of Decent Work in the PRSPs

The CSEND teams' strategy to support the ILO's goals was based on an Advocacy and Development Diplomacy (ADD) strategy consisting of the following nine dimensions, namely:

- *Raising awareness* about the issue of working poor (the great majority of poor people work!)
- *Promoting a sense of urgency* about the social exclusion of the working poor and their vulnerability
- *Campaigning* for the fulfillment of the Millennium Development Goals and Decent Work for All

- *Networking* with like-minded development partners, international NGOs, civil society groups and individuals to strengthen one's power base and to enlarge influence
- *Contributing to the debate* on promoting employment and reducing poverty
- *Influencing the opinions* of potential change agents and decision-makers on the macroeconomic framework and development strategies
- *Negotiating policy changes* which are more consistent with the Decent Work Agenda and poverty reduction
- *Maintaining the coalition and other collaborative partnerships* regarding the Decent Work Agenda and poverty reduction
- *Monitoring the implementation* of policy changes in line with the Decent Work Agenda and poverty reduction
- *Developing and strengthening the capacity of Advocacy and Development Diplomacy within partner organizations and networks*
- *Enhancing capacity in Advocacy and Development Diplomacy*

These dimensions offered a framework to assess the current and future state of a LDC's performance and to assist the ILO in requesting inclusion of employment in their respective PRSP. The Advocacy and Development Diplomacy was needed to assess the current state regarding the following areas of influencing, namely:

a) policy changes in favor of the working poor and more equitable labor market conditions;
b) improved capacities of the social partners in the country;
c) active participation of the marginalized groups and communities in the PRSP and DWA process;
d) improved economic and social benefits of the working people.

Overall goal of CSEND's intervention

The overall goal of the CSEND teams' intervention hence consisted of a capacity-building strategy aiming at "enhancing the ILO's organizational abilities to achieve it its goals. In specific, the strategy was based on advocating, networking, and influencing a variety of stakeholders and constituents"[7] in order to achieve two overall objectives, namely to:

- Ensure incorporation of the Decent Work Agenda into a country's Poverty Reduction Strategy Paper and/or programmers;

- Ensure that operationalization and implementation of PRSP pro-grammers consist of measures that are pro-poor and rights based as encapsulated in the Decent Work Agenda.

This overarching goal of the CSEND team strategy was aligned with the ILO's constituents who share the tasks of effectively advocating the Decent Work Agenda as the fundamental approach to sustained poverty reduction. However, lacking capacities in advocacy has in many cases marginalized the role of the ILO constituents in the PRS process, leaving the vulnerable groups – women, children and minorities – exposed to the structural changes induced by the PRS plan and implementation.

Immediate objectives

The ILO needed to address the *policy causes of poverty* and propose countervailing policy alternatives, i.e., the Decent Work Agenda. The ILO's programs needed to focus on the actions of policy makers, for instance when they draft laws and regulations and allocate resources in general and when they prepare PRSPs and employment policies specifically. The principle aims of Development Diplomacy were to create pro-poor and rights-based policies, to reform policies in line with the Decent Work Agenda and to ensure that these remedial policies were being implemented. Development Diplomacy had to be one of the key competencies of ILO's officials in campaigning for *Decent Work for All* and in making its "working out of poverty" an accepted primary strategy for poverty reduction and international development.

  Some ILO programs already used advocacy/development diplomacy to influence the PRS process with visible success hence the strategy and action plan proposed by the CSEND team was aligned to ILO's general aims while at the same time giving ILO's policy campaigns more institutional support in the LDCs.

Components of CSEND's intervention

The strategy of the CSEND team was further defined and turned into the following actions:

a) Drafting a Guidebook for DAW-PRSP advocacy use of ILO staff in the LDCs
b) Developing a negotiation simulation reflecting the PRSP negotiation process

c) Conducting a pilot seminar to be followed by training and consulting workshops in LDC countries.

d) Strengthening cooperation and alliances of state and non-state actors in the LDCs in favor of inclusion of employment in their PRSPs

The CSEND team was subsequently contracted by the ILO to draft the guidebook, develop a PRSP negotiation simulation and conduct a pilot workshop followed by workshops in the field.

Guidebook[8]

The CSEND team drafted a *Guidebook* which was printed in 2005 and distributed to ILO's staff working in LDCs and to other staff at ILO headquarters in charge of ILO's PRSP-employment strategy.

The guidebook drew on the previous ILO experiences in order to provide concrete examples on how advocacy coupled with other means of action by the ILO officials could achieve pro-worker and pro-growth types of policies in the LDCs.

The guidebook consisted of modules covering the following topics: (1) A Self-Assessment Questionnaire, (2) an overview of the Poverty Reduction Strategy Paper (PRSP), an analysis of PRSP and DWA by sectors, an elaboration of planning and identification of entry points for the ILO's advocacy and influencing, guidelines for advocacy, influencing, networking and negotiations, an in-house case studies of PRSP pilots and advocacy, a PRSP multi-stakeholder negotiation simulation, and conclusions and recommendations for ILO strategies of PRSP/DWA.

Target groups and readership

The ILO constituencies (ministries of labor, employers' associations, and trade unions) were the fundamental stakeholders of the PRSPs process. They needed to be empowered to play a pivotal role in the design and implementation of PRSPs. However, in low-income countries, these social partners are usually not included in the policy-making process which determines employment and poverty reduction policies. Hence, guidebook was intended for three target groups:

- ILO Headquarters staff who have the direct responsibility for poverty reduction-related programs and activities;

- ILO field staff, especially country directors and sub-regional office leaders responsible for ILO's DAW-PRSP strategy;
- Country representatives of the ILO constituencies involved in their country's PRSP process.

The guidebook summarized the salient points concerning the policy environment of the PRSP process and provided concrete tools for advocacy and for managing Development Diplomacy needed to achieve the DWA objectives.

Multi-stakeholder negotiation simulation

The simulation exercise was intended to facilitate the understanding of *advocacy, influencing, networking and multi-stakeholder negotiation techniques,* and how they might be applied in relation to the specific policy-making process of the Poverty Reduction Strategy. Special emphasis was given to the role of the , trade unions, and employers' organizations in influencing the policy formulation in this context.

The simulation allowed participants to engage in a hypothetical negotiation exercise in a fictitious country called "Equatoria" in sub-Saharan Africa. The time of the simulation was situated around the moment when the country's key ministries were drafting the Poverty Reduction Strategy Paper (PRSP). Anticipating the social dialogue part of the process, the Government decided to have initial informal consultations with representatives of the civil society organizations (CSOs) including workers' and employers' organizations. The government would also be holding discussions with joint staff from the World Bank and the IMF as well as with different key donor country representatives.

The simulation consisted of three consecutive phases, namely an initial preparatory stage; three parallel meetings along thematic lines; and a closing session to draft an outline of a PRSP text. Participants were exposed to both the thematic issues of the PRSP and the process of influencing and negotiating the final policy document.

The final PRSP was then to be drafted by the participants playing the roles of government officials within one month following these initial meetings and discussions. It was expected that the ILO and its constituents would try to insert policy recommendations in line with the Decent Work Agenda in the agreed policy matrix and/or the communiqué prepared by the Equatorian government.[9]

Pilot project and workshops in the field

The pilot workshop was agreed to be held in conjunction with an ILO Poverty Reduction Workshop for senior officers and constituencies from ILO's regional offices. The pilot workshop was held in September 2003 and the program consisted of a one-day negotiation skills training and a one-day PRSP simulation negotiation. Sufficient time was provided for the following activities: alliance building, strategy, scenario development and concession making, and dealing with non-traditional counterparts and stakeholders.

As a next step, the negotiation training package together with the Guidebook was used in field workshops in Addis Ababa (Ethiopia) for east African ILO staff. The workshop lasted three days and was designed in cooperation with the ILO department in charge of PRSP-DAW. The negotiation simulation as well as other training inputs was combined with basic inputs by ILO officials on DAW and ILO's PRSP strategy.

Subsequent workshops were held at the ILO sub-regional office for West Africa in Yaoundé, Cameroon in 2006. Workshop was attended by regional ILO staff, ministerial representatives of the sub-regional LDCs, representatives of the regional EU office, and training experts from the ILO training center in Turin, Italy.

The same year, another workshop of similar design like the previous one in Cameroon was held in Antananarivo, Madagascar. The participants for this workshop were government officials of the government's ministries of labor, finance, and economic affairs. Also present were representatives from chambers of commerce, labor unions, and academics from the capital's universities.

Strengthening cooperation and alliances of state and non-state actors in the LDC

The three workshops were very successful. Participants expressed satisfaction to be given support in advancing employment and DAW in their PRSP negotiations. Requests were made for immediate follow-up action in the countries which send participants to the workshop. The message that was conveyed to the CSEND team and their ILO partners was that this workshops should be immediately be followed up to help the countries organized their inter-ministerial coordination and improve on the government to private sector/civil society policy coordination.

Unfortunately, due to lack of financial resources, no more workshops were organized and the call for implementing the action plans developed at the workshop sites were not given follow-up support. As a consequence, the effort of strengthening the LDCs advocacy and negotiation competence in the PRSPs stagnated leaving many of the participants frustrated and disappointed. The frustration and disappointment was shared by the CSEND team and their direct counterparts at the ILO.

Theoretical considerations about large system interventions through capacity building and institution development methods

Designing and implementing large system change and development projects means shifting from a single organization to a multitude of organizations and institutions which in turn means adapting traditional Organization Development concepts to a multi-actor, multi-institutional setting. One major challenge of multi-stakeholder ODSC is the managing of boundaries between international organizations, local authorities, local organizations, NGOs, and international donors. These boundaries are porous and pose a special challenge for ODSC interventions.

Porous Boundaries[10]

Working in LDCs on poverty reduction and inclusive development means facing several IOs who at times do not agree on important economic and social policies. This was particularly evident for the authors when working in the field (Cameroon, Madagascar, and Ethiopia). Relations were at times difficult between the ILO and other IOs or agencies such as the World Bank, the IMF, UNDP, and donors such as the EU, the United States, and Japan. They often had competing strategies and incompatible theoretical understanding as to the development needs to the LDCs. Such lack of policy congruence made project work difficult because the local decision-makers at times exploited the policy disagreement between IOs and donors further aggravating the already difficult challenge of absorbing foreign aid (financial, technical, knowledge expertise) by the local counterparts leading to occasional serious impasses and conflicts.

Experts in charge of multi-actor, multi-institutional development projects have to find solutions to the above mentioned potential conflicts. The following insights from practice were useful for the authors an can be for others working in similar situations. The following insights are suggested:

(a) Public management and public organizations like IOs are character-ized by distinct features. The most commonly known aspects have been summarized by Rainey (1991), namely: reliance on govern-mental appropriations for financial resources; presence of intensive formal legal constraints; presence of intensive external political influences; and greater goal ambiguity, multiplicity, and conflict.

The UN system and international cooperation have to function within similar characteristics. Each specialized UN Agency has its own decision-making body involving a multitude of governments and related con-stituencies, which together approve annual budgets and influence the major directions of the agencies' programs and activities. Hence, the decision-making process can be very complex and presents in itself major obstacles regarding clarity of purpose, effectiveness and efficiency of management, and unity of staff (Sochor, 1989; Saner and Sapienza, 2012).

Continuous external pressures combined with complex decision-making processes weaken organizational boundaries and open the UN Agencies to the power plays of multiple external and internal constituencies.

(b) Power plays an important role in the total management process of the UN system. It cannot be overlooked and needs to be under-stood in its complexity. The factor of political power in private sector organizations has been studied and analyzed by manage-ment scholars, for example, Jeffrey Pfeffer (1981), and especially by Henry Mintzberg (1984), who developed a typology of config-urations of organizational power and proposed one possible rela-tionship between external and internal coalitions, which the author considers fits best the context of the UN system.

Building on Rainey (1991), Sochor (1989), Mintzberg (1984) and Yiu and Saner (2005), the authors proposed a definition of "Porous Boundaries" in Figure 10.3.

Development and change projects, conducted in such a complex and shifting environment are difficult to design and even more difficult to implement successfully (Yiu and Saner, 2006). The relevant fields of knowledge offer little guidance in regard to change projects in such complex and highly politicized environment.

Stakeholders	Multitude of actors, for example, governments, NGO's, intergovernmental institutions, which compete over use of financial and human resources of the organization.
Leadership	Elected or reinstated by members of governing body through process of bargaining and coalition building. Elected leadership enjoying relative autonomy during times of power parity in between budget cycles.
Goals	Negotiated compromises often remaining ambiguous in order to satisfy the needs and objectives of the stakeholders.
Financial Resources	Result of bargaining process, often approved, rejected, altered, or amended on a yearly basis.
Human Resources	Recruitment based on official or unofficial quota system. Standards adjusted to accommodate divergent competence levels of international staff.
Organization	Hierarchical, dominance of legal and bureaucratic measures as a defense against shifting alliances and external pressures.
Culture	Traditional, no innovative, defensive, security-minded, clannish combined with idealism resulting in frequent power fights.

Figure 10.3   Porous Boundaries[11]

Lessons learned and indications for future considerations of large system intervention theory and practice

PRSP-related projects could be designed and implemented at different levels of complexity such as at regional, international, and even global level (meta), for example, PRSP for west African LDCs by the ILO at

(a) national development level (macro), for example, a PRSP project focusing on inclusion of DAW in Cameroon's PRSP;
(b) sector-specific development level (meso), for example, drafting text for Madagascar's PRSP looking at ways to include and implement DAW in the health sector;
(c) institutional or organization level (micro), for example, planning a capacity building and institution development project for Ethiopia's Ministry of Labor to ensure better inclusion of DAW in its PRSP or designing a DAW project for Mali's enterprises to help them apply basic labor laws and labor conventions.

Faced with large-scale social discontinuities typical in international development work as described by the authors in this chapter requires a discussion of the theoretical underpinnings of such large system change projects. Most of existing ODC literature focuses on interventions in private sector for profit oriented enterprises in industrialized and highly developed North American and western European countries. The focus of this chapter's intervention was different as it focused on multi-actor, multi-stakeholder interventions involving various international, national, private sector, civil society actors, and stakeholders.

How can applied psychologists and behavioral scientists contribute to this monumental task? On one hand, the mainstream ODC theories and methods appear well equipped to address the needs of large-scale social intervention. Indeed, many development programs worldwide have already incorporated OD principles and practices into their intervention strategies. On the other hand, social development and social discontinuities in LDCs and low-income countries are characterized by multi-stakeholder – overt and hidden – actors whose' view of the world often differ from Western rational and linear logic.

For instance, most of the premises of classic macro-economic theory are not applicable such as the assumption that people pursue profit maximization, act rationally, and that market information is transparent and available. Some of these assumptions remain valid but other factors of human decision-making enter into play that are not easily understood by Western experts such as deference to elderly leaders, attribution of cause–effect to visible and invisible forces, preferences based on tribal membership to name a few well known relationship, and decision factors unknown to Western ODC-OSDC experts.

The result of these different often not easily identifiable differences means that linear thinking and planning such as the classic "freeze–unfreeze/current–future state" conceptualization of OD intervention needs to be replaced by simultaneous linear–nonlinear reality with more circular change processes involving client system and often multiple shadow social systems which influence the development and change process considerably.

Working as ODC-OSDC expert within non-Western countries and also for IO requires understanding of multi-stakeholder actor networks and their alliance building processes. A very good entry point into such complex ODC change processes is Steve Waddell's description of Global Action Networks (GANs) such as the Global Reporting Initiative (GRI), The Ethical Trade Initiative (ETI), Transparency International (TI), and other such GAN who operate internationally in developed and developing countries.[12] Similarly, OSD experts working in the international development field might benefit from studying the interactions between state, non-state actors (NGOs, MNCs), and IOs.[13] Interactions between these different actors in the field of humanitarian action have also been described as "new diplomacies" and a new group of organizational and industrial psychologists who founded "Humanitarian Work Psychology."

Working in complex social system as OSDC expert

Richard Beckhard reiterated during the last AoM meeting in Chicago in 1999 that he attended a few months before he died that ODC is an interdisciplinary approach combining psychology with sociology and that sociology has been very much absent in contemporary ODC literature and practice. This reminder is very relevant for anybody working in conflict zones and with post-war societies. In such environments, building social fabric is of the essence, not changing them. Inspiration for such OSD work are Durkheim's research on social anomie, Coleman and Bourdieu's research on social capital and Moreno's pioneering work on sociometry, social atom, and sociodrama.[14]

Working at national level and applying ODC-OSDC theory and methods is an even greater challenge since linear processes are not possible due to the multitude of stakeholders involved (overt and covert) hence diagnosis needs more time and experts and clients need to remain open to an emerging approach. ODSC interventions call for large system change architecture and development mechanisms for collective actions at global scale. As a field of specialized knowledge owners, we cannot afford to stick to the old boundary conditions of conventional ODC instead we need to move toward ODSC.

Notes

1. http://www.csend.org/project-samples
2. http://www.unohrlls.org/en/ldc/164/
3. http://www.ilo.org/wcmsp5/groups/public/—asia/—ro-bangkok/—ilo-islamabad/documents/policy/wcms_142941.pdf
4. The PRS process is ongoing. For an update on the countries participating, their timetables and current status of the process, please visit: http://poverty.worldbank.org/files/country_timelines.pdf and http://poverty.worldbank.org/files/prsp_deliveries.pdf
5. Lichia Yiu and Raymond Saner, 2006.
6. Ibid.
7. This advocacy guide is a direct response to the need identified in the ILO governing body report, 2002a: 2.

8. An ILO Advocacy Guidebook: Decent work and poverty reduction strategies (PRS), ILO, Geneva, 2005.
9. For more information see: Decent work and poverty reduction strategies (PRS) An ILO Advocacy Guidebook for staff and constituents; Module 7: PRSP negotiation simulation: PRSP Process in "Equatoria," ILO, 2005.
10. Based on Saner and Yiu, 2009.
11. Saner and Yiu, 2009, Porous Boundaries.
12. Waddell, Steve 2003, "Global Action Networks: Building global public policy systems of accountability," *Account Ability Quarterly*, AQ 20, May 2003, pp. 19–26.
13. Saner, Raymond, & Michaelun, V. (Eds.) (2009). *State actor versus non-state actor negotiations, republic of letters.* NL: The Hague, p. 410.
14. "Reconstructing the Social Fabric of Communities after War Trauma," summary of a workshop with literature reference pertinent for such type of OSD work. Retrieved from http://www.csend.org/conferences/conferences/item/313-1st-introductory-workshop-on-"reconstructing-the-social-fabric-of-communities-after-war-trauma".

References

ILO (2002a). *ILO Governing Body Report in 2002.* Geneva: ILO.

ILO (2002b). *The Decent Work Agenda and Poverty Reduction.* Washington, DC: ILO contribution to the IMF/World Bank Comprehensive Review of the Poverty Reduction Strategy Process. Retrieved from http://www.worldbank.org/poverty/strategies/review/ilo1.pdf.

ILO (2002c). *Poverty Reduction Strategy Papers (PRSPs): An Assessment of the ILO Experience,* 283th Session of the governing body, Geneva, GB283/ESP/3, and March, 2002.

ILO (International Labor Organization) (2003a). *Time for Equality at Work.* Global report of the Director-General as a follow-up to the ILO Declaration on Fundamental Principles and Rights at Work, International Labor Conference, 91st Session 2003, Report I (B). Geneva: ILO.

ILO (2005). *Decent Work and Poverty Reduction Strategies (PRS): An ILO Advocacy Guidebook for Staff and Constituents.* Geneva: ILO.

ILO (2012). Decent work indicators: Concepts and definitions. In *ILO Manual*, 15. Retrieved from http://www.ilo.org/wcmsp5/groups/public/—dgreports/—stat/documents/publication/wcms_183859.pdf.

ILO (2013). Tripartite constituents. In *About the ILO – Structure.* Retrieved from http://www.ilo.org/global/about-the-ilo/who-we-are/tripartite-constituents/lang–en/index.htm.

IMF (2002). *Poverty Reduction Strategy Papers – A Fact Sheet.* Washington, DC: IMF International Monetary Fund. Retrieved from http://www.imf.org/extemal/np/exr/facts/prsp.htm.

Kolb, Darl. G. (2002). *Continuity Not Change: The Next Organizational Challenge, Business Review.* New Zealand: University of Auckland, pp. 2–11.

Maxwell, S. (1999). The meaning and measurement of poverty. In *ODI Poverty Briefing*, February 3. Retrieved from http://www.odi.org.uk/publications/briefing/pov3.html.

Melnick, Joseph, Nevis, Edwin C. (Eds.) (2009). Xlibris corp, pp. 151–180.

Mintzberg, H. (1984). Power and organization life cycles. *Academy of Management Review*, 9(2), 207–224.

Pfeffer, J. (1981). *Power in Organisations*. New York: HarperCollins Publishers.

Rainey, H. (1991). *Understanding and Managing Public Organizations*. San Francisco: Jossey-Bass.

Reichman, W. & O'Neill Berry (2012). The evolution of industrial and organizational psychology. In St Carr, M. MacLachlan, & A. Furnham (Eds.), *Humanitarian Work Psychology* (pp. 34–52). London: Palgrave Macmillan.

Rodgers, G., Gore, C. & Figueiredo, J.B. (Eds.), (1995) Social Exclusion-Rhetoric, Reality, Responses. Institute of International Labour Studies: Geneva: Switzerland.

Saner, R. (1999). The impact of policy and role of donor agencies on small and medium-sized enterprise (SME) assistance projects in Russia. In Paul Trappe (Ed.), *Social Strategies* (pp. 331–346). New York: Peter Lang Verlag, Bern, Berlin, Wien, pp. 331–346.

Saner, R. (2005). Development diplomacy by non-state-actors: Emerging new form of multi- stakeholder diplomacy, diplofoundation, Malta.

Saner, R. (2010). *Trade Policy Governance through Inter-Ministerial Coordination*. Dodrecht: Republic of Letters, pp. 1–142.

Saner, R., & Michalun, V. (2009). Negotiations between state actors and non-state actors: Case analyses from different parts of the world (pp. 1–35), (pp. 119–138), Republic of Letters: Dodrecht.

Saner, R., & Sapienza, E. (2012). Development diplomacy and partnerships for social policy at the time of PRSPs: The case of decent work. *Journal of Poverty Alleviation and International Development*, 3(2), 145–180.

Saner, R., and Yiu, L (2009). A Sisyphean Task: Managing Porous Boundaries During OD Interventions in UN Agencies. In Melnick, Joseph & Nevis, Edwin C. (Eds.), *Mending the World: Social Healing Interventions by Gestalt Practitioners Worldwide*. Xlibris Corperation. Bloomington, IN, pp. 151–180.

Saner, R., & Yiu, L. (2012b). The new diplomacies and humanitarian work psychology. In S.C. Carr, M. MacLachlan, & A. Furnham (Eds.), *Humanitarian Work Psychology* (pp. 129–166). Palgrave Macmillan.

Sochor, E. (1989). Decision-making in the international civil aviation organization: politics, processes and personalities. *International Review of Administrative Sciences*, 55, 241–259.

The General Conference of the International Labour Organisation (1945). Declaration Concerning the Aims and Purposes of the International Labour Organisation (Declaration of Philadelphia). Accessed at http://www.ilo.org/wcmsp5/groups/public/—asia/—ro-bangkok/—ilo-islamabad/documents/policy/wcms_142941.pdf.

The Philadelphia Declaration (1944). www.ilo.org/public/english/support/1.b/century/content/1944.htm

WHO (1986). *Intersectoral Action for Health: The Role of Intersectoral Cooperation in National Strategies for Health for All*. Geneva: The World Health Organization.

World Bank (2013). Defining civil society, July 22. Retrieved from http://go.worldbank.org/4CE7W046K0.

Yiu, L., & Saner, R. (2005). Development diplomacy and poverty reduction strategy papers for least developed countries: Non-state actor advocacy and multi-stakeholder diplomacy. In J. Kobalija (Ed.), *Multistakeholder Diplomacy: Challenges and Opportunities* (pp. 105–121), Malta.

Yiu, L., & Saner, R. (2006). *Poverty Reduction Strategy Paper (PRSP): The Strengths and Weaknesses of its Instrumentality, Diplomacy Dialogue-CSEND*. Geneva.

11

Increasing Resilience Among People Who Are Homeless

Binna Kandola

Peter was homeless. He was not an alcoholic nor was he a drug abuser. He had been a self-employed painter and decorator with a good income and regular business. Married with two children, his life was stable and everything seemed content. With the advent of the global recession, his work dried up, his house was repossessed, and he and his wife separated. Not having close family ties to support him he became one of the invisible homeless, relying on his friends to let him sleep in spare rooms and sofas. This is not the stereotypical image that one has of a homeless person and shows how, because of a coincidence of circumstances, a lot of people could find themselves without a permanent dwelling. Peter was one of the many people that we encountered in our work with homeless people.

According to the DCLG (the Department for Communities and Local Government), there were 55,300 families in temporary accommodation in the United Kingdom in March 2013 (DCLG, 2013). The number of people sleeping rough is estimated to be 2,309 with a significant proportion (24%) being in London (DCLG, 2012). The trend in the United Kingdom from the late 1990s to latter part of the next decade was of a reduction in the numbers of homeless people but since 2009 there has been a 34% increase.

While it may be hard enough to gain an idea of the actual number of homeless people, the task becomes even harder once we consider the hidden homeless defined as: "People who are, arguably, homeless but whose situation is not 'visible' either on the streets or in official statistics. Classic examples would include households subject to severe overcrowding, squatters, people 'sofa-surfing' around friends' or relatives' houses, those involuntarily sharing with other households on a long-term basis, and people sleeping rough in hidden locations" (Fitzpatrick, Pawson, Bramley, and Wilcox, 2012). There was an estimated 1.75 million people in this category of hidden homeless.

Research conducted in the United States revealed that homelessness was related to a number of childhood experiences including separation from parents or caregivers and socioeconomic disadvantage. Other issues related to problems with addiction and mental health (Shelton, Taylor, Bonner, and van den Bree, 2009). However, the majority of people, like Peter, who are homeless do not have substance or alcohol abuse histories nor are they involved in criminal activity.

It is important to make this explicit as it is notoriously difficult to engage people with the topic of homelessness. One study scanned the brains of students at an Ivy League university while they were shown images of different categories of people. The area of particular concern was the medial prefrontal cortex as this activity here relates to thinking about oneself and other people. Some categories (sports people, business people) triggered activity but other categories (drug addicts and homeless people) did not. Homeless people may indeed be viewed as lesser humans, which may be why we feel able to ignore them when we encounter them in the streets.

In 2007, the National Audit Office published a report looking into the barriers faced by workless people when seeking employment. Many of the factors identified were directly applicable to homeless people too and included low skills and poor educational levels; poor health; low confidence and motivation; poor social networks – a lot of people find work through personal contacts the research found; poor job-search skill; and discrimination by employers.

Our work, with what for us was a new and very different client base, was through an organization called British Action on Homelessness (BAOH). BAOH is part of Business in the Community, a business led charity which is "committed to building resilient communities, diverse workplaces and a more sustainable future."

Business in the Community runs a number of programs to support disadvantaged groups into employment. These programs are complementary and build on ten years of experience of delivering its flag ship Ready for Work program. Ready for Work supports people who have experienced or are at risk of homelessness into employment through training, work placements and post-placement support. This long-standing program has supported over 6,000 people in ten years.

BAOH's philosophy is based on the premise that the most significant way that homeless people can achieve independent living is through work that is sustainable. Given the barriers that exist; however, that is no easy task. However, I-O, or as we are called in the UK occupational, psychologists focus is work and its impact on society, organizations, and individuals. The majority of our work however is with people who are employed. This project was involved with a very different client group – people who were unemployed and homeless, which presented us with a different set of challenges than the ones we were used to.

Prior to our involvement the BAOH had commissioned research into the barriers to work for homeless people. These were similar to those identified by the NAO and they were prioritized as

- low self-confidence;
- multiple needs;
- ongoing physical or mental health problems;
- not yet being ready for employment;
- patchy or non-existent employment records;
- age;
- behavioral problems and substance misuse;
- offending and criminal records;
- lack of practical necessities;
- low skill levels, lack of qualifications, and learning disabilities;
- family obligations.

While the bigger part of the report focused on structural and economic factors which impede the search for work (e.g., the way benefits are organized meant that often it was less economic for a person to be in work than out of work) there were four aspects in particular that were psychological and attitudinal.

First, the programs that are designed to help homeless people find work often stop at the point at which the client finds employment. In some respects this is understandable as it may be seen that the objective of the training has been achieved. However, this underestimates the difficulties that the clients face in their first few weeks and months at work.

Second, getting a job could involve relocating, which was disruptive both physically and emotionally. Not only would the person be in a new job, nerve wracking for many of us at the best of times, but they would have the anxiety of making new friends too. The loss of the social network meant that a key aspect of support was lost. The frail economic situation would then have been made worse by the loosening of the immediate social ties that they could call upon within the first two or three months of getting a new job. Support in this early phase was critical in determining whether the person felt able to stick with the job.

Third, lack of confidence is a significant issue and this did not just relate to the skills of the person involved. We found in the interviews that we carried out with clients that things that many of us take for granted represented significant challenges for our clients. Approaching an office building for example would not cause us a moment of hesitation. But it is an entirely different prospect if you have not only been out of work for a significant period but you are homeless too. The office block, from the client's perspective, is not just unfamiliar but alien and forbidding. The reception areas of most organizations may have been purposely designed to be unfriendly with their barriers, security personnel, rituals for entry and the high reception desks with the formal and harried staff behind them. At this point, we discovered, the anxiety is so great that some clients decide not to progress.

Fourth, a poor experience in the first job that the clients experience means that it is less likely that they will try again. Each negative episode will erode their self-belief a little more.

This then was the background to our work with BAOH. Our involvement was to help design a training module for this very specific client group to help them become more confident and resilient. It also involved writing guidance for those who have most contact with clients including key workers, coaches, and employers.

Many homeless people, unsurprisingly, find that the circumstances that led to their homelessness and the experience of being homeless affects their reserve of emotional resilience. A report by St Mungo's, a charity working with homeless people, found that half of respondents to a survey were depressed. Of course, resilience levels may be low before someone becomes homeless, and may be a contributing factor. Importantly, these people found it harder to move on from their homeless situation than those who reported medium to high levels of resilience prior to homelessness.

Other research has also indicated the importance of resilience and has attempted to determine how resilient the individuals were prior to becoming homeless. Joan Smith and her colleagues (Smith et al., 2008) interviewed 87 people in the Spring of 2007 and were able to follow up with 53 of them six months later in the Autumn of 2007. Forty-one of the 53 were interviewed again a few months later. The research was attempting to see type of help clients wanted, what they accessed and the impact it had. Half had had difficult early lives, e.g., abusive parents, parents who had died. The researchers also attempted to see how resilient their interviewees had been prior to being homeless. They found that the majority had led lives which they felt they had some control over. (See Figure 11.1.)

		Number	%
High	People who had led both capable and resilient lives in the past, that is, functioning and self-determining with stable relationships	21	24
Medium	Mostly functioning with or without support and some stability of adult relationships	28	33
Low	Functioning lives but with no stability in their living situation	18	21
Poor	Lives of restricted functioning with no stability	19	22

Figure 11.1   Past capability and resilience
Adapted by the authors from Smith et al. (2008).

The majority of the interviewees therefore (57%) had demonstrated resilience in the past. It would be mistaken then to stereotype homeless people as incapable of leading independent lives. This project was designed to develop greater resilience among this client group and this needed to recognize that for many of them this would involve helping them to recall resilience that they had demonstrated in the past.

Dame Carol Black's 2006 Review of the Health of the Working Age Population and subsequent report, "Working for a Healthier Tomorrow" firmly established that health, work, and well-being are "closely and powerfully linked" and promoted the view that work is good not only for the economic health of the country but for the health of individuals, too. So this project was focused on developing resilience in the client group in order to help them gain meaningful and sustained employment. The formal project aims were to

- advise companies on how to promote emotional resilience for BAOH's clients;
- advise homeless agencies on building resilience for the workplace;
- identify gaps and opportunities for businesses to support the homeless sector in building emotional resilience;
- strengthen the pre- and post-placement support that is offered to Ready for Work clients to further promote emotional resilience.

The phases of the project were

1. understanding the needs of the client group better;
2. designing and drafting the core material;
3. running a train the trainer course;
4. evaluation of the training.

Understanding the needs of the client group better

The project team at Pearn Kandola had access to the research that BAOH had commissioned plus other research that had been conducted in the United Kingdom on homeless people. This material was very useful to provide a backdrop to our work but could not furnish us with the detailed knowledge of the daily experiences of our clients, the type of situations that they found most difficult to deal with and what they personally would value most from some form of training intervention.

Pearn Kandola constructed an interview schedule which was used by BAOH staff to interview a range of people including clients but also key workers who interacted with the clients. This information provided the basis for the materials we developed.

The majority of clients, key workers, and job coaches interviewed felt that emotional resilience was something that is learned over time but there was no easy formula to follow. The key workers interviewed said that enabling clients to develop coping strategies as key life skills was a core focus of their work and that building resilience was embedded into practice. Rather than deal with it separately, boosting resilience was done by stealth in building confidence, capability and through engagement with work preparation activities.

Designing and drafting the core material

Training material was to be provided for a session which was to be of two hours in length. The time constraint was an important one and one that could not be changed. Where training was longer the non-attendance also increased. Train the trainer material was also written as this was always a project that was intended to be sustainable. Guidance was also produced for employers who took on homeless people so that they were better able both to understand the perspective of their homeless colleagues but also to assist them in developing their resilience.

A significant influence to us in designing the materials was the work of the acclaimed social psychologist, Albert Bandura and his Social Cognitive Theory. The theory has, at its heart, the impact of models and the way that they can influence the behavior of others around them. Early theorists claimed that any behavior that people engaged in, after having observed a model, had to be reinforced if it was to be lasting. Bandura, controversially at the time, claimed that observation itself could lead to change without the need for reinforcement (Bandura, 2012).

For the training modules, we created the model character of Toki. This person was essentially a composite of some of the clients that we had met in the course of the project. Toki was having to deal with challenges that the clients face and so was someone that clients could relate to, could think about, advise, and learn from. We encounter Toki in a range of different situations from looking for work, to finding work, to the first few weeks in a new job.

The materials that were developed were intended to be used flexibly: from more formal training situations to one to one advice provided by a key worker for example.

One immediate casualty of the consultation phase was the term "emotional resilience" itself which did not mean much at all to clients or key workers. Consequently the program was renamed Positive Thinking. It is important to recognize however that this did not change the content of the material but it did ensure that we had the attention of or target audience. Strong emotional resilience is considered by homeless people and the people working with them as crucial to whether or not someone thrives or fails in work. This is because it is largely felt that people with a homeless background can be more vulnerable to setbacks and lack the coping mechanisms needed to adapt when things go wrong. The definition of emotional resilience, or positive thinking was to help people cope better when things do go wrong or they are facing change.

Four modules were designed focusing on areas that would help to build resilience in participants:

A. Thinking Positively. This module covers self-talk and the impact that positive or negative thoughts can have on our feelings and actions. The participants are given practical actions that they can take to be positive in their thinking. In this module participants are introduced to Toki for the first time. He has an interview coming up with a local authority and participants learn about the thoughts that are running through his head. Their task is to help him convert the negative thinking to positive thinking. We also learn that Toki has been successful in his interview but he needs assistance again with the negative thoughts that again have intruded.

B. Dealing with Change. Establishing routines, developing new habits and establishing new patterns of behavior are important ways of coping with change. It is the same with our clients. However when they had found ways of settling into a new role and organization any further change could be extremely disruptive. This was the reason for this second module. Once again tips and techniques were provided to help the participants deal with change. On this occasion we found Toki in his new job and doing well after the first few weeks. He then discovers that due to a reorganization, his job has been relocated to a different department. His negative thoughts re-appear and the participants must help him with these as well as helping settle into the new department as quickly as possible. The module then reinforces the learning from the first one as well as re-introducing new elements.

C. Responding to feedback. Negative feedback can be challenging for any of us and our clients were no different in this regard. However more surprising to us was that positive feedback was often just as challenging. The clients had been out of work for extended periods and had got out of the habit of having any feedback either positive or negative. Positive feedback was treated warily if not outright suspicion. A seemingly simple statement designed to be encouraging, such as: "You're doing a great job. Keep it up" could set up a complex chain of thoughts – why is the person saying this, what do they want, are they saying this to disguise some bad news that they are about to deliver? So this session helped participants to evaluate and understand what feedback is and how it can be used constructively to improve performance at work. In this module we learn that Toki has feedback about use of language, swearing especially, and poor timekeeping, two issues that come up regularly with homeless people who have been out of work for a while. The participants must help Toki deal effectively with the feedback, to use it as a means of improving performance.

D. Getting positive support from others. The final module shows the importance of getting support from others and that we can be more successful when we help others and when they help us. The participants are asked to think about their own personal network, how close they feel to each of the people identified and the type of support they can count on getting from them, for example, knowledge and information, practical help, advice. They are shown Toki's support network and to provide advice on how to make best use of it.

As I hope can be seen the materials are designed to be practical, involving and enables clients to see that they do know how to be more resilient, it is a question of accessing this knowledge.

Running a train the trainer course

Once the materials had been developed we then set up a train the trainer course. A detailed manual was created which showed what each component was designed to do and how it should be delivered. The workshop was held at a solicitors office in Birmingham, Britain's second city with the trainers coming from a range of organizations. Some were from BAOH, others were involved in the support of homeless people from other charities for example, and others were BAOH's corporate supporters who will take in the clients for training or for employment, typically on short contract. The training lasted a day and was well received.

Evaluation of the training

Having completed the project, we felt it was very important to see whether the training had made a difference to or clients' lives – that after all was the point of the work. It proved more difficult than anticipated to conduct the research and in the end only 18 people who attended the training were interviewed, six each from three different locations where the training had been run.

The evaluation of the resilience training was based around evidence gathered from interviews demonstrating whether clients had improved in three key competencies related to resilience:

- *Thinking positively* – the client has improved in his or her ability to recognize and turn negative thoughts into positive ones and visualize success.
- *Dealing with change* – the client has improved in his or her ability to deal with setbacks and take action to make the best of a situation.
- *Receiving and responding to feedback* – the client is better able to deal with feedback in a constructive manner.

The fourth key component of resilience, "Getting positive support" (which focused on the clients recognizing their current support structure and making efforts to build on them), was covered in the training, but due to the sensitive nature of the topic this was not covered during the interviews.

However, interviews with clients only took place *after* the training. Therefore, there was no data against which to independently measure resilience before training. Clients were thus asked to self-rate their ability on a scale of one to ten before and after training for each competency (see rating scale below).

Rating scale	Level of ability
0–2	Very weak
3–4	Weak
5	Moderate
6–7	Strong
8–10	Very strong

The difference between the two ratings would then give an impression of the impact of the training on the client.

I will firstly address the successful aspects of the resilience training, highlighting the key findings from the clients' self-rating scores and include some examples of how the clients managed to use the training in their own experience (as well as including some useful quotes as to the effectiveness of the training). The following section focuses on potential areas for improvement, which are identified as being (1) the difficulties clients found in visualizing success; (2) the role of the "Ready for Work" scheme in fostering clients' belief in their ability to succeed at work; (3) integrating interview skills training into the resilience training; and (4) the dangers of repeated rejection.

Successful Aspects

Thinking positively

Examples of clients using the training

One client described his experience undertaking two weeks of initial training with a possible employer. He waited for several weeks for a response but they did not get back to him. As time went on, still with no response, negative thoughts started to creep in. He remembers being able to tell himself to just "stop it." He made the conscious decision to be proactive and decided that if they didn't call in the next week, he would call *them*. Eventually he did, but on several occasions he was told that the person he needed to speak to was busy. In the end his persistence paid off and he was told he had the job.

Another client explained how prior to the training, waiting to be called in for an interview in reception with other candidates for the job was an incredibly daunting experience. She found herself thinking about the qualities in these other people that she might not have and how they were more likely to get the job than her. So, on more than one occasion, before even being interviewed, she would feel nervous and negative of the outcome. The training had helped her to keep telling herself that she had been capable at these types of jobs before and that she *could* do it since she has the experience.

The training has helped me to look at the brighter side of things and not to dwell too much on the negative.

The training has definitely helped me when facing a difficult situation to slow down, come back ten steps and stop it [thinking negative thoughts].

I have been able to apply the training to other aspects of my life. Thinking about being with my family is not automatically negative. Before I felt it would all fall apart, when now I think it can be okay.

I had not come across the visualization technique before and before the training I hadn't been able to visualize anything. But now I can see the success I want to do.

Before the training I didn't do visualization at all. But now I'm more focused on getting a job and one day getting my own place.

My goals have never been so clear in his mind since the training. He knows where he wants to be in four years and come hill or mountain I know I'll get there.

I sometimes think back to that guy in the training, who came from nothing and set up his own business ["Toki"]. That was really inspirational. I think "if he can do it, why can't I?"

Dealing with change

Examples of clients using the training

A client described a situation where he set up a meeting for a service committee that he was a part of. He felt he had so much to contribute, but when it was cancelled twice, he became very upset and negative. He says where previously he would have let the negative thoughts play on in his head, since the training, despite feeling very frustrated, he had learnt to use his support network, talk to his manager, to his social support worker, to his job coach, whoever it may be. If he could not get in touch with any of them, he had learnt how to relax and take things in perspective. For instance, he now enjoys going for a walk with his dog or will go fishing and sit by the lake and it will calm him down.

Another client described a situation where he injured his ankle while tyre fitting at his last job. He had to take leave and came back eight weeks later and was told that he was being fired. He felt "gutted" and felt like he has been treated very unfairly and "used." He did feel very depressed, but after a week he realized that he had to get "back on the horse" and look for employment:

> I've learnt that the way people treat you is out of your control, because you can't control the way they are. Some treat you unfairly and can treat you like you're nothing. You just have to avoid people like that. At the end of the day it's their loss and my gain because I wouldn't want to work for someone that treated me that badly.

One client described a situation since the training where he was working in a café clearing tables. A new employee then joined and worked with him, however he clearly was not working as hard as the client. This resulted in the client then having to work even harder than previously. He began to grow increasingly frustrated with his work situation because he did not feel that this was fair. Despite being mild mannered and the type of person that avoids conflict as much as possible, he realized that if he did not take control of the situation, he would end up feeling more frustrated. So, eventually after several weeks, he took the opportunity to take this issue up with his work colleague. Previously he felt he may have just carried on as normal, but he demonstrated an ability to take control of a new situation that clearly was affecting him negatively. He now has a much better working relationship with his new colleague having approached him.

Receiving and responding to feedback

Examples of clients using the training

When he could not think of a situation since the training where he has reacted positively to being criticized, one client described two instances where in retrospect (having been through the training) he would have dealt with the situation differently. In a previous job in London, his manager criticized him for not completing his stock take properly. He reacted quite confrontationally, even though he knew that the manager was right to be annoyed. He now realizes that he doesn't always need to react so defensively and by doing so things don't have to escalate to anything more (as they have done in the past).

At another job, he arrived ten minutes late to a shop where he was supposed to fit a glass washer. The shop keeper had a funeral to attend to in the afternoon and wanted the washer fitted as soon as possible and was very angry at the client for having been late. However, by his own admission he was quite confrontational with the shopkeeper, despite him having a valid reason to be angry. If that situation were to occur now, he would have dealt with the situation far differently by simply apologizing straight away and ignoring the client's aggressive demeanor.

> The training has helped me to step back and actually think about what's being said. Even if I don't agree with everything being said, I respect my manager and my support worker and so I respect what they say. Before the training, without a doubt I react more negatively.

> Overall, the training couldn't have been any better. The 'pulling back and thinking' aspect of dealing with a bad situation was really helpful. I'm more likely now to sit back and take it on the chin.

> It has helped. Before if someone approached me aggressively, then I would react aggressively back at them. But now I'll show a bit more restraint. Don't get me wrong, I still have a limit, but I feel I can hold myself back a little more.

Comments about the overall value of the training

> The training couldn't have been any better. It was set at the right level. It always felt like everyone was on the ball. The pace was just right and everyone had the opportunity to fully understand the training.

> Nothing else was really needed in the training. It just added to my resilience.

> Being able to share the training with other people like me and going through it with them is very helpful. Like they say "a problem shared is a problem halved".

> The training has really helped me to go for jobs that I might not have applied to before.

> I wouldn't have changed anything about the training, it was exactly what I needed.

Areas of improvement

Difficulties in visualizing success

The principal idea behind this technique is that individuals are more driven to succeed when they have something they are striving toward. Despite acknowledging that the visualization technique was very useful, clients' descriptions of their vision of success were often quite vague. Descriptions often entailed "having more money" or "having a better job," but the exact nature of their goals was generally unclear. Those that did demonstrate some sort of vision of success in the future (say for example one year from now) were still often unclear on the smaller steps needed to eventually reach the longer term goal.

Despite this, those that were in paid employment certainly had a *more* developed vision for the future than the two that were not. I can only speculate that having a more present orientation will help those struggling for employment deal with the anxieties and struggles on a day to day basis. However, the concern is that this may not provide a foundation for motivating positive and proactive behaviors in the client that come with setting goals and developing strategies to achieve stable employment. Job coaches could play a crucial role in developing long term goals with the client over time, as well as helping clients to understand the smaller steps necessary along the way.

"Ready for Work" developing self-efficacy

Self-efficacy is a person's *belief* in his or her ability to successfully perform a particular task and it is something that can be developed in individuals. This in turn has the effect of promoting resilience since when facing adverse events, those who have the belief that they can exert control over a given event are more likely to succeed in their efforts. Therefore, unless people *believe* they can produce a certain outcome (for example, the belief that one can actually perform well at a job) they will have very little incentive to persevere in the face of adversity.

One very interesting aspect from the interviews was how useful many of the clients found the "Ready for Work" scheme as a strong source of confidence in their ability to do a particular job. For example, one client describes how he was very apprehensive at first when applying for retail work. But having secured a two week placement through the Ready for Work scheme he went ahead with it. Once he had the training to help him deal with customers he gained a lot of confidence to the point where he now does not have any anxieties about doing the job anymore and feels very capable in his position. The placement has clearly given him the confidence in his ability to work in retail and deal effectively with customers. He readily admits that if it was not for the Ready for Work scheme he would not have applied for the job, simply because he did not believe he could do it.

Another client commented that since the experience from the Ready for Work scheme, he has found confidence in his ability to learn, not just for the job that he was applying for, but more generally that he is capable of doing something new, if only he is *given the chance* to learn:

> I would always prefer being given feedback. It will only help me to do my job properly. If someone tells me I'm doing something wrong, then next time I know I'll do it right. The only real way you can make progress is to look, listen and learn.

It appears that the level of "self-mastery" achieved when clients experience success at performing at least portions of a task through the "Ready for Work" program, can serve to convince them that they have what it takes to achieve increasingly difficult accomplishments of a similar kind. Most of the clients clearly found the "Ready for Work" program not only practically valuable, in terms of a logical step closer toward paid employment, but also serves a second, equally important role, in helping build clients' confidence in their own abilities to perform successfully in a job. The positive knock-on effects of work experience are thus likely to be seen in more proactive efforts to seek employment and also searching for wider-ranging job roles, as their belief in their ability to *learn* how to successfully perform is strengthened.

Interview skills training

One of the main issues that clients found difficult to deal with was being interviewed:

> I get quite anxious before interviews. Will they take me on? Do I have enough experience?

> I really don't' like being talked down to. And as soon as I meet someone for a job, I already know they're looking down on me and it doesn't feel good.

> I always worry about what type of questions they will ask at interviews. I just don't know what I'm going to say.

> It's just so easy to create a negative atmosphere when they are interviewing me. I already know I'm not going to get the job as soon as they ask me anything about my past work experience.

It is clear that the job interview is a very stressful and difficult situation for many of the clients. However, in the same way that the "Ready for Work" program has aided in developing the confidence in clients' ability to perform a job, focusing some of the training on interview skills may help clients to overcome this important hurdle in the search for employment.

In fact, a couple of clients already addressed the fact that their job coaches' help in this area has proved invaluable:

> One of the most useful things I did with my job coach was a mock interview. That was really helpful. I want to take useful elements from any feedback and put them into action. Even if it is something like keeping the right posture for interviews, I would be able to put this into practice on my own.

It may be useful to integrate some interview skills training as part of the resilience program to develop the clients' *belief* in their ability to perform successfully at interviews and alleviate the anxiety and pressure of a situation that is clearly very difficult for them.

The dangers of repeated rejection

A common theme from the interviews was the difficulty in overcoming negative emotions that accompany rejection. Here are a few responses from clients when asked to describe the negative thoughts they found most difficult to overcome:

> Getting knockbacks from interviews is very difficult to deal with. I even ask for feedback from them [the potential employer] but they never get back to you. You just end up waiting.

> Going to the job centre for months and months on end and thinking that there really are no jobs that will ever become available

> When I'm applying for jobs and I don't hear anything back after the interviews I can get really sad and frustrated.

> I have to admit, there was a time when I just thought of giving up entirely.

In the same way that offering clients the opportunity to work in a placement program and develop confidence in their ability to perform a particular job, there is a potential phase in the job hunt that can be extremely damaging to a client's belief in their ability: repeated rejection. Faced with the prospect of not finding a job and constantly being rejected will gradually chip away at any self-efficacy beliefs the client may have. There is certainly a danger if a client already has a low belief in his ability to find a job, because a negative outcome (e.g., from an unsuccessful interview) will be seen as confirming the incompetence they perceive in themselves.

It is clear that programs like the resilience training, "The Ready for Work" scheme and even the support network of job coaches can help in building belief in clients' ability to succeed at work and ultimately foster positive behaviors like sustained search for employment. However, the experience of repeated rejection has the risk of producing the opposite effect and research has shown that such experiences can lead individuals to become more inclined to pass their time away unproductively and give up far more easily in search of employment. Therefore, it is suggested here that more time is invested in identifying those clients who may need extra guidance and support to restore some self-assurance and focus attention in developing their search skills to increase their chances of finding stable employment.

What we learned

This was a fascinating project for a group of occupational psychologists to be involved with.

The greatest learning for me was to understand the assumptions that we take for granted in the way we habitually work. For example, the modules we developed had to be delivered in one two hour session, which was always going to be tall order. On looking at the proposed timetable given to us by our colleagues at BAOH we saw that within the two hours time had been set aside for a break. Our initial response was that we felt that this was unnecessary and we expected them to agree as our clients are quite happy to use such limited time completely for learning. We came to understand two things: first this was a group that was not used to sitting in a training room for two hours. Second, many people would be attending for the food and refreshments available, which to be honest was something that we have not encountered before nor had expected.

The other key learning was that no matter how hard we tried at simplifying the language that we were using, it was never clear enough. Our colleagues at BAOH were incredibly patient and helpful in working with us to put these psychological concepts into language that would have the greatest impact with our clients.

The project, as always, demonstrated the importance of evaluation. The program was a partial success; it seemed to develop resilience in the participants. The evaluation led to changes in the program that were instituted the following year. Ultimately, we are unsure as to whether it has led to more people staying in employment and clearly this is something that we need to assess in future years.

Finally, it demonstrated not to underestimate the client. We know this. We practice it every day with our multinational clients. But did we, as a project team, have a slightly patronizing approach to the clients in this work? Did we, unconsciously, apply a different set of standards to our work? It is not easy to acknowledge this but I feel that may indeed have been the case. Closer involvement with the clients themselves corrected any sense of complacency that may have been present. It is not enough to work with the underserved if the quality of work that is produced is not to the standard of the work that is delivered to the regular client group.

References

Dame Carol Blacks (2006). Review of the Health of the Working Age Population: Working for a Healthier Tomorrow, 17 March, 2008. London. TSO, pp. 1–24.

DELG (2012). https://www.gov.uk/government/publications/dclg- staff- survey-2012 retrieved 6/1/14.

DELG (2013). www.gov.uk/government/organizational department-for-communities- and -local-government 2012 retrieved 6/1/14.

National Audit Office (2007). Helping people from workless households into work. Report by the comptroller and auditor general HC 609 session 2006–2007, July 19, 2007.

New Economics Foundation (2008). *Work it Out: Barriers to the Employment of Homeless People*. BAOH.

Shelton, Katherine H., Taylor, Pamela J., Bonner, Adrian, & van den Bree, Marianne (2009) *Risk Factors for Homelessness: Evidence from a Population-Based Study Psychiatric Services 2009*. doi: 10.1176/appi.ps.60.4.465.

St Mungo (2009). Happiness matters: Homeless people's views about breaking the link between homelessness and mental ill health.

Smith, J., Bushaq, H., Campbell, A., Hassan, L., Pal, S., & Akpadio, S. (2008). *Valuable Lives: Resilience amongst Homeless People*. London Metropolitan University and Crisis.

12
In the Wake of Disaster: Facilitating Business Recovery

Vicki V. Vandaveer and Tracey E. Rizzuto

On August 29, 2005, Hurricane Katrina, one of the five deadliest hurricanes in US history, slammed into the Louisiana coast – with sustained winds during landfall in southeastern Louisiana of 125 miles per hour. Psychologists in the Society for Industrial and Organizational Psychology (SIOP), Division 14 of the American Psychological Association (APA), jumped into action to do what they could to help the people and businesses that had been ravaged and/or destroyed by that storm. We hope that by sharing the story of what we did, and how we overcame various barriers encountered, other professional organizations that plan disaster relief outreach will benefit from our experience.

This chapter has four sections: (1) a description of the KARE (Katrina Aid and Relief Effort) professional volunteer effort that was mobilized to respond to the Gulf Coast's desperate needs; (2) a case study of one KARE consulting project; followed by (3) a post-hoc scientific analysis of the work and outcomes associated with the volunteer effort; and (4) lessons learned from the KARE experience.

Mobilizing the Katrina Aid and Relief Effort

In the early weeks after the storm, KARE's initial goals were to support and assist SIOP members and student affiliates affected by the storm. We contacted colleagues in affected GulfCoast areas, offering whatever we could in the way of help. Those with whom we were able to connect expressed gratitude for our outreach. However, they all had already evacuated to higher ground, staying with relatives or friends and not needing immediate help. What people most appreciated at that time was our concern and outreach – very simply the human touch. While our expertise as industrial and organizational (I-O) and consulting psychologists was not immediately needed (we specialize in human behavior, effectiveness, and performance in organizations), just being there for them was, they said, invaluable. It was becoming clear that we are second responders, not first. As we later learned, the importance of our work a year after the disaster was significant and valued.

SIOP was soon joined by the Society of Consulting Psychology (SCP), Division 13 of APA; and that collaboration significantly expanded our capabilities, including experience in disaster response. All of our volunteers were passionate, energetic, and eager to help.

Early action steps

We engaged five early steps to put the KARE into action: recruitment, organization, initial action, comprehensive planning, and execution of plans. We recruited volunteers via our professional association members' ListServe; created a database with volunteer information, such as demographics, areas of expertise, licensure status, availability, contact information, etc.; and developed a Volunteer Communication Plan, using all available technology. A Web-based help and response center allowed people needing help to post their needs which were triaged to the most appropriate volunteer(s). Having done all that we could do for our colleagues at the moment, KARE focused its efforts on a comprehensive plan of support for the New Orleans area – the most population dense region experiencing the greatest storm impact. For more than six months after the storm, the people who lived in the storm's path were still operating in survival mode. Many people who lost everything decided to leave New Orleans. Others committed to stay and rebuild, but as widely reported in the media, they faced unimaginable delays and bureaucratic hurdles to receiving promised-but-very-slowly-delivered insurance and disaster relief funds.

We decided to take advantage of the American Psychological Association's (APA) annual convention that was being held in New Orleans (NOLA) August 10–13, 2006 (one full year after Katrina). A good opportunity for our volunteers to come together (as many were going to the convention anyway), the convention also provided a good platform for visibility and outreach to the NOLA community. KARE's strategy was twofold: (1) identify GulfCoast businesses in need and match their needs with the most appropriate volunteers; and (2) conduct workshops, seminars and consultations at the APA Convention to help businesses rebuild and recover. We submitted a proposal to APA, requesting a place on the program and space for providing our services. Our proposal included a diagram of a metaphoric MASH tent with round tables inside – each dedicated to a specific type of assistance.

The APA proposal was well received in concept. And, although we quickly found plenty of willing volunteers, numerous legal, professional, cultural, and logistical obstacles presented themselves. Our role as second responders was met with many delays. It took many months to get to the point of *plan execution* where we *could* help. The next pages describe these barriers to service and how the KARE team managed and overcame them.

Finding our way and dealing with challenges

APA legal concerns and Louisiana psychologist licensure law

APA's Legal Department initially rejected our proposal due to potential Association liability concerns. However, after many weeks of conversations with them about possible risk mitigation actions, legal eventually approved of our work provided that we keep good documentation, obtain signed release-from-liability waivers from everyone, and comply with Louisiana licensing law, rules, and regulations for psychologists. They, too, wanted to help.

The next hurdle was the psychologist licensing law in Louisiana, which required, for some of the services we intended to offer, that providers be licensed in Louisiana or, if licensed in another state, sponsored and supervised by a psychologist licensed in Louisiana. For other services (e.g., training), licensure was not required if provided under the auspices of a university. Very fortunately, one volunteer was licensed in Louisiana and was also a past Chairman of the Louisiana State Board of Examiners of Psychologists. He worked with the Louisiana legislature and Licensing Board, and they were all very helpful in paving the way for us to serve. We were ready to go. However, there was a traffic jam at the NOLA border; and soon our green light turned to yellow.

Barriers to NOLA entry

NOLA cultural issues. Our New Orleans university-based colleagues were happy to join us and serve as local advisors, as well as sponsors of the training and educational seminars. Their seeing our plan, however, resulted in our next yellow light. The MASH tent was unacceptable – would be insensitive, they said, to New Orleans people, who had had their unfair share of tents for a year now. We abandoned the MASH tent concept and found a hotel that provided a large ballroom for our use at a considerably reduced rate.

Access to people, the press, and businesses. We forged ahead, submitting press releases to the local newspapers and other community and regional periodicals announcing workshops, private consultations, helpful tools, etc. during the APA convention. Alas, none of our press releases were published. And no one from the newspapers would talk with us. It seems that everyone from someplace else was descending on New Orleans to help, and our voices were lost among bigger and recognized names – none of whom, however (as far as we could discern), did what we were trying to do. An I-O psychology graduate student from New Orleans came to our rescue. He advised that we were going to need local communications/public relations professionals if we were to have any hope of getting our press releases and announcements into print in NOLA, and he connected us with two of the best in New Orleans. However, we had no funding for what we were doing.

Funding. With the deadline approaching for confirming and securing the hotel ballroom, and needing to get the word out to New Orleans businesses and people who could benefit from our services, we scrambled to figure out how to raise money quickly. We wrote letters to our larger consulting firms and corporate clients of some of our volunteers, and soon had collected $18,000 in donations, in return for which we happily displayed donors' company names and logos as sponsors on our announcements and at our convention outreach event.

Our light had definitely changed to green – bright green. Turnout was good even though many people had still not returned to New Orleans.

The KARE response team

A critical element to success was that KARE operated as a strategically organized team and not just a group of volunteers. Each team member contributed unique and valuable resources for carrying out KARE's mission. Team members possessed multidisciplinary (and often multientity) affiliations that became useful for helping to navigate many operational challenges. KARE consulting project teams ranged in size from one to five volunteer "consultants." and varied in the amount of time they could contribute to project work. Consulting team members rarely had prior working relationships with each other or with the client organizations, so volunteers had to quickly become oriented to their team members' expertise, styles of practice, and professional capabilities.

Somehow this collection of individuals proved to be very resourceful in overcoming challenges to the outreach effort.

Professional volunteers. Assistance from the public relations and communications professionals was invaluable. We could not have done what we came to do without them. They had excellent and long-standing relationships in the media, community, and government. Once they learned of KARE's mission, they too wanted to help us help – significantly discounting their fees and convincing hotels and vendors to do the same. Immediately our press releases got into all of the major newspapers and media, including four radio announcements, a local television news spot that ran for several days prior to and during the days of our APA convention workshops, seminars and consultations. Our PR experts introduced us to the chair of NOLA tourism board and other key local officials, who in turn helped spread the word about our outreach. People began to sign up for our workshops and consultations.

APA assistance. APA Staff advised KARE leaders on speaking to media and provided guidelines for hosting outreach programs; and they helped us with publicizing our event during convention. They had first contact with the media, opening the door for us to work with them directly after training our volunteers.

A little help from our friends. As we were setting up for the first day of our convention initiative, two managers from one of our KARE clients, the Louisiana SPCA (description of that work in next section of this chapter) appeared with a surprise gift for us. They had created a wonderful slideshow presentation to display at our workshops to communicate what I-O psychologists could do for people and businesses working to recover. It was titled "Overcoming our Challenges/Unleashing our Strength," and told the story of what we and they had done together for their organization – complete with pictures and illustrations (see excerpts – Figures 12.1–12.4).

Key collaborations. As soon as we began working with New Orleans business owners and professionals, we saw that even after many months since Katrina, emotions were still raw and stress was very high. Help from many different areas of Psychology was needed. We reached out to clinical and counseling psychologists who lived and worked in Louisiana, and established referral sources for people who were having great difficulty coping with everything that had happened to them and/or their businesses.

The relationships formed across areas of psychology as a result of this crisis have been very healthy for the very large APA, and enhanced communication has continued since that time.

Lending a KARE-ing hand

Industrial organizational psychology

Industrial organizational (I-O) psychology is concerned with the scientific structuring of organizations and helps organizations develop strategies to improve the productivity and quality of life of people at work.

* In response to Hurricane Katrina, the Society of Industrial and Organizational Psychology, in collaboration with the Society of Consulting Psychology, formed KARE – Katrina Aid and Relief Effort – to provide support to organizations, businesses workers, and workplaces damaged by Hurricane Katrina.

* KARE contacted the LA/SPCA and generously offered its professional expertise and service to assist the LA/SPCA in its team-building work in the midst of the organization's catastrophic losses. The staff also suffered deep personal and professional losses.

Figure 12.1 About I-O Psychology and what we did to help them recover – in LA/SPCA management team's own words

The first steps to moving forward

Louisiana SPCA takes part in a two-day management team rebuilding workshop

Figure 12.2 First steps: I-O and Consulting Psychologists Begin to Help

Importance of volunteer self care and team building. The KARE team itself was not immune to stress. As the reader can imagine, working with clients who are themselves very highly stressed, with scarce resources, all with regular "day jobs," and encountering so many hurdles and barriers to helping, our team of 35 highly educated, strong, passionate volunteers had its own internal challenges. Typical of diverse and geographically dispersed teams whose members are working together for the first time – all with the best of intentions – there were predictable disagreements and strained interactions. That the severity of the devastation lingered on for many months, and that there were so many barriers to service, meant that tensions were exacerbated as everyone strived to help – and all were not pulling in the same direction. Time and attention must be devoted to team building with the volunteers.

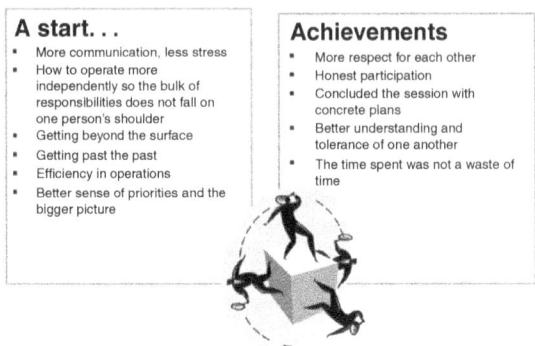

The workshop's impact on
rebuilding the strength of the team

A start. . .
- More communication, less stress
- How to operate more independently so the bulk of responsibilities does not fall on one person's shoulder
- Getting beyond the surface
- Getting past the past
- Efficiency in operations
- Better sense of priorities and the bigger picture

Achievements
- More respect for each other
- Honest participation
- Concluded the session with concrete plans
- Better understanding and tolerance of one another
- The time spent was not a waste of time

Figure 12.3   LA/SPCA Management Team's own words: What we accomplished in the first two days

Just a few examples of areas of fierce disagreements that we experienced include the following:

- Whether to approach client organizations for donations
- Whether to reach out to clinical and counseling psychologists
- Methods of communicating with each other
- What to do with the leftover donations

We learned to apply our processes and tools to ourselves in this initiative to achieve a strong, aligned, high-spirited Volunteer Team.

APA convention initiative

The official program for our two-day convention initiative is shown in Figure 12.5.

Each KARE Volunteer on site at the convention was given a "Guidelines and Procedures for KARE Volunteers" booklet, which provided instructions and guidelines on everything from sign-in to sign-out, including the following:

- Do's and Don'ts in greeting attendees
- Intake, triage and record-keeping procedures
- Guidelines and talking points for speaking with the Media
- Volunteer roles and responsibilities chart

Figure 12.4 Discovering and Recapturing our Strength and our Spirit

Approximately 35 volunteers provided consulting services to affected businesses, parts of city government and individuals. The feedback we received from the organizations served was uniformly positive.

KARE case study of the LA/SPCA

Three I-O psychologists, the authors and another colleague, were privileged to get to work with the Louisiana Society for the Prevention of Cruelty to Animals (LA/SPCA).Two of us were full-time consulting practitioners and one is an academic researcher and consultant – from three different states (Louisiana, Texas, and Arizona).

The LA/SPCA responded to our offers of help to businesses affected by Hurricane Katrina, and our work with them began in March, 2006 – seven months after the disaster. Their shelter in the Gentilly section of New Orleans had been demolished – swept away in the storm.

KARE

Katrina Aid and Relief Effort

**Business consulting psychologists
offering free help and seminars to
help businesses recover**
Azalea Room
Wyndham Canal Place
100 Rue Iberville
Friday, August 11 – 8:00 am–8:00 pm
Saturday, August 12 – 10:00 am–5:00 pm

Division 14	Division 13
Society of Industrial and Organizational	Society of Consulting Psychology

American Psychological Association

KARE schedule of events

Friday, August 11 Free consultations and/or referrals	Saturday, August 12 Free consultations and/or referrals
• Managing change • Managing stress • Selecting and hiring employees • Employee training – building job skills • Motivating employees and boosting morale in difficult times • Managing a diverse workforce • Healing wounds and taking control • Leader development • Management team rebuilding • Turning adversity into advantage and strength • General consultation – organization effectiveness	• Managing change • Managing stress • Selecting and hiring employees • Employee training – building job skills • Motivating employees and boosting morale in difficult times • Managing a diverse workforce • Healing wounds and taking control • Leader development • Management team rebuilding • Turning adversity into advantage and strength • General consultation – organization effectiveness
Free seminar: Selecting and retaining employees	Free seminar: Managing a diverse workforce
Free seminar: Managing stress	Free seminar: Managing change in turbulent times

Figure 12.5   APA convention program of KARE activities

Thankfully – and to the credit of the management team and staff – all of the animals in their care had been safely evacuated.

Working with the Management Team to help them rebuild their organization, we drew on every bit of knowledge, skills, abilities, Life experiences, and motivation to help that we had – powered by the energy that came from our love for the animals and the strong bonds we developed with the animals' remarkable management team of rescuers and caretakers.

The "Present state" in 2006

At the time of our engagement, LA/SPCA was operating out of a temporary shelter in Algiers that the organization rented from a New Orleans businessman. It was a 40,000 square feet commercial steel building, the inside of which had been partitioned into separate sections for dogs, cats (in sound-proof rooms); and offices for management and staff were in a separate adjacent temporary building. Seven months after Katrina, their staff numbered 40, down from previous 60. Of the 40, 15 were former staff members who had returned; and many were shelter staff from other states and a Director of Operations from the ASPCA, based in New York City[1] – all now deployed to deal with the largest animal disaster in U.S. history. The animals were receiving good, compassionate care.

Meanwhile, plans were under way for developing a new home for LA/SPCA – even though the future was uncertain and funding was seriously diminished, as many donors had left the area for higher ground. Rebuilding the donor base was a critical and top priority.

A few characteristics of the "present state" in March 2006 were the following:

Advantages

- The Executive Director of LA/SPCA was a very effective leader, very experienced in non-profit animal organizations. Highly respected in the community, she had been very effective in development and organization change initiatives, bringing a strategic focus, business acumen, and strong networking and community relations orientation to her role.
- The staff were all hard-working and committed to the organization.
- The board was very supportive.
- Operations and facility were working well.
- Animal care was good. Everyone expressed and demonstrated love for the animals.
- Staff genuinely liked each other (even though emotions and irritability ran high).

Challenges

- Fiscal challenges were daunting, with the donor base eroded and the city looking to cut animal control funding significantly.
- The organization was facing the need for layoffs in the face of its financial distress, while at the same time needing to hire and train new staff for key positions.
- Morale was very low; and felt stress and anxiety were extremely high – manifesting in behaviors symptomatic of extreme stress, including quarrels and some in-fighting among staff.
- The New Orleans population was predicted to be significantly smaller with increased poverty increasing – conditions which correlate with poor animal care.
- The Executive Director was pulled in many different directions and she and the staff felt a need to be better connected with each other.

The KARE consulting team

Initial conversations by telephone with the Executive Director indicated that there were a number of possible ways that we might help, as they worked to re-focus; rebuild their donor base; re-establish operations, infrastructure and staffing; adapt to the significant changes in the community; reduce stress; strengthen their teamwork; and effectively manage all of the changes.

Our work began with a thorough assessment of the "present state" and most pressing needs by way of management and staff confidential interviews, the results of which formed the basis of our proposed plan of action for comprehensive change management consulting, which was accepted by the Management Team. The plan included

A. Facilitating the management team's

- **Updating its vision** for LA/SPCA, and renewing their commitment to the Mission
- Preparing for **leading and managing big change**

B. **Leader development coaching**
C. Advising **on recruitment, selection** and **succession planning**
D. **Team development** to strengthen working relationships and teamwork
E. Serving as advisors for all **organizational behavior and performance** issues that arose

Our meetings with the management team took place in an air conditioned wooden building-within-the-building, adjacent to several hundred dog kennels; and we were "serenaded" by the dogs continually as we worked. Our first management team meeting had the following purposes:

A. Strengthen working relationships
B. Clarify LA/SPCA's Vision for the future
C. Identify the Critical Success Factors (CSF) to achieve the Vision
D. Learn how to manage and reduce stress
E. Figure out what must be done – individually and as a team – to ensure the CSF's were solid and to be more effective together as the management team

We arrived early for this first visit with the Executive Director and her Management Team in order to set up the room and become oriented to the surroundings. Upon entering, we saw that at each place around the U-shape conference table, in addition to notepads and pens, were boxes of tissue! Tissue was the most needed and used office supply at that time, as we soon learned.

After introductions of the consultants and review of the meeting Objectives, Agenda, and Meeting Rules (which included, among other things, "all make it safe for each other to express candid thoughts and feelings"), we conducted a meeting "check-in" process in which each person introduced themselves – describing their job and roles, challenges they were facing, and what they hoped to get from this meeting. Very early in the "check-in" process the tears began flowing. Stress was obviously very high, and people were exhausted from many months of hard work and some horrifying experiences.

One of the managers had been sitting back with arms crossed over her chest, looking very skeptical and uneasy. When her turn came to "check in," she bluntly asked us, "What are you going to do for us?," followed by, "I have a lot of work to do and don't have time to sit in a meeting." Appreciating her honesty and straightforwardness, for she was expressing what others were probably thinking, we replied, "We don't know exactly. But we are here. We have come to help you figure out what to do – and to do whatever we can to help you improve the current situation and figure out how to create LA/SPCA's bright future." She obviously remained unconvinced that what we were doing was not a waste of time. However, as the session unfolded, she gradually began to participate; and she had some very valuable insights, understandings and ideas – some of which seemed to pleasantly surprise some of her co-workers. She was one of the "most valuable team members," serving as the Devil's advocate, the group's conscience, and naysayer-turned-advocate for positive change. Another team member who was very bright and also had keen insights and perspectives, happened to also be fairly negative in what she said and how she said it. As a result, her teammates tended to tune her out – so they didn't hear the nuggets of wisdom that she had and tried to share. Every team member had a story – the rest of which we cannot share for reasons of confidentiality – but experiences had affected their personal and professional lives, and they would never be the same. However, they all did rise to their challenges and turned adversity into great strength.

It became obvious early on in the meeting that stress levels were so high that we would not be able to accomplish the other objectives until stress levels were lessened and manageable. On a measure of individual stress level, the average score was at the 100th percentile of all norms available. The boxes of tissue were nearly all empty by the end of the first day, and were replenished with new boxes for Day two.

At the end of the first day, the three consultants convened to debrief and re-focus the workshop. It was clear to us that we needed to marshal additional resources – counseling and/or clinical psychologists – to work individually with a couple of members of the management team who were all but paralyzed by their trauma, grief and stress. We found counseling psychologists in Baton Rouge who were willing to help, and our work with the team continued simultaneously with their individual work. Over that summer we had several team development meetings. By August, the team had renewed its Vision for LA/SPCA and was well on its way to accomplishing the goals identified for the year. The new shelter was in the process of being designed; stress levels were down sufficiently that they were manageable, the management team was working better together, and there were fewer tears in meetings by August.

We continued to work with the management team for approximately 18 months, at first monthly – then every two or three months. The management team members often expressed to us how grateful they were for our help and for what they had all learned; and it was from that gratitude and their renewed spirit that the surprise gift of their slideshow presentation was conceived and developed.

Results of KARE work and outcomes

- LA/SPCA was soon back up on its feet, with a new, very nice shelter and its donor base rebuilding and including national donors

- Leadership Team members were working well together, and the atmosphere when we arrived for meetings was very different – people laughing, joking, cooperating – and everyone was eager to give us a tour of the new facility. The dogs continued to serenade us. The cats loved their new (soundproof!) digs. We took several tours – each time, hearing new stories. Of course, there were always new challenges, problems, frustrations, and controversies; but Team LA/SPCA's spirit was back. No one had ever joined and stayed with the LA/SPCA because it was easy and always fun. It wasn't easy and not always fun. People are with the LA/SPCA for the love of the animals and their connection with their mission: "to improve the quality of life of all companion animals." Guided by that mission, they worked tirelessly to:

1. Educate the community about issues affecting animals;
2. Advocate and lobby for improved local and state animal protection laws;
3. Reduce animal overpopulation through aggressive spay/neuter programs;
4. Investigate animal cruelty cases;
5. End dog fighting in Louisiana;
6. Promote the human/animal bond;
7. Find loving families for displaced and homeless animals

Especially noteworthy is that their efforts succeeded in successfully getting passage of Louisiana State Senate Bill 607, dubbed the "Pet Evacuation Bill," which contains mandated emergency operation plans for the humane evacuation, transport, and temporary sheltering of service animals and household pets in times of emergency or disaster.

- Individuals who had received consultations did find employment.
- The Louisiana Senate issued a resolution commending SIOP and SCP for our humanitarian help, and presented us with the document beautifully framed.

One goal of this chapter is to demonstrate that professional associations can play a pivotal role in helping individuals, businesses, and communities plan for and respond to disasters (Rizzuto and Vandaveer, 2013). In addition, we hope to have offered actionable suggestions for mobilizing critical resources and developing the logistical pathways for undertaking similar outreach efforts. In the section that follows, we reflect on the KARE experience to encourage additional research and future linkages between organizational science and practitioner expertise in order to benefit disaster recovery.

Post-hoc scientific analysis

In order to best leverage the KARE work, lessons, and contributions to continually improve the role of second responders in disasters, we undertook a post-hoc analysis of the scientific underpinnings of our work.

Our literature search revealed that due to the increasing occurrence, severity, and diversity of crises in our society (Schouten, Callahan, and Bryant, 2004), organizational researchers and practitioners have begun to explore planning and recovery strategies to assist disaster-affected businesses (e.g., Corey and Deitch, 2011; Quarantelli, 2001; Riebeek, 2005; Rizzuto, 2008, 2009). There is an emerging emergency organizational development (EOD) literature that is still in its infancy.

Traditional Organizational Development (OD) interventions, designed to facilitate planned organizational change, assume an adaptive approach that allows for iterative feedback and adjustments to optimize the intervention process over time; whereas Emergency OD (EOD) interventions usually necessitate just-in-time fixes to short-term needs, learning from and adapting those practices happening later and over time (Guastello, Koopmans, and Pincus, 2009; Kotter and Schlesinger, 1979; Pascale, Milleman, and Gioja, 2000; Schneider and Somers, 2006).

Post-crisis organizational environments can be chaotic, intensely stressful, and unpredictable, evading traditional OD approaches (Dolan, Garcia, and Auberbach, 2003; Piotrowski, 2006). Given the state of organizational fragility and EOD literature limitations, professionals who provide disaster response and recovery services must draw upon tacit knowledge and professional intuition accumulated over years of professional practice and grounded in their knowledge of the science base of organizational change dynamics in non-disaster situations.

The KARE experience may offer an example to help guide future EOD interventions.

Science behind KARE emergency organizational development

Much of the disaster literature focuses on individual-level clinical interventions and community-level policies and programs (e.g., Comfort et al., 1991) rather than group and organizational level work. Very little empirical research systematically examines the implementation and assessment of EOD in disaster contexts. The intervention practices implemented by KARE were guided by the knowledge and experience bases of the consultants, which included evidence-based research in traditional OD strategic change interventions, leadership development, team dynamics, and team development; and which were grounded in organizational, social-psychological, cognitive, and leadership theoretical frameworks.

The empirical foundations of the consulting techniques implemented with Katrina-affected businesses included human, operational, and technical workplace structures, which are the "life" functions of the organization and that demand attention in the aftermath of disaster. Much of the crisis management literature focuses on technical (i.e., facilities, tools, materials) aspects of work (Fleming, 2006; Smith, 1990; Turner, 2007), while published research on the human component regarding employee health and organizational well-being is scant to nonexistent. KARE focused its efforts on the human (performance, behavioral, relational) and operational (job tasks, roles, processes, etc.) EOD. Results from the intake assessment from the APA convention in New Orleans in August of 2006 are presented below (Figure 12.6). Stress management was reported as the primary need by business representatives, as it was by LA/SPCA management.

EOD is a rapidly evolving non-linear process (Rizzuto, 2009). Although human components are acknowledged as primary needs

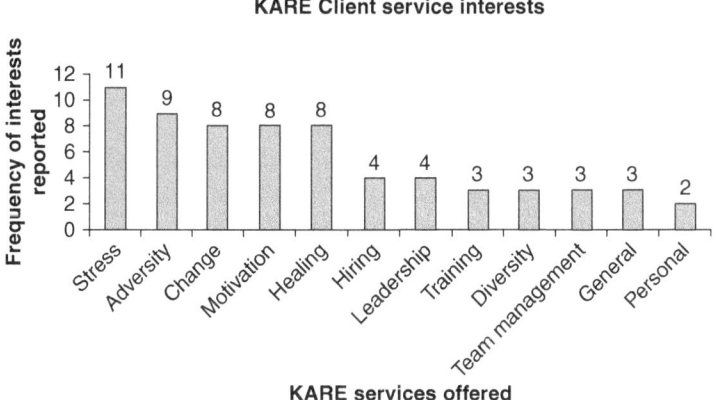

Figure 12.6 Workplace recovery needs noted by KARE

within the first six to nine months of the disaster, the operational needs were shown to be critical in subsequent assessments conducted nine months to a year after Hurricane Katrina. It is also important to note that organizations are organic and dynamic networks of interconnected relationships, and therefore severe stress and trauma experienced in one part of the system ripples throughout the system (Senge, 1990). Improvements to operational workplace functions can provide psychological benefits that can boost the human workplace functioning and vice versa. An organization is healthiest when all three components are optimally functioning.

Stress management

"Bleed over" effects from crises have been shown to permeate and transfer from one life domain to another (Barnett and Hyde, 2001), compounding negative disaster effects on individuals. Galea and colleagues (2008) found that people who faced economic and employment instabilities in addition to lacking social support were more prone to Post Traumatic Stress Disorder (PTSD) two years after Hurricane Katrina. Employees who endure personal losses and injuries as the result of a disaster are likely to experience high stress and time pressure across personal, work, and family life domains, and therefore are at an increased risk for PTSD, burnout, lower job satisfaction, role conflict, and other precursors that ultimately lead to job turnover (Milano, 2005). Everyone in the organizational system feels the impact of the disaster, even to the extent that indirectly-affected individuals approximate PTSD symptoms in a phenomenon referred to as "survivor syndrome" (Wilson and Raphael, 1993). Organizations that provide timely and tangible relief services (Sanchez, Korbin, and Viscarra, 1995), such as housing, transportation, and flextime may not only improve organizational functioning but also remove obstacles to establishing workplace routines and alleviate inter-domain conflicts (Rizzuto and Maloney, 2008). Healthy social relationships among co-workers and a satisfying work life can help employees manage inter-domain stress (Hulin, 2002).

Relationship management

Not only do individual employees experience their own psychological discomforts, the organization as a whole experiences increased levels of stress and anxiety that impact interpersonal interactions and emotions among employees (e.g., Rizzuto and Maloney, 2008), as we witnessed so clearly in our work with LA/SPCA. Yet, at the same time, a common disaster experience creates the opportunity for enhanced interpersonal bonding through shared struggles for survival. Using formal and informal social networks to provide support, and providing information and key resources to help with mental health challenges and facilitating effective coping strategies for dealing with difficult circumstances is well advised (Green and Solomon, 1995).

Leadership development

The actions organizational leaders take in response to, and in the aftermath of, a disaster can help return businesses to normal operations (Junglas and Ives, 2007). Best practices for change management frequently advocate employee participation in knowledge capturing activities that can increase access to valuable information to aid crisis planning and prevention, and build confidence and trust in the managerial leadership (Shrivastava and Shaw, 2003). Creating a workplace culture that encourages leadership behaviors from all hierarchical levels in the organization, in order to build trust and shared understandings about workplace changes (Bordia et al., 2006), are important for navigating unpredictable organizational change (Karaevli and Hall, 2003; Stock and McDermott, 2001).Therefore, OD interventions should emphasize information and leadership sharing throughout the organization during disaster recovery.

Recent applications of chaos and complexity theory to organizations (along with related new models of leadership) show promise for increasing effectiveness in leading change, such as in disaster recovery. Leaders working to harness the "distributed intelligence" across the organizational system, and serving as catalysts for "emergence" of spontaneous groups to resolve the organization's most challenging problems go a long way toward building a more nimble and adaptive organizational system capable of surviving and thriving in a fast- and ever-changing world (Guastello et al., 2009; Pascale et al., 2000; Schneider and Somers, 2006).

Future directions for practitioners and researchers

Traditional OD practice assumes an *adaptive* approach that allows for iterative feedback and adjustments to optimize the intervention process. Complexities of EOD often necessitate just-in-time fixes to short-term needs, learning from and adapting those practices happening later and over time. To date, little is known about organizational practice in the context of large-scale disasters. Two examples of how this affected KARE services are provided. First, although intake assessment processes used by KARE were well established and commonly used by practitioners in *typical* intake settings, their usefulness in *atypical* (disaster) settings is less reliable. Most KARE clients found it difficult to assess the magnitude of damage to their organizations because the workplace damages caused by Katrina were embedded within the context of a larger humanitarian disaster. While the data gathered during the initial intake assessments provided a helpful glimpse of the needs in the affected region, in some cases inaccurate data from intake assessments affected KARE's ability to broker well-fit consultant–client relationships, which led to inaccurate estimates of project timelines and priorities for organizational needs, and distorted perceptions of organizational support for KARE projects. As a result, some projects were subject to scope creep, exceeding the commitment expectations and bandwidth of project members, and ultimately contributed to some instances of member burnout, fatigue, and withdrawal from project teams.

A second example is that typical benchmarks and indicators of challenges, progress, and/or success may be difficult to interpret in the disaster context. Issues pertaining to disaster recovery timelines (e.g., how soon after crisis can organizations absorb consulting services?), typical recovery needs (so many needs, too little time), and the applicability of ordinary business practices and tools remain unexplored. Consultants had to rely on intuition and experience to guide decision making and service delivery under these unpredictable circumstances.

From a scientific perspective, more research is needed to examine the utility and/or validity of various methodological designs, measures, approaches, and tools in the disaster contexts.

Lessons learned and future directions

Lessons that we learned from the KARE experience included:

1. The knowledge, skills, and abilities that our professionals can offer are greatly needed and valued as part of crisis management and disaster recovery – as evident in the continued interest KARE has received from local businesses, state officials, and national crisis management groups.

2. A seemingly simple vision (i.e., mobilize volunteers and render services) involves a number of logistical "start-up actions and costs" that cannot be quickly established. Thus, future emergency outreach efforts would be best served by an intact team that preserves an organizational structure, volunteer network, professional partnerships, financial base, and an institutional knowledge for navigating legal and logistical challenges.

3. Diversity of expertise and experience was critically important to the success of KARE, as it increased the capability for creating a strong consultant–client fit. Teams comprised of both local and non-local volunteers benefitted from fresh ideas for problem solving and insights into local values and business norms.

4. Local volunteers can inform the remote team members of broader recovery efforts in the region and enable frequent in-person contact with client organizations, facilitating trust, rapport, and communications with the client organizations.

5. Future outreach efforts would benefit from strengthened ties to regional professional association chapters, other professional business and psychology associations, and psychologists in other areas (e.g., clinical, counseling). Research on effective social movements cites the need for connected networks to "seed" and spread ideas and information about the need to mobilize action (Liu-Thompkins, 2012). The ability to seed communities can be achieved in part by educating business and government about the relevance of our expertise toward disaster response, recovery, and planning.

6. While there was an abundance of support and willingness to help among KARE volunteers, particular experience was at times in short (or over-)supply. As a result, project workloads were unevenly distributed contributing to strain and fatigue among some project members. Better strategies are needed for: (1) utilizing the expert knowledge of seasoned practitioners and the willingness of early-career professionals; (2) brokering consultant–client matches; and (3) collaborating across disciplines.

7. Establishing relationships with key professionals locally (i.e., Public Relations, community leaders) is imperative for success, as they have the knowledge of the community and connections with media and community leaders that is so important. In addition, supporting local businesses still in operation to produce materials (e.g., printing of announcements, posters; T-shirts with logo for the volunteers...) is hugely beneficial for getting the word out about volunteers' available services.

8. Ongoing work to raise the professional association's national visibility relative to skills and expertise that are useful in recovering from disasters, and having a geographically distributed network of volunteers, will be very helpful in aiding outreach efforts.

9. Investing the time and energy to "build"/align the Volunteer team is very important to the effectiveness of the effort. The demands of each situation were typically so intense that volunteers had to "hit the ground running" and took little-to-no time to properly form their consulting team. When conflicts arose, and time out was required, we learned that the investment of time up front to align and get to really know each other is time/investment well spent.

Finally, two key lessons not to be overlooked nor underestimated were:

10. Irrespective of our professional expertise, one of the most valued and therefore valuable contributions that we made was simply being there with caring hearts and willing hands. That we KARE'd and were there with them was what those we helped said helped them the most to recover, renew, and re-energize to rebuild – their businesses, their lives, and their spirits.

11. Benevolence begets benevolence; our clients and the local professionals we partnered with KARE'd about us and actively worked to help our outreach be successful. These were mutually reinforcing circles of humanity that left each of us volunteers also forever changed by our KARE experience!

Note

1. The ASPCA is based in New York City and does national advocacy and outreach. Although many people believe local SPCA's are part of a national organization, each SPCA operates independently as private non-profits. The ASPCA is not a national organization.

References

Barnett, R. C., & Hyde, J. S. (2001). Women, men, work, and family: An expansionist theory. *American Psychologist*, 56, 781–796.

Bordia, P., Jones, E., Gallois, C., Callan, V. J., & Difonzo, N. (2006). Management are aliens!: Rumors and stress during organizational change. *Group & Organization Management*, 31, 601–621.

Comfort, L. B., Wisner, S. C., Pulwarty, R., Hewitt, K., Oliver-Smith, A., Wiener, J., Fordham, M., Peacock, W., & Krimgold, F. (1991). Reframing disaster policy:

The global evolution of vulnerable communities. *Environmental Hazards*, 1, 39–44.

Corey, C. M., & Deitch, E. A. (2011). Factors affecting business recovery immediately after Hurricane Katrina. *Journal of Contingencies and Crisis Management*, 19, 169–181.

Dolan, S. L., Garcia, S., & Auberbach, A. (2003). Understanding and managing chaos in organizations. *International Journal of Management*, 20, 23–35.

Fleming, C. (2006). After the rescue workers go home. *Public Management*, May, 6–10.

Galea, S., Tracy, M., Norris, F., & Coffey, S.F. (2008). Financial and social circumstances and the incidence and course of PTSD in Mississippi during the first two years after Hurricane Katrina. *Journal of Traumatic Stress*, 21, 357–368.

Green, B. L., & Solomon, S. D. (1995). The mental health impact of natural and technological disasters. In J. R. Freedy and S. E. Hobfoll's (Eds.), *Traumatic Stress: From Theory to Practice* (pp. 187–298). New York: Plenumn Publishing Corporation.

Guastello, S. J., Koopmans, M., & Pincus, D. (2009). *Chaos and Complexity in Psychology: The Theory of Nonlinear Dynamical Systems*. New York: Cambridge University Press.

Hulin, C. L. (2002). Lessons from industrial and organizational psychology. In J. M. Herman, & F. Drasgow (Eds.), *The Psychology of Work* (pp. 3–22). Mahwah, NJ: Erlbaum.

Junglas, I., & Ives, B. (2007). Recovering IT in a disaster: Lessons from Hurricane Katrina. *MISQuarterly Executive*, 6, 39–51.

Karaevli, A., & Hall, D. (2003). Growing leaders for turbulent times: Is succession planning up to the challenge? *Organizational Dynamics*, 32, 62–79.

Kotter, J. P., & Schlesinger, L. A. (1979). Choosing strategies for change. *Harvard Business Review*, 57, 106–114.

Liu-Thompkins, Y. (2012). Seeding viral content: Lessons from the diffusion of online videos. *Journal of Advertising Research*, 52, 465–478.

Milano, C. (2005). The benefits of post-crisis counseling. *Risk Management*, 52(5), 12–17.

Pascale, R. T., Milleman, M., & Gioja, L. (2000). *Surviving the Edge of Chaos*. New York: Three Rivers Press.

Piotrowski, C. (2006). Hurricane Katrina and organization development: Part 1. Implications of chaos theory. *Organizational Development Journal*, 24(3), 10–19.

Quarantelli, E. (2001). Another selective look at future social crises: Some aspects of which we can already see in the present. *Journal of Contingencies and Crisis Management*, 9, 233–237.

Riebeek, H. (2005). The rising cost of natural disasters. *NASA Earth Observatory*, *March* 28, 2009. Retrieved from http://earthobservatory.nasa.gov/Features/RisingCost/.

Rizzuto, T. (2008). Katrina aid and relief effort (KARE) lesson: Looking back and moving forward (Feature article). *The Industrial-Organizational Psychology*, 45(4), 11–26.

Rizzuto, T. (2009). Human dimensions of workplace disaster recovery. In K. Cherry's (Ed.), *Lifespan Perspectives on Natural Disasters: Coping with Katrina, Rita and Other Storms*. New York: Springer Inc. pp. 261–280.

Rizzuto, T., & Maloney, L. (2008). Organizing chaos: Lessons from successful crisis management in the wake of Hurricane Katrina. *Professional Psychology: Research and Practice (Special Issue: Hurricane Katrina)*, 39, 77–85.

Rizzuto, T., & Vandaveer, V. (2013). Mobilizing action through professional societies. (Chapter 17). Using I-O psychology for the greater good: Helping those who help others. In J. B. Olson-Buchanan, L. L. Koppes Bryan, & L. F. Thompson (Eds.), *Frontiers Series of the Society for Industrial and Organizational Psychology*. New York: Routledge, 529–556.

Sanchez, J. I., Korbin, W. P., & Viscarra, D. M. (1995). Corporate support in the aftermath of a natural disaster: Effects on employee strains. *The Academy of Management Journal*, 38, 504–521.

Schneider, M., & Somers, M. (2006). Organizations as complex adaptive systems: Implications of complexity theory for leadership research. *The Leadership Quarterly*, 17, 351–365.

Schouten, R., Callahan, M. V., & Bryant, A. (2004). Community response to disaster: The role of the workplace. *The Harvard Review of Psychiatry*, 12, 229–237.

Senge, P. M. (1990). *The Fifth Discipline: The Art and Practice of the Learning Organization*. New York, NY: Doubleday Publishing Group.

Shrivastava, S., & Shaw, J. B. (2003). Liberating HR through technology. *Human ResourceManagement*, 42, 201–222.

Smith, D. (1990). Beyond contingency planning: Towards a model of crisis management. *Industrial Crisis Quarterly*, 4, 263–275.

Stock, G., & McDermott, C. (2001). Organizational and strategic predictors of manufacturing technology implementation success: An exploratory study. *Technovation*, 21, 625–636.

Turner, A. (2007). US critical infrastructure in serious jeopardy. *CIO Magazine*. Retrieved June 2007 at http://www.cio.com/article/107904/US_infrastructure_in_serious_jeopardy.

Wilson J. P., & Raphael, B. (1993). Theoretical and conceptual foundations of traumatic stress syndromes. *The International Handbook of Traumatic Stress Syndromes* (pp. 226–243). New York: Plenum Press.

13

Service Learning in Developing Nations

Daniel Sachau, Carol Lynn Courtney, Dick Olson, Julene Nolan, and Scott Fee

In this chapter, we discuss two short-term, international service-learning trips where US graduate students, faculty and program advisors (I-O-trained management consultants) traveled to developing nations to complete projects in local schools. Drawing from these experiences, we discuss lessons we have learned regarding the challenges and benefits of the trips. Although it may be easier to imagine how people from nursing, construction, or education might serve the disadvantaged, we have found that the skill set of I-O psychologists can be of great benefit to people who need to manage their way out of poverty. I-O psychologists can, for instance, teach job search, interviewing, and supervisory skills. They can help the agencies who serve the poor by providing organizational development, managerial and problem-solving expertise. The skills of researchers and grant writers can be of immense help to those who serve and those who are served. Service learning is of growing interest to I-O psychologists and our hope is that the chapter will be useful as a resource for professionals who would like to start an international service-learning program.

Service learning

Service learning is a form of experiential education (Dewey, 1938) that integrates coursework and community service (American Association of Higher Education, 2003).

The proponents of service learning suggest that good projects will foster a sense of caring for others and will heighten self-reflection. Service-learning projects can also enrich learning, teach civic responsibility, and strengthen communities (Fiske, 2001). Ultimately, service learning benefits both the providers and the recipients of service.

While many educators have commented on the benefits of domestic service-learning experiences, a growing number of educators are advocating international programs (Bringle and Tonkin, 2004; Kiely, 2005). International service-learning projects combine the benefits of study abroad with the benefits of service learning (Parker and Dautoff, 2007). Study abroad programs can increase cultural sensitivity (Anderson, Lawton, Rexeisen, and Hubbard, 2006), improve student self-confidence, heighten an appreciation for other cultures (Pence and Macgillivray, 2008), increase international functional knowledge (Chieffo and Griffiths, 2004), and deepen an understanding of global interdependence (Sutton and Rubin, 2004).

Eden campus, South Africa

Eden Campus was established in 2005 to help disadvantaged black and *colored* students (a technical term in South Africa meaning *mixed race*) gain the entrepreneurial skills they need to return to their communities and start small businesses. Students live on campus for two years during which time they complete courses and work as partners in their own campus-based businesses. These ventures include a small organic farm, a bee keeping business, a hair salon, a laundry service, a car wash, a jewelry shop, a mountain bike rental/tour service, and a video production company. While students are running campus businesses, they are also incubating ideas for new enterprises they can take back to their communities after graduating. For example, the Eden Campus founders are especially interested in eco-friendly businesses. One of the most promising ventures on campus is an innovative project that combines tire recycling, worm farming, and composting. This business can open in any community with virtually no start-up costs.

With leadership from entrepreneur Steve Carver, the campus was established as part of a Black Economic Empowerment (BEE) program. Except for nominal registration fees, students attend the campus free of charge. All students come from impoverished townships in the region and they gain admission by being nominated by their community leaders.

In February of 2011, Eden began its sixth year of operation by instituting the Mini-Enterprise curriculum developed by Junior Achievement (JA) and Cambridge University. The school leaders had struggled with developing new curriculum and the JA model solved a variety of problems related to course content. The new curriculum requires coursework in financial planning, general management, stock control, pricing, marketing, and sales. Upon completion of the Mini-Enterprise Program, students are offered an opportunity to take the Cambridge Examination, an internationally recognized entrepreneurial qualification underwritten by Cambridge University. In the near future, students will specialize in either eco-agribusiness, eco-construction, or eco-tourism.

The campus is located in the town of Karatara in the Western Cape Province of South Africa. The town was originally established as a welfare community to house White displaced forestry workers. In 2006, faculty and students moved into an abandoned retirement home. Because the campus enrolls black and colored students, there was immediate tension between the community and campus. The campus has gone through additional growing pains as campus leaders have had to build virtually every component of a modern campus with minimal money, labor, and time.

Pre-trip. We recruited students from three departments on campus – construction management, clinical psychology, and industrial/organizational psychology. Our plan was the construction management students would assist with construction/landscaping projects; the psychology students would assist with job-seeking skills, business planning, and resume writing. Once we filled our roster, we set up three campus orientation sessions and we assigned readings. We used the sessions to set expectations, answer questions, and provide background information.

Six months before the trip, our students initiated fund-raising projects for Eden Campus. First, students mailed alumni donation requests. Second, students and faculty in the industrial/organizational psychology program completed a project for Minnesota State University's (MSU's) on-site consulting practice. Students donated all the proceeds of the project to the trip. Third, students asked regional business leaders to donate outdated laptop computers. The students asked for computers that were too old to run the most recent version of Windows, but new enough to run Ubuntu. Ubuntu is a freeware operating system based on Linux. Ubuntu is popular in developing nations. This computer recycling project yielded 22 laptops.

One unusual aspect of the program is that US management consultants traveled with our students. We did this for two reasons. First, most of the students on the trip were enrolled in the industrial/organizational psychology graduate program at MSU. We thought that the consultants would be good role models for our students (which turned-out to be the case). Second, we wanted the consultants to work on an organization development project on campus.

On-site. Once we arrived in Karatara, we spent two days doing group process exercises to help our students get to know the Eden Campus students. Nidhi Chaitow, a South African educational consultant, served as group process facilitator. Nidhi was one of the founding instructors at Eden Campus. Although she is no longer employed on campus, she is intimate with the ideals, history, and politics of the campus. Nidhi arranged nightly team building exercises including discussion circles, drumming sessions, and group music programs. The team building sessions helped all of the students get to know each other. The sessions created a sense of trust and openness and they refocused student attention on the mission of the trip. In addition, Nidhi met one-on-one with our students throughout the 16 days and asked students to discuss their perceptions of South Africa.

Having professional contacts in the Capetown area, we met with local consultants in Capetown. The work we were engaged in was not their focus, yet we learned about issues and problems in South Africa. They described challenges in selection and leadership development with the relatively recent racial integration required by law with the large business clients with whom they work.

Service projects. Students completed a variety of projects including painting, construction, and landscaping. Some students remodeled a storage room to create a spa/salon that will serve the local community. Others remodeled the campus store. Still others completed landscaping projects on campus. One group of students built playground equipment for the local grade school. Technically speaking, this was not an Eden Campus project but Eden Campus ran the project as an outreach to local community leaders.

In keeping with Eden Campus' goal of training leaders, an Eden Campus student was assigned to manage each project. Many of the Eden Campus students had never had a job of any kind. Further, many of the Eden students had grown up in families where parents and siblings were unemployed. Thus, some of the Eden Campus students lacked many of the basic knowledge, skills and values that come with holding a job. Organizing service learning projects provided valuable learning experience for the Eden students.

While these construction projects were in progress, MSU faculty and the management consultants completed an organization development project where we interviewed the staff, faculty, and students. We then provided a detailed report to the campus leadership that included suggestions for organizational change. For example, with some recent staffing changes, leadership roles were not clear and this created confusion. We made several recommendations to clarify and strengthen leadership.

In addition to the projects above, the management consultants on the trip also held an interview skills workshop. During the sessions, Eden Campus students participated in role-playing sessions and received feedback about their performance.

Yachana technical high school, Modana Ecuador

Douglas McMeekin moved to Ecuador in 1986 and worked as an environmental consultant for the oil industry. He quickly realized something had to be done to help people living in the Amazon region where poverty, environmental degradation, and poor quality public education are all inextricably linked. Thirty percent of children in the Amazon region do not finish sixth grade, and only 15% finish secondary schooling. Students often drop out because they feel the current public education available in their remote communities is irrelevant to their everyday lives.

In 1995, McMeekin opened the Yachana Eco Lodge, and used the proceeds from the lodge to establish the Yachana Technical High School. Like Eden Campus, Yachana Technical School integrates academic and hands-on learning. All the students come from the Amazon region and attend school on a rotational schedule of three weeks at school and three weeks at home. The idea is to prepare the students to become entrepreneurs in their communities focusing on environmental conservation and management of small businesses.

Pre-trip. Students in the graduate program in industrial/organizational psychology program participated on the trip. We met on the months leading up to the trip. Students were assigned to read: *Savages* by Joe Kane (1995). Two themes emerged in this book. One was a more thorough understanding of the indigenous culture. Second, the book described the invasiveness and environmental damage created by the development of oil production in the Amazon basin. We could see the clash of cultures as indigenous workers earned what to them was a great deal of money as a laborer in the oil industry. The substandard construction by the oil companies of pipelines through the jungle provided numerous locations where pollution occurred. This pollution ultimately flowed into the rivers, which are the lifeblood of the indigenous people. We could see firsthand how the conflict between economic development, and the associated greed conflicted with protection of the environment as well as the long-standing cultures of the indigenous people.

On-site. To get to the school, our group had to take a one hour flight from Quito, the capital of Ecuador. Then we boarded motorized canoes and traveled two hours up the Nampo River to reach the village of Modana. Modana has a few buildings including a church and a small medical clinic. The Yachana Technical High School sits near Modana, the eco-lodge and across the river from a large jungle preserve that is also owned by the Yachana Foundation.

The founder and leader at Yachana, Mr McMeekin, is a study in successful entrepreneurship. He has the interpersonal charisma that many successful entrepreneurs possess, including the ability to influence and persuade. He is a conceptual thinker who effectively lays both tactical and strategic plans. The dedication and long hours he commits to all aspects of Yachana are his primary focus and consume his life. Mr McMeekin has been honored for his social entrepreneurialism. We learned that he had created the Yachana non-profit foundation with a number of subsidiaries. In addition to non-profit initiatives, for-profit initiatives were designed to be supportive of and integrate with the non-profit work. The enterprise that Mr McMeekin has created in the jungle and in Quito is highly sophisticated and effective, having won awards from National Geographic Society as well as other organizations.

Service projects

We made arrangements for the management consultants to provide executive coaching with Mr McMeekin. This was to affirm and support his leadership, and his ongoing growth and success. Unlike many entrepreneurs who have carved their own path, Mr McMeekin was very open to interacting and working with the consultants to better understand how he could be a stronger leader. He quickly pointed out that succession planning for the organization was one of the areas of concern. Early in the process, the consultants were able to describe and document the much strength he provided in his leadership. As with many entrepreneurs, Mr McMeekin needed to delegate even more responsibility in order to develop and grow others to run the organization. While extremely healthy and vigorous at 68 years of age, he wants the organization to thrive long past his leadership. To arrive at this goal, developing ongoing leadership succession within the organization is critical. Various structures were discussed with him as well as methods by which he could be even more effective in this area.

While some of the details involved in the executive coaching process are confidential, this provided an opportunity to discuss with the students the process of executive and leadership coaching within the context of Yachana, a successful entrepreneurial venture. The consultants are continuing the coaching experience with a few of the key leaders within the operations at Yachana. This can be done remotely as Yachana is well equipped with communications equipment.

It was a valuable experience for the students, faculty, and consultants to observe a well-run, successful operation in the Amazon jungle. The well-defined roles, the overall strategy and business plans and goals, and the successful operation of the various initiatives provided a great learning experience for everyone. Many of these concepts are critical to the success of entrepreneurial organizations in North America. Incorporated into all this experience was the variety of cultures represented by the indigenous peoples and the constraints and restrictions of a remote location.

Service-learning lessons

Trip goals

We established learning objectives for each trip. Typical goals included: (1) to help our students understand the complexities of culture, (2) to help our students better understand the complexities of race and poverty problems, (3) to help our students develop an interest and competence in service work, (4) to help our students better understand their own culture, (5) to help indigenous students gain project management skills, and (6) to help students gain a better understanding of the skills that are necessary to compete in business. We found that these goals help define the planning and implementation of a trip.

Sustainability

The Eco Lodge and Technical High School provided a study in sustainability. There were numerous examples, which range from raising animals and crops for food to incorporating water power and solar power for energy. Use of animal waste and food waste was creatively used for a variety of purposes. There were times solar energy was not available creating a problem for the computer lab. A small hydroelectric plant was installed in a creek to provide a continuous supply of energy to the computer lab, even when there were long rainy periods, limiting the sunshine. The graduate students could see that this environmentally sound approach was done on a sound economic basis.

Dealing with crisis

During our stay in South Africa, violence broke-out in townships surrounding Johannesburg. South African citizens were targeting refugees from Zimbabwe. The locals complained that the Zimbabweans, who were willing to work for food rather than money, were taking work away from already poor South Africans. Within two days, rioting spread to many townships in South Africa including the very townships where our students had just visited. This rioting lead to 62 deaths and displaced more than 20,000 people (Mail and Guardian, 2008). The violence, described by the local media as "xenophobic," was a wake-up call for our students. The students realized that, "South Africa is not as calm as it appears on the surface." Some students expressed surprise that violence could occur in a town where they felt, "welcomed and safe." Others expressed embarrassment about, "feeling naïve."

Although the violence was tragic, the students did learn a valuable lesson: things can change very quickly in communities where people are desperately poor. The violence also drove home the point that even though apartheid ended without a bloody struggle, racial and international tensions could still boil over. As one student noted, "South Africa is not out of danger yet."

The crisis was also a wake-up call for those of us who lead the trip. The riots highlighted the dangers of taking students to communities with high crime rates and minimal law enforcement. This risk can certainly be an issue when providing services in the communities that need it most. For more about this issue see Nelson and Ornstein (2002), and Stevenson (2008).

Facing health care problems

AIDS is ravaging sub-Saharan Africa. As of 2005, over 30% of all pregnant women were HIV positive (Actuarial Society of South Africa, 2005). Over 1,200,000 South African children (aged 0–17) had been orphaned by AIDS. Nineteen percent of all South Africans aged 15–49 are HIV positive (UNICEF, 2008). During our stay, we had the opportunity to meet with Heidi Sonnekus who had served as an AIDS researcher for UNICEF. Heidi spent an afternoon talking about a large-scale project where she and her colleagues gathered attitude data from 5,162 classes in 1,418 South African schools (Andersson et al., 2004). Heidi discussed the scope and complexity of the AIDS problem in South Africa. She noted that there has been progress in slowing the spread of HIV but AIDS workers and social service workers are so busy dealing with the spread of AIDS that they have not had time or the resources to plan for a generation of orphans. No one is quite sure how the deaths from AIDS will affect the South African economy and labor markets.

The service-learning environment made the AIDS issues very real for our students. All of the Eden Campus students had lost friends and family to AIDS. All of the students could talk about the issue in a very personal way. Oddly, some of the Eden students had heard so much about, and lost so much to AIDS, that they were developing what Heidi referred to as *AIDS compassion fatigue* – a tendency to become numb to the AIDS warnings and AIDS statistics. When our students discussed the AIDS issues in South Africa, their comments reflected both, "a sorrow seeing how close AIDS is to the Eden Campus students," and a surprise that "some Eden Campus students seemed to be bored by the topic."

New models for education

Eden Campus and Yachana are unusual because the campus leaders are not tied to traditional models of education. For example, students do not receive degrees. Students work in campus businesses and they are expected to start their own business. Campus leaders expect students to return to their communities and help others start small enterprises. Students are admitted based on their perceived potential as community leaders. The campuses are managed without any government support, and campus leaders have a long-term goal for the campus to be financially self-sustaining. Although neither Steve Carver nor Douglas McMeekin use the term, Eden Campus and Yachana could be called *service-learning academies*.

The role of technology

Because one of our goals was to help students form meaningful friendships with Eden Campus students, we started an internet correspondence project. Each MSU student was paired with an Eden Campus student. The students were then given short assignments where they became acquainted with their partner. We started by exchanging email addresses but the correspondence quickly shifted to Facebook. Facebook allowed the students to exchange pictures and film clips, to form discussion groups, to post biographical information, and to use free live chat. Facebook also has a *people you may know* feature which records interconnections between networks of friends. Facebook then suggests people a user may want to connect to because of common links among friends. This feature quickly expanded the interconnection of Eden Campus and MSU students.

Ultimately, Facebook allowed students to get to know each other very quickly. As a student mentioned, "Every student was nervous about meeting students from half-way around the world. During our initial e-mail introductions, everyone was so focused on cultural differences that we were all walking on eggshells. When we saw each other's Facebook pages, many of our cultural assumptions disappeared." The students are still interacting over Facebook. This medium allowed them to stay in contact in ways that letter, the telephone, and even email would not allow.

Status differences

In a service-learning environment, the service providers often enjoy a higher socioeconomic status than the people they are helping. This disparity means that providers need to be thoughtful about the way they serve. For instance, a long history of research in social psychology suggests that one of the best ways to break down stereotypes and prejudice is to increase social contact between groups (Myers, 2005). However, contact must be close, long term, and on equal status (Pettigrew, 1998; Stephan, 1987). An issue with our trips is the MSU students were not on equal footing with the students from the various schools. The MSU students were much wealthier, had much greater professional opportunities, and were in the role of helper or "academic missionary," as one student put it. The danger is this, if students with higher socio-economic status interact as "helpers" to students in lower socioeconomic status, the act of helping may reinforce stereotypes and status differences. Thus a *White Knight syndrome*, as Hondagneu-Sotelo and Raskoff (1994) call it, can exacerbate social problems and slow change.

Another problem that can arise in a service provider relationship is passivity on the part of the service recipients. For instance, on the trip to South Africa, there were a few MSU students who had a difficult time dealing with what they perceived as apathy from the Eden Campus students. The Eden Campus students worked at a slower pace than the MSU students and they were more likely to take breaks to talk to their classmates. Further, many of the Eden Campus students simply did not have work experience so they were less confident than the MSU students. Thus, for a few MSU students, the Eden Campus students were perceived as under-motivated. Interestingly, this lack of motivation may have been an example of the conspiracy of courtesy (DiPadova-Stocks and Brown, 2006):

> In gratitude to those providing service, recipients try to please them by going along with whatever the service providers seem to want to do. The recipients may trust the providers more than they trust their own experiences and judgment. Also, those who render the service might be uncomfortable with their role, and not find ways to press the recipients for needed information. This conspiracy of courtesy, which occurs in interpersonal interaction, nullifies reciprocity and destroys the service credibility of the experience. (p. 137)

A third problem related to status inequality was evident when the MSU students were interacting with local students in social settings where the disparity in wealth could be embarrassing for both groups. The MSU students are generous but many local students are not financially able to reciprocate. In some cases, this generosity caused students to feel indebted. One MSU student wisely pointed out to his colleagues how the Eden Campus were sensitive to the language that Americans use regarding giving and helping. He noted, "The Eden Campus students do not like it when I say, 'Can I give you this shovel?' They would rather we say, 'Do you want me to share this shovel with you?' They are also uncomfortable when I use the words, 'Can I buy you a drink?' They would feel more comfortable if we asked, 'Shall we have a drink?'."

Overall, neither the White Knight Syndrome, the conspiracy of courtesy, nor the embarrassment of riches were big problems, but in a long-term stay they could be. People considering service-learning trips should keep these potential roadblocks in mind.

Who's helping whom?

In contrast to the White Knight syndrome, many of our students suggested that they learned more from the trips than the local students could have learned from them. As one student put it, "Are we helping them or are they helping us?" For example, in South Africa, US students appreciated the South African students' spontaneous dancing and singing and their ability to, "have fun with nothing," the way they, "are happy in the face of adversity" and are, "joyful and exuberant at the drop of a hat!" Our students learned that happiness may be less closely related to income, iPods, cars, and designer labels than they once thought.

Who are we?

An interesting aspect of international trips is that travelers often learn a great deal about their own country by leaving it. One student mentioned, "It is difficult to understand my own culture when I have never had anything to compare it to." For example, students often finish the trips with a better appreciation of their own wealth. The trips to the townships and villages gave students exposure to a level of poverty that they have never witnessed in the United States. Beyond wealth, our students express an appreciation of the freedoms they enjoy in the United States. In addition, students gain a sense of the extent to which US media spreads US culture all over the world. Students express a concern that, "the local students expect us to be like the people they see in U.S. reality shows and sitcoms."

In as much as the trips highlight the cultural differences, the trip also made many students aware of the commonalities. Most students are surprised to find that the basic values of people across nations are remarkably similar. That South African's and Ecuadorians, like Americans, are proud of who they are. As one student noted, "college students, no matter what background they come from, share similar hopes and fears, joy and sadness."

Distance and momentum

Leaders in each of the remote schools noted that there seem to be a large number of people who are willing to visit and offer assistance. The leaders also noted that most of the people who visit are excited about helping and most make plans to return and/or arrange financial support. However, all of the leaders stated that few of these promises pan out. As Douglas McMeekin noted, "I have heard a lot of promises but people go home, and then nothing happens."

We suspect that plans fall through not because people who make the promises are callous or self-interested. If our own experiences are any indication, returning to the United States and our daily routines insulates us from news and thoughts about the schools. Because the schools are so remote, and because they are in places that are so starkly different from our lives at home, we are not faced with daily reminders of the needs in the schools. It is interesting, and tragic, that this problem is directly proportional to the need of the schools. US news and media outlets are more likely to run stories about geographically, economically, and culturally close countries than distant countries. Without reminders of the plight of these nations, it is easy let a busy schedule move plans to help on the back burner.

Aware of this problem, we have worked to keep momentum for each of the service projects. After the South Africa trip we arranged for one of the Eden Campus students to be enrolled at (MSU). He was given financial support by MSU and the local community. This student's transition into the university was made easier because of the friendships he developed with students and staff during the trip to South Africa. Another development was another group of MSU students returned to Eden Campus to work on additional projects the following summer. Third, one of the MSU faculty members decided to take a sabbatical in South Africa where he is working with students from Eden Campus and Nelson Mandela University.

As a follow-up to the Yachana trip, with help from one of the consultants, an MSU student started a master's thesis investigating the predictors of indigenous student performance in non-traditional school. He traveled back to the school eight months later to collect data. Mr McMeekin and his team were interested in identifying and selecting indigenous students who represent the greatest potential for contribution to their communities. As a result, research is being completed on a work habits questionnaire, which is to be completed by applicants based on key characteristics that students need to be successful (not only at school but also back in their communities). A graduate student, fluent in Spanish, has taken this project as a master's paper. He will complete a follow-up visit to the Yachana campus, and with the cooperation of Yachana staff, this student will complete the necessary research to assure the effectiveness of this selection tool, designed to be one part of the overall selection process. Further, the management consultants who traveled with the students continued leadership coaching and succession planning for the Yachana staff. In addition to these efforts, the trip leader paid for a well-connected professional fund-raiser to travel to Yachana and meet the staff. The trip leader did not put any stipulations on the trip other than if the fund-raiser liked what he saw, he would encourage his contacts to visit the school and provide financial support.

We have done follow up evaluations with MSU students to better understand the learning and value of these trips. We have found perspectives have been broadened and appreciation for other peoples' experiences enhanced. We have followed up, as previously described, with ongoing work, even after returning to the United States. A formal evaluation of our work at the sites visited would be a good idea, yet has been beyond the scope of our projects to date.

Conclusion

International service-learning experiences have been identified as a valuable resource to help students gain a myriad of skills, competencies and confidences (Anderson et al., 2006; Pence and Macgillivray, 2008). Nowhere is this more important than in the field of psychology. Because psychologists and the clients they serve are culturally and linguistically different from each other, it is vital that psychologists gain the training and experience necessary to become multiculturally competent practitioners (Loe and Miranda, 2005). Research indicates that the three most important components of training programs noted for educating from a multicultural perspective include the opportunity to work with diverse clients, experience with diverse faculty and colleagues, and coursework that includes issues of diversity (Coleman, 2006; Rogers, 2006; Rogers, Hoffman, and Wade, 1998). International service-learning opportunities provide these experiences and should be made available to students in order to produce university graduates who are global citizens.

Overall, these international service-learning trips have been very successful. The students were able to make meaningful contributions. As importantly, students formed friendships with people they would never otherwise get a chance to meet. The trips changed attitudes and increased student confidence. They opened students' eyes to the complexities of racism, class, AIDS, language, and poverty. These trips helped students see how traditional models of education may not be the best solution in all settings. They gave students a firsthand look at the way that technology is shaping culture and a shrinking the world. Finally, the trips caused students to wrestle with the realistic yet conflicting feelings of hope and discouragement, charity and partnership (King, 2004), commonality and differences.

References

Actuarial Society of South Africa (2005). *ASSA 2003 AIDS and Demographic Model*. Retrieved September 15, 2008, from www.actuarialsociety.co.za/aids/content.asp?id=1000000449.

American Association of Higher Education (2003). *Service-Learning*. Retrieved September 15, 2008, from http://www.aahe.org.

Anderson, P. H., Lawton, L., Rexeisen, R. J., & Hubbard, A. C. (2006). Short-term study abroad and intercultural sensitivity: A pilot study. *International Journal of Intercultural Relations*, 30(4), 457–469.

Andersson, N., Ho-Foster, A., Matthis, J., Marokoane, N., Mashiane, V., Mhatre, S., Mitchell, S., Mokoena, T., Monasta, L., Ngxowa, N., Pascual Salcedo, N., & Sonnekus, H. (2004). National cross sectional study of views on sexual violence and risk of HIV infection and AIDS among South African school pupils. *BMJ*. Retrieved September 15, 2008, from www.bmj.com/cgi/reprint/bmj.38226. 617454.7Cv1.pdf.

Bringle, R. G., & Tonkin, H. (2004). International service-learning: A research agenda. In H. Tonkin, S. J. Deeley, M. Pusch, D. Quiroga, M. J. Siegel, J. Whiteley, & R. G. Bringle (Eds.), *Service-Learning Across Cultures: Promise and Achievement* (pp. 365–374). New York, NY: International Partnership for Service-Learning and Leadership.

Chieffo, L., & Griffiths. L. (2004). Large-scale assessment of student attitudes after a short-term study abroad program. *Frontiers: The Interdisciplinary Journal of Study Abroad*, 10, 165–177.

Coleman, M. N. (2006). Critical incidents in multicultural training: An examination of student experiences. *Journal of Multicultural Counseling and Development*, 34, 168–182.

Dewey, J. (1938). *Experience and Education*. New York, NY: Collier Books.

DiPadova-Stocks, L., & Brown, V. (2006). Service-learning and the conspiracy of courtesy. *International Journal of Case Method Research and Application*, 18(2), 136–147.

Fiske, E. B. (2001). *Learning in Deed. The Power of Service-Learning for American Schools*. Battle Creek, MI: W. K. Kellogg Foundation.

Hondagneu-Sotelo, P., & Raskoff, S. (1994). Community service-learning: Promises and problems. *Teaching Sociology*, 22(3), 248–254.

Kane, J., (1995). *Savages*. New York: Knopf.

Kiely, R. (2005). Transformative international service-learning. *Academic Exchange Quarterly*, 9(1), 275–281.

King, J. (2004). Service-learning as a site for critical pedagogy: A case of collaboration, caring, and defamiliarization across borders. *Journal of Experiential Education*, 26(3), 121–137.

Loe, S. A., & Miranda, M. H. (2005). An examination of ethnic incongruence in school-based psychological services and diversity training experiences among school psychologists. *Psychology in the Schools*, 42, 419–432.

Mail & Guardian (2008), Xenophobia deaths. Retrieved September 1, 2008, from http://www.mg.co.za.

Myers, D. (2005). *Social Psychology*. 7th Edition. New York: McGraw-Hill.

Nelson, T. and Ornstein, S. (2002). Preparing for the unexpected: Managing low probability, disruptive events in student international travel courses. *Journal of Management Education*, 26(3), 259–273.

Parker, B., & Dautoff, D. A. (2007). Service-learning and study abroad: Synergistic learning opportunities. *Michigan Journal of Community Service-Learning*, 13(2), 40–52.

Pence, H. M., & Macgillivray, I. K. (2008). The impact of an international field experience on preservice teachers. *Teaching and Teacher Education*, 24(1), 14–25.

Pettigrew, T. F. (1998). Intergroup contact theory. *Annual Review of Psychology*, 49, 65–85.

Rogers M. R. (2006). Exemplary multicultural training in school psychology programs. *Cultural Diversity and Mental Health*, 12, 155–133.

Rogers, M. R., Hoffman, M. A., & Wade, J. (1998). Notable multicultural training in APA- approved counseling psychology and school psychology programs. *Cultural Diversity and Mental Health*, 4, 212–226.

Stephan, W. G. (1987). The contact hypothesis in intergroup relations. In C. Hendricks (Ed.), *Group Processes and Intergroup Relations* (pp. 13–40). Newbury Park, CA: Sage.

Stevenson, D. (2008). Sending students, faculty to study abroad opens door to both opportunities, risks. *National Underwriter/Property & Casualty Risk & Benefits Management*, 112(21), 28–31.

Sutton, R. C., & Rubin, D. L. (2004). The GLOSSARI project: Initial findings from a system-wide research initiative on study abroad learning outcomes. *Frontiers: The Interdisciplinary Journal of Study Abroad*, 10, 65–82.

UNICEF (2008). South Africa statistics. Retrieved September 19, 2008, from http://www.unicef.org/infobycountry/ southafrica_statistics.html.

14
Industrial and Organizational Psychology and Community Service Involvement: Students Helping Locally

Kristie Campana

As noted by my colleagues Sachau, Courtney, Olson, and Fee (Chapter 13), I-O graduate students gain many useful insights into the field by participating in service learning. As a faculty member at a Midwestern State University who has participated in a number of these international service trips, I too have seen the growth among students within the few weeks they are involved in the service-learning trip.

In this chapter, I build on their points about the value of service learning for students. However, for this chapter I have slightly different goals. First, I will emphasize the importance of getting new I-O psychologists involved in using their skills to educate and support organizations and people in the community who are typically not served by I-O psychology. A case study from my own experiences with community-based service in the classroom will serve as an example of how this process might unfold. I will also provide suggestions for future avenues that other instructors and mentors can pursue easily within their own communities and professional organizations, and how these experiences can be mutually beneficial. I should note, however, that helping young practitioners and scientists to engage in their communities need not be limited to academic settings – organizations can also make community involvement part of employee development and mentorship, which I will discuss toward the end of this chapter.

The value of community involvement for I-O students

I-O psychology has been widely criticized as being focused on the goals of the organization at the expense of the individuals within the organization (Weiss and Rupp, 2011). As early as 1965, I-O psychology has been identified as the handmaiden of management, whereby the use of psychology in the workplace focused primarily on the needs of the organization, and interventions are typically designed to protect the interest of the company by studying how workers can help or hurt the organization (cf. Baritz, 1965). As noted by Lefkowitz (2011), this overemphasis on organizational concerns has left I-O, as a field, with an identity crisis. When I-O practitioners and researchers focus heavily on an organization's goals, they are less able to focus on the individuals who work within the organization.

In fact, the mission statements of our professional organizations reflect this divide. Connecting to the greater community and helping individuals is highlighted in American Psychological Association's ethical principles. As psychologists, we are meant to use our competencies and skills to better the communities around us, and to fight for social justice. Meanwhile, SIOP's mission statements are fairly bereft of any discussion of service to the community, beyond educating others about what I-O psychology is. Unfortunately, when coursework is focused primarily on performance (or how to ensure employees are satisfied enough to perform well), students are left with the impression that I-O psychology is a value-free endeavor – when in fact, I-O psychology is often used to put productivity and profitability above all other values (Lefkowitz, 2005). It is not surprising, then, that on a survey of SIOP practitioners, *increasing effectiveness and efficiency, enhancing productivity,* and *promoting quality of products and services* were considered to be the three most important values for I-O psychologists. Meanwhile, *humanizing the workplace* ranked 17th out of 31 values in terms of importance (Church and Burke, 1992). As a result of this narrow focus, many graduating I-O psychologists are not exposed to more person-centric practices, nor are they necessarily cognizant of the disconnect between the goals of I-O psychology and the more humanistic values associated with psychology as a broader field.

During my tenure as a professor, I have worked with I-O students (both graduate and undergraduate) on a number of different service projects. Some of these projects included:

- designing materials for a local women's shelter to help clients improve their interview and resume-writing skills;
- working with the local Salvation Army to conduct customer satisfaction surveys, and using general principles from consumer psychology to help them reorganize their store;

- working with local small businesses to help them devise more effective training programs, communication systems, and performance evaluations;
- guiding a local assisted living organization on selecting and training caretakers (this project was completed in conjunction with our clinical psychology program);
- assisting a reproductive health-care organization in managing and analyzing data from surveys (this project will be the subject of the case study I present later in this chapter).

Although each organization gained something from my students' expertise, my students also had an opportunity to learn and grow from their work in these organizations. First, community service has helped my students feel more connected to the university and its surrounding community. My university is located in a mid-sized Midwestern city. Many students come from more urban areas, and can have a tendency to be dismissive of people who live and work in small towns. Having students work with local businesses has helped them learn about the people behind the small businesses they patronize, and illustrates that the problems that large companies face are similar to those experienced by smaller businesses. Furthermore, an adversarial relationship between universities and their surrounding communities is not uncommon (Torres, 2002). There is mounting evidence that suggests that community-based learning partnerships between universities and local communities can have noted positive effects on the community itself, as well as on the students (Eyler, Giles, Stenson, and Gray, 2001).

Additionally, I-O students in particular can gain some important experiences from working with community organizations. Colleges and universities have come under fire for failing to produce graduates who have practical knowledge and skills (Casner-Lotto and Barrington, 2006; Ward, 2003). I-O students are no exception to this critique; Fink et al. (2010) conducted a survey examining new graduates' competencies in consulting skills. In general, the findings elucidated three important points: (1) both faculty and students believed students should get more consulting/practical experiences in their education, (2) consulting skills were primarily taught using formal coursework, and (3) employers consistently reported that consulting skills possessed by new graduates were significantly lower than what was expected. As noted by Thomas, Downey, and George (2013), I-O graduate students in particular can benefit from these types of partnerships, as they get feedback from client partners as well as from faculty. In fact, sometimes these experiences can be particularly informative for students, as it can demonstrate the complexities of applying in-class learning to an organizational context (see Casile, Hoover, and O'Neil, 2011). Most for-profit organizations have return-on-investment as the ultimate goal; this is not the case for non-profit and volunteer organizations, so working with these organizations can help students engage in critical thinking about how a different goal might change which intervention they choose or how that intervention is applied. These types of experiences are also helpful for students because they tend to be of low risk, so they can work on their consulting and networking skills in a safe environment. Furthermore, these types of experiences allow students to try out their career path and learn what they do and do not like in a consulting context, which can help them identify what other learning experiences they want before they graduate (Thomas and Landau, 2002). Some students may learn that they would prefer to pursue a non-traditional career path, such as working with unions or the unemployed.

Finally, working with underserved populations can help students to understand how I-O psychologists can influence the lives of others, for better or for worse. For example, when students have the opportunity to work with people who are living in poverty, it can help them recognize the influences that contribute to the marginalization of groups within society (Seider, Gillmor, and Rabinowicz, 2012). When students gain these experiences, it can help them think through their own values and ethics as psychologists, and how as future practitioners they can continue to do work that contributes to the greater good. It also can encourage students to give back to the I-O community that has invested in their education and development by providing meaningful mentoring experiences to future I-O psychologists.

Case study: Training assessment for Planned Parenthood Minnesota, North Dakota, South Dakota

In order to illustrate some of my own experiences with working with a local organization for service learning, I will go in depth on a training evaluation project I did with my I-O graduate students for Planned Parenthood Minnesota, North Dakota, South Dakota parentheses (referred to as "Planned Parenthood" hereafter). In this case study, I've provided some background into the project, some of the practical steps I took to ensure this would be an effective learning experience for my students, and some of the surprises that happened along the way.

Background on Planned Parenthood Federation of America

Planned Parenthood Federation of America (PPFA) is one of the most well-known reproductive health-care providers in the United States. Currently, they have over 700 health centers throughout the United States, and they serve nearly 3 million patients each year (Planned Parenthood, n.d.). The services they provide are quite varied. More than a third of their clientele seek birth control services. PPFA also does a great deal of health screening; they provide cancer screenings such as Pap smears and breast exams, and affordable STI testing and treatment. In addition, PPFA health centers offer comprehensive sex education to adults and adolescents.

Some PPFA locations also provide abortions. Although this makes up only about 3% of their services nationally, it is focused on heavily advocates, religious groups, and politicians that oppose abortion. As a result, PPFA and its affiliates have recently experienced a number of challenges with regards to their funding. For example, in 2011, six states (Wisconsin, Indiana, Kansas, North Carolina, Texas, and Tennessee) attempted to deny access to federal and state funding for preventive health services and education to PPFA affiliates within their states (Planned Parenthood, 2011). In 2012, this trend continued, with Texas and Tennessee attempting to remove PPFA from more public health programs (Planned Parenthood, 2012).

In fact, attempts to defund PPFA and its affiliates are not limited to family planning funds; in September of 2012, two professors at North Dakota State University (NDSU) won a $1.2 million federal grant to develop a sex education program for teenagers in conjunction with Planned Parenthood. However, in response to pressure from legislators, NDSU placed a freeze on the grant (Nelson, 2013). The freeze was later lifted after an outcry of public support for Planned Parenthood and academic freedom. As these developments illustrate, PPFA and its affiliates, as non-profit organizations, face unique challenges in obtaining funding.

Although PPFA affiliates are fully staffed and have the benefit of many volunteers, not all locations have resources to devote a skilled worker to tasks such as training, evaluation, and similar I-O relevant topics. As a new faculty member, I was eager to get more involved in the community using my degree to help others, and I thought that Planned Parenthood might be a fruitful avenue to pursue.

Creating the project with Planned Parenthood

One thing that is often surprising about volunteering I-O services is how strangely difficult it is. For most organizations, the skills provided by I-O psychologists can be easily related to the bottom line. However, for non-profits and volunteer organizations, the "bottom line" is no longer profits; instead, it might be something like placing pets into loving homes, helping their clientele obtain jobs, or educating community members. As a result, the link between good I-O practice and organizational success is more circuitous, and requires a different and more convincing sales pitch and consulting approach. Planned Parenthood was more amenable to working together than I have found to be the case with other organizations. All the same, it did take some research, footwork, and negotiation to solidify a project. Through my own research on the local Planned Parenthood affiliate's website, I was able to focus in on their educators as a group that would be more likely to understand how measurement and assessment could contribute to their mission. I was able to contact one of the lead educators at a nearby location and schedule a meeting with her to learn more about her education programs.

We briefly discussed what I-O psychology was, and what services I could offer pro bono to Planned Parenthood. The lead educator suggested that we work with a program called "Making the Connections, A Day of Discovery for Mothers and Daughters." This program is an all-day retreat in which pre-adolescent girls and their mothers (or other important adults) spend time examining changes that come with puberty and adolescence, while working together to enhance positive communication and connection and recognize the healthy nature of developing sexuality. Over the course of a day, participants engaged in active learning, discussions, and projects that allowed both mothers and daughters to learn about how to communicate well with each other about the feelings and events associated with the onset of puberty.

From a training perspective, the program was quite well designed. The materials provided a "logic model" that provided activities, learning goals, and long-term outcomes. The documents were explicit about what participants should gain through the program, and how each component contributed to overall learning goal. The Planned Parenthood educators, with the help of an Evaluation Coordinator in the Healthy Youth Development-Prevention Resource Center at the University of Minnesota, had also done an impressive job at designing tools to help them assess training effectiveness of the program. Specifically, the material designers had created a pre-retreat evaluation (given immediately before the retreat began), a post-retreat evaluation (given at the end of the day) and a follow-up evaluation (mailed to participants six months following the retreat). However, the lead educator shared that Planned Parenthood did not have the resources to analyze and summarize most of the program data they had collected. At the time, their data recording consisted primarily of a form where educators would provide tally marks indicating how many participants had selected, for example, "strongly agree" in response to a question, as well as recording qualitative responses to survey questions. As a result, the recorded quantitative data provided no information about how an individual rated across different items. Furthermore, although the data had been coded to allow mothers and daughters to be matched, this coding had not been leveraged to help Planned Parenthood understand how mother and daughter variables correlated.

Through our discussions, I also learned that Planned Parenthood still had the hard copies of the data. Thus, my needs as an educator and their needs as a non-profit matched perfectly – my students could gain experience entering data, analyzing it, and creating presentations based upon that data, while Planned Parenthood would be able to use the data and presentations to gauge the success of their program and apply for future funding. We agreed that Planned Parenthood would provide the hard copies, and would provide feedback on what the students produced. Meanwhile, my students and I would provide them with data reports and presentations that could be useful to Planned Parenthood.

Getting students involved

Although my department has a student-run consulting firm, I chose to incorporate this project into a training course for several reasons. First, the training course at my institution was one of the few classes in our program that has first- and second-year I-O master's degree students in mixed company. In this context, the second year students would be able to guide the newer students with their more advanced knowledge of statistics and research methodology. However, both classes could gain experience applying the content they were learning in the course. It also provided all students with an opportunity to see how messy and complex actual organizational data is compared to some of the cleaned or generated data sets they had worked with previously.

During our first class section on the topic, I presented the project to the students. First, I separated students into ten groups of two, with each first-year student matched randomly with a second-year student. We signed confidentiality agreements, and I handed out packets of hard data to the groups. Each group was responsible for creating separate SPSS files for mothers and daughters, and separate files for pre-retreat, post-retreat, and follow-up evaluations. The students were instructed that we would be merging the files (something they had not done previously), so they needed to be careful to put in mother and daughter codes exactly how they were written on the forms. Once all the data were entered, I planned to show them exactly how to merge the data sets. With this final data set, each team would create a technical report conveying key findings, a presentation with a script that could be used internally at Planned Parenthood (to inform colleagues about the program) and a presentation with a script that could be used externally (to help gain additional funding, or to share information with community members). I provided students with a rubric that I planned to use to evaluate their performance. I also let students know that our clients at Planned Parenthood would be evaluating their presentations as well; the winners would work with me to hone their draft of the report into a final report for Planned Parenthood.

Unexpected challenges

As with any consulting project, my students and I faced some interesting and educational challenges during the project. In fact, one of the first challenges occurred right as I ended my introduction to the project. Two students in the class brought up concerns about the project. One student was politically conservative, and was bothered by the use of tax dollars to fund Planned Parenthood. Thus, although we were doing the work pro bono, this student knew that the results of our work could potentially be used to garner additional funding for Planned Parenthood. The second student was a devoted Mormon who was opposed to abortion, and was troubled by Planned Parenthood's provision of birth control to young, unmarried adults.

These concerns led to a fruitful discussion on the nature of I-O work. I noted that, as I-O psychologists, they would likely be faced with ethical dilemmas of their own – perhaps working for a client whose philosophy they disagreed with, or being asked to use statistics they knew were misleading or incorrect. I discussed some of my own experiences with unethical behavior in other workplaces, and how I made decisions about how to behave. We also spent some time exploring the difference between having an ethical concern on a class assignment, versus having one on the job. I noted that the consequences for not participating in the class assignment were relatively minor; the students would miss out on a learning experience, and would either miss some points or would have to come up with an alternative assignment. However, in the real world, refusal to take part in a project could potentially lead to negative consequences for their career, their company, or their families and they would have to think carefully about the costs and benefits of their response to an ethical dilemma. I also presented my perspective on the project – tax dollars were not funding our work directly, and we were working on an educational program targeted at helping mothers and daughters improve their communication, not a program that provided any information or direction on premarital sex or contraception. Ultimately, both students who spoke up agreed to do the project despite their initial misgivings. However, both the students and I gained some perspective about potential ethical issues that can and do occur even when work is humanitarian in nature. It was also a good reminder for all of us that we should be prepared to make some tough decisions when faced with work that goes against our personal ethics.

Another interesting dilemma involved working with the data itself. My goal in assigning second-year students with first-year students was to help bolster the first-years' confidence in data analysis. In fact, I found the second-years' sophistication in statistics to be a disadvantage for them. The data collected by Planned Parenthood was fairly simple – the surveys contained a number of items asking the daughters about how much they thought they knew about puberty, and whether they could envision their mothers as young teenagers experiencing many of the same things. Likewise, the mothers' surveys asked questions about what they knew about puberty, if they felt they trusted their daughters, and if they could empathize with what their daughters were going through. For the most part, these types of questions could be analyzed using repeated ANOVAs or t-tests, but because the intended audience was not likely to be well versed in statistics, a focus on descriptive statistics and practical significance was key. Interestingly, the second-years had just learned about factor analysis, and as a result, they attempted to build scales out of the items included in each evaluation. This led to a number of groups devising scales that made little practical sense in the context of the evaluation materials. We discussed this issue as students were working with the data, and had some interesting exchanges about tailoring analyses and explanations when a lay audience is involved. A number of students noted that they had not thought about using descriptive results to help build a data-driven story for a lay audience. We also reviewed the differences between results that are practically significant versus statistically significant. Hence, this project also helped them see some of the reasons a scientist-practitioner gap exists in the field, and how to address this gap.

One final challenge that occurred with this project had to do with how I graded the assignment. As noted earlier, my contacts at Planned Parenthood had generously agreed to provide feedback through ratings on a rubric, and selected a winner. I also conducted my own ratings on the rubric. When my contacts provided their ratings, I found that their ratings correlated −.20 with my own ratings! Ultimately, I stayed true to my word and had the students who were chosen the winners by the client work with me to complete a final report for Planned Parenthood. However, it was instructive for me as a professor to see how a rubric, which I thought had been well designed and clear, could be used so differently by raters within the organization. At this point, the class was completed, and I did not have any formal meetings with students to talk about this issue; however, I did share this information informally with some of the students, and this led to some interesting conversations about the nature of performance measurement when subjective ratings are involved. It also reminded me of the importance of keeping in touch with clients, to ensure that what is delivered is what was expected.

I know that our contacts, ultimately, were very pleased with the materials we provided to them. They incorporated a number of our recommendations, adapting their evaluation survey tools with clear language that has been used since the 2009 project. The project materials are still housed in Planned Parenthood's administrative offices and referenced regularly by program staff. I can also say that the project continues to benefit students – I have had several students from that class reminisce fondly about the project, and a version of the data we collected is still being used in the training class to illustrate how to analyze, summarize, and report training evaluation results.

Future avenues

If anything, opportunities to involve students in community projects will become more numerous in the future. As income inequality grows (Weeks, 2007), non-profits and volunteer organizations will have a greater need for skilled volunteers. In addition, I-O professional organizations are becoming more clearly supportive of humanitarian initiatives. There has been a recent upswing in interest in humanitarian work psychology (HWP), decent work, and serving the underserved (see Carr et al., 2013 for a review). SIOP has also started to coordinate I-O psychologists on service projects; as of this writing, Nathan Ainspan is spearheading an effort to provide resume assistance to veterans who are returning to the workforce (Below, 2012), and recently Koppes (2007) highlighted SIOP members' contributions to non-profits. As noted by Lefkowitz (2005), many relevant groups have been consistently over-looked by I-O psychologists, such as unions, non-profits, the working poor, the unemployed, recently released prisoners, and non-traditional workers. There are many organizations that work with these groups, and these groups would likely benefit from I-O expertise. Likewise, students can learn a great deal from these groups about the nature of I-O work, and how I-O might fit into society in the future. I have provided a few suggestions below.

Small businesses

Several of my own projects have involved local businesses that were facing difficulties, but did not have funds available to hire a consultant for help. This environment is an ideal place for students to begin their consulting career, and I have found a number of benefits from these projects. First, small businesses have needs that closely mirror larger corporations, but are less complex. In some of the projects I have worked on with local businesses, the interventions can be basic enough that undergraduate students in an I-O course can provide some solid recommendations. Second, students have an opportunity to interact with clients on a more personal basis. Thus, students can personally interview clients for more information and practice their professional communication skills. Third, students can get fast and relevant feedback from the client on whether the intervention is appropriate, and whether the intervention worked. In fact, in one project I worked on with students with a local restaurant/bar, students were thrilled to see the effect a training intervention had on the business – when students visited the bar, they could see new servers being trained using materials and techniques they had recommended. They were also able to see a new training schedule posted at the server station. On another of my service projects, the business owner chose not to implement our intervention, and ultimately closed down her business. This was a good lesson for students that clients sometimes do not take consultants' advice, despite our best efforts. Finally, partnering with business owners can lead to future collaborations. Often, once business owners learn about what I-O is and how it can help them, they are eager to engage with students and professors. Working on service projects is also a way for faculty and students to give back to the field – when I-O is well regarded, it benefits the field as a whole.

Non-profit organizations

As noted by Thomas et al. (2013), non-profit organizations can also be excellent partners for community service projects. These projects can be particularly beneficial to students in several ways. First, given that a small percentage of I-O psychologists ultimately work for non-profits, this type of experience can provide students with a realistic job preview for the benefits and difficulties of this type of work. Second, some of the unique challenges faced by non-profits can provide students with challenging but valuable experiences.

For example, Schmidtke and Cummings (2013) note that because incumbents are expected to fulfill several organizational roles, role conflict and role overload are common problems. Funding can also be an added difficulty for these organizations. Under poor economies, non-profits will be hit hard by cutbacks in government funding and private donations. Because pay is often low in non-profits, attracting and maintaining talent is also challenging (Thomas et al., 2013). Even leadership takes on a different tone; because the CEO must be responsive to the board of directors, the hierarchy within non-profits can be more complex and nuanced than in for-profit organizations (Jacobs and Johnson, 2013). Many non-profits depend heavily on volunteers, and hence issues such as absenteeism and turnover are still present, but cannot be dealt with by financial incentives or promotions as they can in for-profit organizations. Ensuring that volunteers are appropriately socialized into an organization can have beneficial effects on their engagement, fit, and performance (Lopina and Rogelberg, 2013).

Working with non-profits is also an excellent opportunity for individual student projects. Because non-profits often have a clear service mission, students can pick an organization with a mission they feel passionate about. This way, they can develop their consulting skills, work for a cause they find personally meaningful, and use their expertise to perform tasks that might be beyond the skill level of a typical volunteer. My own passion for feminism has led me to my work with women's shelters; a number of my students have begun working with humane societies, youth programs, and similar organizations after graduation.

Schools

In my own experiences, I have donated my time to programs at my universities that have little funding; for example, I have educated student organizations on how to survey their members effectively, and I have helped school districts design parent satisfaction surveys. Educational institutions are often interested in getting community members' involvement; interested I-O psychologists can provide guidance on conducting surveys for school districts, teaching adult education seminars, or coordinating efforts for fund-raising or similar endeavors. These types of collaborations can also allow I-O psychologists an opportunity to engage with young children and emphasize the importance of education for their futures.

Conclusion

It is my hope that this chapter can serve as an inspiration for all I-O psychologists to engage in their communities. Although I've framed this from my own viewpoint as a professor, I think that many of these suggestions could be tailored for many organizational positions. For example, imagine how powerful mentorship could be if the mentor and his or her protégé worked together on a service project such as this one. I-O psychologists who are working in the non-profit sector could also initiate some projects with local I-O students and faculty. Ultimately, we all gain from recognizing that I-O is not a value-free endeavor; we learn and become better scientists and practitioners when we work to serve the underserved in our own communities. As noted by Koppes (2007), we are responsible for creating great places to work *and* live. We owe it to future generations to fight for social justice and ensure that I-O is not a servant of power, but a servant of people.

References

Baritz, L. (1965). *The Servants of Power: A History of the Use of Social Science in American Industry*. New York, NY: John Wiley & Sons.

Below, S. S. (2012). From civilian to soldier. *SIOP Newsbriefs*. Retrieved from http://www.siop.org/article_view.aspx?article=978.

Carr, S. C., Thompson, L. F., Reichman, W., McWha, I., Marai, L., MacLachlan, M., & Baguma, P. (2013). Humanitarian work psychology: Concepts to contributions. [White paper]. Retrieved from http://www.siop.org/WhitePapers/White%20Paper%20Series%2020122013HumanitarianWorkPsychology.pdf.

Casile, M., Hoover, K., & O'Neil, D. (2011). Both-and, not either-or: Service learning as a tool for moral development and intellectual learning. *Education and Training*, 53, 129–139.

Casner-Lotto, Jill, & Barrington, Linda (2006). *Are They Really Ready to Work? Employers' Perspectives on the Basic Knowledge and Applied Skills of New Entrants to the 21st Century U.S. Workforce*. Retrieved May 31, 2013, from http://www.conference-board.org/pdf_free/BED-06-Workforce.pdf.

Church, A. H., & Burke, W. W. (1992). Assessing the activities and values of organization development practitioners. *The Industrial-Organizational Psychologist,*
30, 59–66.

Eyler, J., Giles, D., Stenson, C., & Gray, C. (2001). *At a Glance: What We Know
About the Effects of Service Learning on College Students, Faculty, Institutions, and
Communities, 1993–2001.* 3rd Edition. Nashville, TN: Vanderbilt University.

Fink, A. A., Guzzo, R. A., Adler, S., Gillespie, J. Z., Konczak, L. J., Olson, T., Beier,
M. E., & Dickson, M. W. (2010). Consulting and business skills in industrial-
organizational psychology graduate education. *The Industrial-Organizational
Psychologist,* 48, 34–46.

Jacobs, R., & Johnson, J. (2013). Nonprofit leadership and governance. In
J. Olson-Buchanan, L. K. Bryan, & L. F. Thompson (Eds.), *Using Industrial-
Organizational Psychology for the Greater Good* (pp. 325–354). New York, NY:
Routledge.

Koppes, L. (2007). SIOP members as citizen leaders. *The Industrial-Organizational
Psychologist,* 44, 25–33.

Lefkowitz, J. (2005). The values of industrial-organizational psychology: Who are
we? *The Industrial-Organizational Psychologist,* 43, 13–20.

Lefkowitz, J. (2011). The science, practice, and morality of work psychology.
Industrial and Organizational Psychology, 4, 112–115.

Lopina, E. C., & Rogelberg, S. G. (2013). Recruitment, retention, and motivation
of volunteers in the nonprofit sector: A volunteer socialization perspective.
In J. Olson-Buchanan, L. K. Bryan, & L. F. Thompson (Eds.), *Using Industrial-
Organizational Psychology for the Greater Good* (pp. 239–264). New York, NY:
Routledge.

Nelson, L. A. (2013). Planned Parenthood, political pressure. *Inside Higher Ed.*
Retrieved from http://www.insidehighered.com/news/2013/01/18/legislator-
pressure-leads-north-dakota-state-freeze-planned-parenthood-grant.

Planned Parenthood (n.d.). Planned Parenthood at a glance. Retrieved
from   http://www.plannedparenthood.org/about-us/who-we-are/planned-
parenthood-glance-5552.htm.

Planned Parenthood (2011). *Planned Parenthood Condemns Wisconsin Governor for Cutting Off Health Care for Women.* [Press release]. Retrieved from
http://www.plannedparenthood.org/about-us/newsroom/press-releases/
planned-parenthood-condemns-wisconsin-governor-cutting-off-health-care-
women-37132.htm.

Planned Parenthood (2012). *Annual Report: 2011–2012.* [Annual Report].
Retrieved from http://issuu.com/actionfund/docs/ppfa_ar_2012_121812_vf/1.

Schmidtke, J. M., & Cummings, A. (2013). Salient challenges of staffing and man-
aging employees in the nonprofit sector. In J. Olson-Buchanan, L. K. Bryan, &
L. F. Thompson (Eds.), *Using Industrial-Organizational Psychology for the Greater
Good* (pp. 325–354). New York, NY: Routledge.

Seider, S., Gillmor, S., & Rabinowicz, S. (2012). The impact of community service
learning upon the expected political voice of participating college students.
Journal of Adolescent Research, 27, 44–77.

Thomas, K. M., & Landau, H. (2002). OD students as engaged learners and reflec-
tive practitioners: The roles of service-learning. *Organizational Development
Journal,* 20, 88–99.

Thomas, K. M., Downey, S., & George, K. E. (2013). I-O psychology education and the nonprofit context. In J. Olson-Buchanan, L. K. Bryan, & L. F. Thompson (Eds.), *Using Industrial-Organizational Psychology for the Greater Good* (pp. 325–354). New York, NY: Routledge.

Torres, J. (2002). *Benchmarks for Campus/Community Partnerships.* Providence, RI: Campus Compact.

Ward, K. (2003). *Faculty Service Roles and the Scholarship of Engagement* (ASHE-ERIC Higher Education Report, Volume 29, Number 5). Indianapolis, IN: Jossey-Bass.

Weeks, J. (2007). Inequality trends in some developed OECD countries. In J. K. S & J. Baudot (Eds.) *Flat World, Big Gaps* (pp. 159–174). New York, NY: ZED Books.

Weiss, H. M., & Rupp, D. E. (2011). Experiencing work: An essay on a person-centric work psychology. *Industrial and Organizational Psychology*, 4, 83–97.

Index

Printed and bound by CPI Group (UK) Ltd, Croydon, CR0 4YY